Ibrahim Elsayed

Dataspace Support Platform for e-Science

Ibrahim Elsayed

Dataspace Support Platform for e-Science

Dataspace-based Preservation of Scientific Studies

Südwestdeutscher Verlag für Hochschulschriften

Impressum/Imprint (nur für Deutschland/only for Germany)
Bibliografische Information der Deutschen Nationalbibliothek: Die Deutsche Nationalbibliothek verzeichnet diese Publikation in der Deutschen Nationalbibliografie; detaillierte bibliografische Daten sind im Internet über http://dnb.d-nb.de abrufbar.
Alle in diesem Buch genannten Marken und Produktnamen unterliegen warenzeichen-, marken- oder patentrechtlichem Schutz bzw. sind Warenzeichen oder eingetragene Warenzeichen der jeweiligen Inhaber. Die Wiedergabe von Marken, Produktnamen, Gebrauchsnamen, Handelsnamen, Warenbezeichnungen u.s.w. in diesem Werk berechtigt auch ohne besondere Kennzeichnung nicht zu der Annahme, dass solche Namen im Sinne der Warenzeichen- und Markenschutzgesetzgebung als frei zu betrachten wären und daher von jedermann benutzt werden dürften.

Coverbild: www.ingimage.com

Verlag: Südwestdeutscher Verlag für Hochschulschriften GmbH & Co. KG
Heinrich-Böcking-Str. 6-8, 66121 Saarbrücken, Deutschland
Telefon +49 681 37 20 271-1, Telefax +49 681 37 20 271-0
Email: info@svh-verlag.de

Approved by: Wien, TU, Diss., 2011

Herstellung in Deutschland (siehe letzte Seite)
ISBN: 978-3-8381-3157-3

Imprint (only for USA, GB)
Bibliographic information published by the Deutsche Nationalbibliothek: The Deutsche Nationalbibliothek lists this publication in the Deutsche Nationalbibliografie; detailed bibliographic data are available in the Internet at http://dnb.d-nb.de.
Any brand names and product names mentioned in this book are subject to trademark, brand or patent protection and are trademarks or registered trademarks of their respective holders. The use of brand names, product names, common names, trade names, product descriptions etc. even without a particular marking in this works is in no way to be construed to mean that such names may be regarded as unrestricted in respect of trademark and brand protection legislation and could thus be used by anyone.

Cover image: www.ingimage.com

Publisher: Südwestdeutscher Verlag für Hochschulschriften GmbH & Co. KG
Heinrich-Böcking-Str. 6-8, 66121 Saarbrücken, Germany
Phone +49 681 37 20 271-1, Fax +49 681 37 20 271-0
Email: info@svh-verlag.de

Printed in the U.S.A.
Printed in the U.K. by (see last page)
ISBN: 978-3-8381-3157-3

Copyright © 2012 by the author and Südwestdeutscher Verlag für Hochschulschriften GmbH & Co. KG and licensors
All rights reserved. Saarbrücken 2012

*In the Name of God, Most Gracious, Most Merciful.
All praise is due to God, Lord of the Worlds.*

Preface

Scientific data, collected in various research domains are made accessible for significant analysis through portals by the means of e-Infrastructures. Managing the outcome of these analyses in conjunction with its corresponding input data, by enriching the existing relationship with semantics to facilitate reuse of data and analytical methods is nowadays more important than ever. Systems providing advanced integrated view to large-scale and distributed scientific data are described in the literature to a great extent, however the key (dataspace) feature *managing semantic relationships* is not well considered and thus it represents an open research challenge to be addressed in this book. The work presented in this book focuses its effort on scientific dataspaces, which, if applied in e-Science applications can provide a highly efficient and powerful scientific data management solution for e-Infrastructures. The authors approach is to semantically enrich the existing relationship among primary and derived datasets and to preserve both, relationships and datasets together within a dataspace to be reused by owners and others. This approach is shown to significantly improve assisted publishing, discovery, and reuse of primary and derived data used in scientific studies within e-Infrastructures. To enable reuse, data must be well preserved, which can best be established if the full life cycle of data is addressed. A novel OWL ontology for the creation of semantically rich relationships among primary and derived datasets in scientific studies is presented. The major contributions presented in this book include: (1) *e-Science life cycle model*, a specific model addressing the complete data life cycle to provide well-preserved scientific studies, (2) *Semantic markup for scientific studies* enabling to describe relationships among datasets of scientific studies with a semantic model, (3) *Long-term preservation framework* providing preservation of the complete life cycle of data in scientific studies, (4) *Large-scale scientific dataspace platform - jSpace* integrating the achievements presented in this book enabling to interconnect multiple dataspace instances from various domains, and (5) *jSpace Java API* providing all needed methods to construct semantic data about scientific studies and a model for their management within a distributed data environment.

This book summarizes scientific contributions made by the author during his research in the context of his PhD study. Most of the research has been carried out at the Research Group Scientific Computing of the Faculty of Computer Science, University of Vienna.

Acknowledgements

All praise is due to God, who gave me the chance to thank Him and my parents.

I extend my warmest thanks to my supervisor, Prof. Dr. Peter Brezany. He initiated and supported this work with his long standing experience and the organizational background and gave me the opportunity to work on this challenging topic. Without the inspiring, productive and supportive working environment, he created in the scientific computing research group, this work could never have come into existence. I am also very grateful to Prof. Dr. A Min Tjoa for his interest in my work and his immediate willingness to act as the second referee.

I am thankful for the friendly working relationship I have with my colleagues in the scientific computing research group. The fruitful cooperation and discussions with my colleagues in the group have helped developing this work. Special thanks to Prof. Dr. Siegfried Benkner for providing an excellent working environment in his function as head of the research group.

Last but not least, I want to thank my family and friends for their support and encouragement during the time that I was engaged in this study. In particular, I thank my parents who always supported my career and encouraged me to follow the straight path in my life.

Vienna, Austria Ibrahim Elsayed
October 17, 2011

Contents

Preface iii

Acknowledgements v

List of Figures xii

List of Tables xvii

I Introduction and Research Background   2

1 Introduction   4
   1.1 Motivation 4
   1.2 Research Approach 6
   1.3 Research Questions, Goals, and Methods 9
       1.3.1 Semantic Relationships among Dataspace Participants 9
       1.3.2 Establishing Data Preservation Spaces 9
       1.3.3 Realizing Large-Scale Dataspaces 10
   1.4 Organization of the Dissertation 10

2 Research Background and Context   16
   2.1 Introduction 16
   2.2 e-Science and e-Infrastructures 17
   2.3 e-Science Portals 18
   2.4 Service Oriented Architectures (SOA) 19
   2.5 Key Data Management Tasks in e-Science 20
       2.5.1 Determining of What Data Exists and Where it Resides ... 21
       2.5.2 Searching for Answers to Specific Questions 23

		2.5.3	Discovering Interesting New Datasets and Patterns	24
		2.5.4	Assisted and Automated Publishing	25
	2.6	\multicolumn{2}{l}{Data-Management Requirements on Scientific Dataspaces . . . .}	25
	2.7	\multicolumn{2}{l}{Summary . . . .}	28

3 Related Work — 30

	3.1	\multicolumn{2}{l}{Large-Scale Data Management Systems . . . .}	31
		3.1.1	DSpace	31
		3.1.2	Storage Resource Broker	34
		3.1.3	iRODS - integrated Rule-Oriented Data System	37
		3.1.4	IBM Webshpere Information Integrator	41
		3.1.5	Chimera	45
		3.1.6	myExperiment	47
		3.1.7	PAYGO	50
		3.1.8	Linked Data	52
	3.2	\multicolumn{2}{l}{Small-Scale Data Management Systems . . . .}	54
		3.2.1	SEMEX Personal Information Management Platform	54
		3.2.2	*iMeMex:* A Personal Dataspace Management System	57
		3.2.3	Google Desktop Search	59
		3.2.4	Phlat and Windows Desktop Search	60
	3.3	\multicolumn{2}{l}{Summary . . . .}	62

II Methodology and Concepts — 68

4 Semantic Relationships among Dataspace Participants — 70

	4.1	Introduction	70
	4.2	Scientific Dataspace Model	72
		4.2.1 e-Science Life Cycle Activities	73
		4.2.2 The Scientific Resource Space Model	75
		4.2.3 The Environment of Dataspaces in e-Science	81
	4.3	Relationships in the Scientific Dataspace	84
	4.4	Related Work	90
	4.5	Summary	92

5	**The e-Science Life Cycle Ontology**		**94**
	5.1 Introduction		94
	5.2 Applied Methodology		96
	5.3 e-Science Life Cycle Ontology Development		98
		5.3.1 Feasibility study	98
		5.3.2 Kickoff	99
		5.3.3 Refinement	102
		5.3.4 Evaluation	110
		5.3.5 Maintenance and Evolution	115
		5.3.6 Life Cycle Ontology Properties	115
	5.4 Reasoning the e-Science life cycle ontology		118
	5.5 Scope of the e-Science life cycle ontology		120
	5.6 Alternative Approaches to develop an Ontology		124
		5.6.1 Unschold and King's method	125
		5.6.2 Grueninger and Fox's Methodology	125
		5.6.3 Methontology	126
	5.7 Summary		127
6	**A Dataspace-Based Support Platform jSpace**		**130**
	6.1 Introduction		130
	6.2 Generic Use Cases		131
		6.2.1 Search&Query Dataspace	131
		6.2.2 Browse Dataspace	133
		6.2.3 Create Life Cycle Resource	133
		6.2.4 Visualize Life Cycle Resource	134
	6.3 jSpace System Architecture		135
		6.3.1 Search&Query Processor	136
		6.3.2 RDF Store	139
		6.3.3 e-Science Life Cycle Composer	140
		6.3.4 Dataspace Indexer	143
		6.3.5 e-Science Life Cycle Visualizer	146
		6.3.6 Dataspace Browser	146
	6.4 Reference Implementation		148
	6.5 Summary		154

7	**Realizing Large-Scale Scientific Dataspaces**		**158**
7.1	Introduction		158
7.2	Scalability in Scientific Dataspaces		161
7.3	Semantic Data Infrastructure		165
	7.3.1	Software Architecture Design Overview	166
	7.3.2	Discussion	170
	7.3.3	Prototypical Implementation	171
	7.3.4	Multi-Disciplinary Scientific Dataspace	172
7.4	A Synthetic Large-Scale Dataspace		173
7.5	Towards Cloud-Enabled Dataspaces		175
7.6	Performance Evaluation		179
7.7	Alternative Solutions for Distributed SPARQL Query Processing		183
7.8	Summary		185

III Evaluation and Conclusions   186

8	**Experimental Evaluation in e-Science Applications**		**188**
8.1	Introduction		188
8.2	Non-Invasive Health Parameter Prediction based on Traditional Chinese Medicine		189
	8.2.1	NIGM Use Case Scenarios	190
	8.2.2	NIGM Dataspace Participants	191
	8.2.3	NIGM Example Life Cycle Resource	193
8.3	Breath Gas Analysis for Detection of Minimal Diseases		195
	8.3.1	BGA Use Case Scenario	196
	8.3.2	BGA Dataspace Participants	199
	8.3.3	BGA Example Life Cycle Resource	201
8.4	jSpace Experimental Evaluation		204
	8.4.1	Experimental Setup	205
	8.4.2	jSpace Performance Evaluation on NIGM	207
	8.4.3	jSpace Performance Evaluation on BGA	208
	8.4.4	Impact of Large Values of Dataspace Participants in jSpace	211
	8.4.5	Dataspace Reusability Measures	212
	8.4.6	Experiences	215

	8.5 Summary	217
9	**Conclusions**	**220**
	9.1 Summary of the Research	220
	9.2 Research Contributions	221
	9.3 Open Issues and Future Research Directions	225
	9.4 Research Publications	226
	Bibliography	**230**

IV	**Appendices**	**250**
A	**A concrete Breath Gas Analysis Life Cycle Resource**	**252**
	A.1 Life Cycle Activities	254
	A.2 Individuals of the e-Science life cycle ontology	254
	Index	**274**

List of Figures

1.1	Dataspace research extension.	7
1.2	Book overview - Dataspace support platform for e-Science.	12
2.1	Small-scale research lab.	21
2.2	Key components of a scientific dataspace support platform.	26
3.1	Ingest process in DSpace.	34
3.2	SRB architecture.	35
3.3	InQ SRB Client.	38
3.4	The architecture of the iRODS system.	40
3.5	WebSphere Information Integrator data federation	42
3.6	WebSphere Information Integrator components.	43
3.7	Chimera architecture.	46
3.8	The myExperiment user interface.	49
3.9	An instantiation of the PAYGO data integration architecture.	51
3.10	Linked Data publishing options and workflows.	53
3.11	The architecture of SEMEX.	55
3.12	A sample screenshot of the Semex interface.	56
3.13	The architecture.	58
3.14	Heterogeneous personal information iDM.	58
3.15	The Google Desktop interface.	60
3.16	The Phlat interface.	62
4.1	The e-Science life cycle.	73
4.2	The *"goalSpecification"* dimension of the *SRS*.	76
4.3	2-dimensional scientific resource space.	77
4.4	3-dimensional scientific dataspace.	78

xiii

4.5	5-dimensional scientific dataspace.	79
4.6	Environment of a scientific dataspace.	82
4.7	Three layers of abstraction for e-Science life cycles.	83
4.8	Semantic relationship in e-Science applications.	85
4.9	Organization of dataspace participants.	87
4.10	Relationships among dataspace participants.	89
4.11	Abstraction layers of scientific dataspaces.	91
5.1	Main concepts of the e-science life cycle ontology.	95
5.2	Methodology for On-To-Knowledge.	97
5.3	Identified people involved in the e-Science life cycle ontology.	99
5.4	Lice cycle activity concept taxonomy.	100
5.5	Dataspace participant concept taxonomy.	101
5.6	Publication mode concept taxonomy.	102
5.7	Generic metadata concept and example.	103
5.8	e-Science life cycle - activity relations.	104
5.9	e-Science life cycle - publication mode.	105
5.10	OWL classes and properties of the dataspace.	107
5.11	Data description concept in the e-Science life cycle ontology.	108
5.12	OWL classes and properties regarding EPRs.	110
5.13	Instances and properties of a concrete EPR example.	111
5.14	SPARQL query example 1 results in Protégé.	112
5.15	SPARQL query example 2 results in Protégé.	113
5.16	SPARQL query example 3 results in Protégé.	114
5.17	SPARQL query example 3 results in Protégé.	115
5.18	Environment of the e-Science lifecycle ontology.	123
5.19	Ontology prefixes.	124
6.1	Overview of the use cases of the system.	132
6.2	Holistic view of the system architecture [EB10].	135
6.3	IGT of a concrete example.	137
6.4	UML activity diagram of the IGT implemented in jSpace.	138
6.5	Activity diagram 'Create Life Cycle Resource"	141
6.6	The Welkin RDF Visualizer visualizing three life cycle resources	147
6.7	Semantic markup and physical dataset layer.	150

6.8	The e-Science life cycle composer GUI.	151
6.9	Global centralized RDF store.	152
6.10	The jSpace Search and Query Panel showing the *SPARQL-tab*.	153
7.1	Large-scale scientific dataspace architecture overview.	160
7.2	Levels of abstraction of breath gas analysis dataspace participants.	162
7.3	Middleware connecting two local RDF stores.	165
7.4	Layered architecture of the scientific dataspace support platform.	167
7.5	Sequence diagram showing a search request.	168
7.6	Overview of the components of a single dataspace instance.	169
7.7	LCR Preserver and e-Science Search&Query Panel.	172
7.8	Large-scale scientific dataspace infrastructure.	174
7.9	An e-Science cloud.	176
7.10	The scientific dataspace cloud.	178
7.11	LCR dataset (1-5) load times of the local and global RDF store.	180
7.12	LCR dataset (6,7) load times of the local and global RDF store.	181
7.13	Response times of query answering in the local RDF.	182
7.14	Response times of query answering in the global RDF store.	182
7.15	Total response times of query answering.	183
8.1	The Non-Invasive Glucose Measurement Service (NIGM-Service).	192
8.2	Goal specification activity of an example NIGM LCR.	194
8.3	Use case depicting the current sequence of events.	197
8.4	Main entities of a breath gas analysis experiment.	201
8.5	Snapshot of an RDF graph of a sample breath gas experiment.	203
8.6	Screenshot of the Matlab-template for BGA studies.	204
8.7	Web portal for breath gas analysis researchers.	206
8.8	Distribution of the performance overhead in NIGM.	208
8.9	Distribution of the performance overhead in BGA.	209
8.10	Performance overhead in relation to execution time.	210
8.11	Performance overhead with reused LCA.	211
8.12	Performance with different input data sizes.	213
9.1	Realization of the scientific dataspace paradigm.	222
A.1	Classes and properties of a single LCR.	253

A.2	Classes and properties of the goal specification activity.	255
A.3	Classes and properties of the data preparation activity.	256
A.4	Classes and properties of the ask selection activity.	257
A.5	Classes and properties of the ask execution activity.	258
A.6	Classes and properties of the esult processing activity.	259

List of Tables

3.1	DSpace object with concrete examples.	33
3.2	Supported data sources in WebSphere IBM Information Integrator.	46
3.3	Traditional data integration vs. PAYGO.	50
3.4	Data management systems providing dataspace features.	63
3.5	Dataspace features comparison matrix.	66
4.1	Definition of the *SRS axes* names and their mapping.	75
4.2	Dimensions of the scientific dataspace.	76
5.1	Object properties.	117
5.2	Data type properties.	118
6.1	Description of the use case *"Search&Query Dataspace"*.	139
6.2	Description of the use case *"Create Life Cycle Resource"*.	143
6.3	Flat table storing indexes of individuals.	145
6.4	Example flat table storing LCR indexes.	146
7.1	Individuals in the synthetic LCR datasets.	175
7.2	LCR datasets file and database sizes.	180
8.1	Dataspace participants in a typical NIGM study.	193
8.2	Individual axiom counts of the NIGM LCR.	195
8.4	Dataspace participants in a typical BGA study.	199
8.3	Definition of breath gas analysis actions.	199
8.5	Individual axiom counts of the BGA LCR.	205
8.6	Performance overhead in the NIGM application.	207
8.7	Performance overhead of jSpace in the BGA application.	209
8.8	Performance overhead in the BGA application with reused LCA.	210

Part I

Introduction and Research Background

Chapter 1

Introduction

> *"A dataspace is everything that is not only in a single DBMS."*
>
> In the keynote to the 15th International Conference on Database Systems for Advanced Applications in Tsukuba on April 1st, 2010
> given by
> GERHARD WEIKUM

1.1 Motivation

Scientific instruments and computer simulations are creating vast data stores that require new scientific methods to analyze and organize data. Data analysis tools have not kept pace with our ability to capture and store data [GLNS+05]. However, access to and analysis of scientific data within a short period of time is a crucial factor in achievements of scientific discoveries. New research challenges are brought about by the emergence of data-intensive scientific discovery [HTT09], which is a rapidly emerging methodology, introduced as "The Fourth Paradigm" by Jim Gray. Researchers will gain from an increased ability to make discoveries that are hidden in the huge amount of their data. There are many excellent examples of long-term use of data in different research domains, however, these are not detailed in publications, because they are part of a researcher's work. This has as a consequence that the ideas behind them are not made accessible to others by publishing a scientific paper. Increased use of data will be a persistent feature of future research, business, government and discussion making [AR10].

e-Science refers to the large-scale science that will increasingly be carried out through distributed global collaborations enabled by the internet. In many e-Science applications relevant scientific data is typically collected at different participating research centers. This distributed and often heterogenous data is made accessible for significant analysis through portals by the means of e-Infrastructures. Scientific data can be categorized into three major categories: (1) primary data, (2) derived data, and (3) background data. Data items of each category are interacting within scientific experiments. Typically, a *primary data* set is accessed and analyzed by some kind of analytical methods, which produce a set of *derived data* products. Analytical methods are often composed into scientific workflows represented by a workflow language and executed by a workflow enactment engine. *Background data* typically represents such scientific workflows, but is not limited to it. Also provenance data[1] [SPG05] is regarded in this context as background data. In general any data item corresponding to a scientific experiment that does not represent primary or derived data, is classified as background data. Managing the outcome of scientific experiments in conjunction with its corresponding input data by enriching the existing relationship among primary and derived data with semantics to be searchable and following to be discovered and further used in other research areas represents an open research issue to be challenged by the work presented in this book.

The distributed space of primary, background and derived data can, if managed by semantically rich relationships among participating data items support scientists in organizing and preserving their scientific experiments in the long-term to be re-used by owners and others.

Institutional repositories are clearly and broadly being recognized as essential infrastructure for scholarship in the digital world. Consequently, it seems highly probable that the next few years will see growing connections between institutional repositories as infrastructure and the broader issues that are emerging about strategies and infrastructure necessary to support the management, dissemination and curation of research data [LL05].

Today, there are powerful systems for managing data at the level of a single database system (whether relational, XML, or in some other model). While the commercial world has standardized on the relational data model and SQL, no single standard

---

[1] Provenance data is referred in the literature to a description of the origins of a dataset and the process that led to that specific dataset, such as a workflow description.

or tool has critical mass in the scientific community [GLNS+05]. There are many parallel and competing efforts to build scientific data management solutions - at least one per discipline. Data interchange outside each group is problematic, and therefore an open research issue and probably a never-ending story faced by the data management community .

A much greater challenge facing the data management community is to raise the abstraction level at which data is managed in order to provide a system controlling different data sources, each with its own data model [Hal05]. The goal is to manage a dataspace, rather than a database. A dataspace consists of a set of participants and a set of relationships among participants [FHM05]. A participant can be any element containing data in some way. Relationships describe how two participants are related to each other. Relationships can be expressed by single word-relationships, such as *replica-of, related-to, view-of*, etc. In the extreme example they can be semantic mappings of database schemas. Systems providing the required services over dataspaces are considered to be Dataspace Support Platforms (DSSPs) [HFM06]. In [EBT06] we have defined such a system as:

> "A set of software programs that controls the organization, storage and retrieval of data in a dataspace. It also handles the security and integrity of the dataspace."

We are aware that the security of the dataspace represents an important challenge, however it is not addressed in this book. Besides authentication, encryption and privacy requirements on the infrastructural layer [DFL+09] main security issues in this context deal with retaining data control to the client with multiple organizations involved [DMF+09].

1.2 Research Approach

The initial ideas on managing dataspaces have started to evoke interests of the data management community, however most effort is related to the database research and application mainstream and so far not considered for advanced scientific data management. Furthermore, most of the approaches towards realizing a dataspace system that were presented at international conferences to date, focus on personal information management. In Figure 1.1 we illustrate our extension to the mainstream dataspace

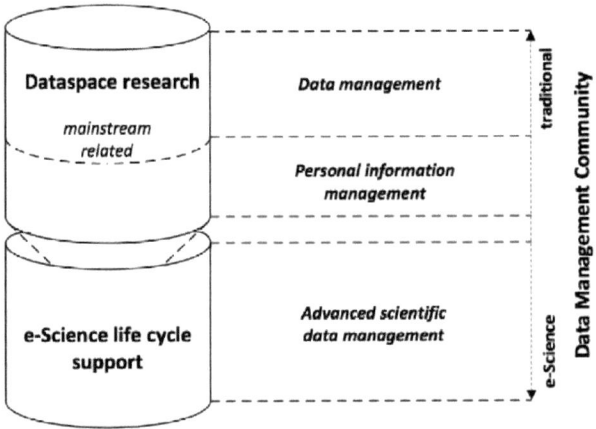

Figure 1.1: Dataspace research extension.

research providing advanced scientific data management. The mainstream dataspace research can be summarized as the research direction focusing on the realization of dataspace concepts for an on-demand data integration, which is referred in literature as pay-as-you-go data integration [DSDH08].

Scientific dataspaces aim at providing associated mechanisms for managing semantically rich relationships among scientific data resources as well as to keep track of scientific experiments - independent of the e-Science application domain - that are being conducted by members of a scientific community and to link these experiments with user information i.e. institutional affiliation, email address, working field, etc. of the scientist who conducted the experiment.

The work presented in this book intends to provide novel data management solutions based on the concepts of dataspaces for large-scale and long-term management of scientific data, and we also utilize several concepts from knowledge management technologies . Our approach is to investigate how the creation of the relationship between dataspace participants can be semi-automatized, how to semantically enrich existing relationships among primary and derived data items, and how to preserve both relationships and data together within the dataspace to be reused by owners and others. To enable reuse, data must be well preserved. Preservation of scientific data can best be established if the full life cycle of data is addressed [Lyn08]. The effects of data loss can be economic, because the experiments have to be re-run, but in some cases data loss represents an opportunity lost forever. Therefore, the preservation of scientific data (primary, background, and derived datasets), including semantic relationships among them providing knowledge, such as why and how a specific study was conducted, represents an important challenge to be faced in this work.

Main objective is to link derived data with their corresponding primary data by providing semantically rich relationships. Further, to make both relationships and data available within the dataspace for scientists from various groups of organizations who might have use of it and who want to collaborate by the means of virtual organizations in the context of an e-infrastructure. We present the key concepts of dataspaces and its environment in e-Science - the life cycle of scientific data[2] - as classes of an ontology expressed in OWL [W3C04], and we use this ontology to provide semantics about iterations in the life cycle for creating semantically rich relationships among life cycle iterations and its corresponding primary, background, and derived data.

The success of a dataspace will be highly dependent on the power of the used relationship concept as well as its flexibility. Rich relationships between participants are going to be the backbone of such a system, with the basic necessity to support their semi-automatically creation of them as well as their improvements and maintenance. The development of a suitable relationship framework customizable towards various application needs is an important issue, to be solved by the scientific dataspace paradigm presented in this book.

The dataspace paradigm is being evaluated in the context of two real world e-Science applications:

1. Non-Invasive Health-Parameter Prediction based on Traditional Chinese Medicine - conducted within the CADGrid bilateral research project [cad11].

2. Breath Gas Analysis for Molecular-Oriented Detection of Minimal Diseases - conducted within the Austrian Grid [agr10] project. The follow up project Advanced Breath Analysis [aba11] builds upon the dataspace paradigm and further develops the platform addressing security and autonomous features for execution of breath gas analysis experiments.

---

[2]The life cycle of scientific data covers all steps in the process of conducting a scientific study. It is further described in Section 4.2.

Moreover, to evaluate performance and scalability of our solutions, we build a synthetic large-scale dataspace. This approach is shown to significantly improve assisted publishing, discovery, and reuse of primary, background, and derived data used in e-Science applications.

1.3 Research Questions, Goals, and Methods

Our research questions and goals are explicitly and systematically described in the following subsections.

1.3.1 Semantic Relationships among Dataspace Participants

Research Question A: How can semantically enriched relationships among data items, described by an ontology support discovery of scientific datasets in a dataspace?
Research Goals are:

- to define a measure for semantic richness of dataspace participants,

- to link participants of a scientific dataspace by providing semantically rich relationships among derived data products with their corresponding primary and background data,

- to invent a suitable relationship paradigm for the creation, representation and advanced searching of relationships among participants of a scientific dataspace,

- to apply the relationship model in a prototype implementation of a scientific dataspace support platform offering semantic search&query interfaces,

- to evaluate the model on top of several real world and modeled e-Science applications.

1.3.2 Establishing Data Preservation Spaces

Research Question B: How can an ontology that addresses the full life cycle of data support long-term preservation of scientific data in a dataspace?
Research Goals are:

- to develop an OWL ontology that addresses the full life cycle of data in scientific experiments considering accessed and derived, as well as background datasets,
- to dispose single instances of scientific experiments as individuals of that ontology to be represented in RDF graphs linking to involved scientific datasets (resources),
- to provide an appropriate indexing mechanism for uniform organization of scientific data life cycle resources,
- to preserve those RDF graphs together with its corresponding scientific resources within an adequate physical storage system.

1.3.3 Realizing Large-Scale Dataspaces

Research Question C: Are large-scale dataspaces the next generation knowledge- and data management paradigms replacing data grids and what requirements (performance, scalability, usability, etc.) should they fulfill?
Research Goals are:

- to analyze most recent developments in the area of scientific data management systems and other large-scale data and knowledge management solutions including data grids taking into account the defined measure for semantic richness,
- to elaborate and experimentally implement large-scale dataspace scenarios with geographically distributed scientific data resources and collaborating scientists on top of a real world e-Science application,
- to differentiate those existing systems with the scientific dataspace support platform in terms of multi-disciplinary virtual organizations,
- to define how the process of scientific collaboration should be organized, in order to efficiently affiliate existing dataspaces of different domains into a large-scale and multi-disciplinary scientific dataspace.

1.4 Organization of the Dissertation

This book is organized into three major parts. Part I introduces the problem area, provides the background knowledge and an extensive related work chapter. Part II deals with the methodology and concepts applied. Its three Chapters (4, 5, and 6) elaborate the scientific data life cycle in e-Science applications, present the system architecture of our Scientific Dataspace Support Platform , and discusses large-scale dataspace scenarios. Part III finally describes the prototypical implementation, the system usage and interaction, and the experimental evaluation in two real world e-Science applications. It also concludes the work presented in this book and gives suggestions for future research. A visual overview of the organization of this book is given in Figure 1.2.

In the following an outline of this book is given with a brief description of each chapter.

Chapter 2 This chapter introduces an appropriate research background and introduces the research context of the work in this book. In particular, it describes the terms e-Science and e-Infrastructure, e-Science Portal, and Service Oriented Architecture. Furthermore, it defines four supreme disciplines of data management in e-Science and discusses their corresponding key data management tasks. Finally, the chapter provides an overview of the data-management requirements of e-Science applications on dataspace systems and gives a general summary of data management solutions for e-Science.

Chapter 3 represents a comprehensive work to survey the state of the art in dataspace features to date. It describes in great detail how dataspace features were considered in the current research projects and enterprise solutions of the data management community. Its sections cover research projects and enterprise solutions including data preservation systems that provide at least some of the features a dataspace system should offer.

Chapter 4 This chapter discusses the development and evaluation of the scientific dataspace model and elaborates what data items are considered as dataspace participants in the scientific dataspace. It demonstrates the approach for creation, representation, and maintaining of semantically enriched relationships among distributed dataspace participants.

Chapter 5 This chapter introduces the e-Science life cycle ontology. It describes how relationships among dataspace participants can be semantically enriched by the use of an ontology. This chapter also describes the methodology that was applied for building the e-Science life cycle ontology and outlines the major classes and

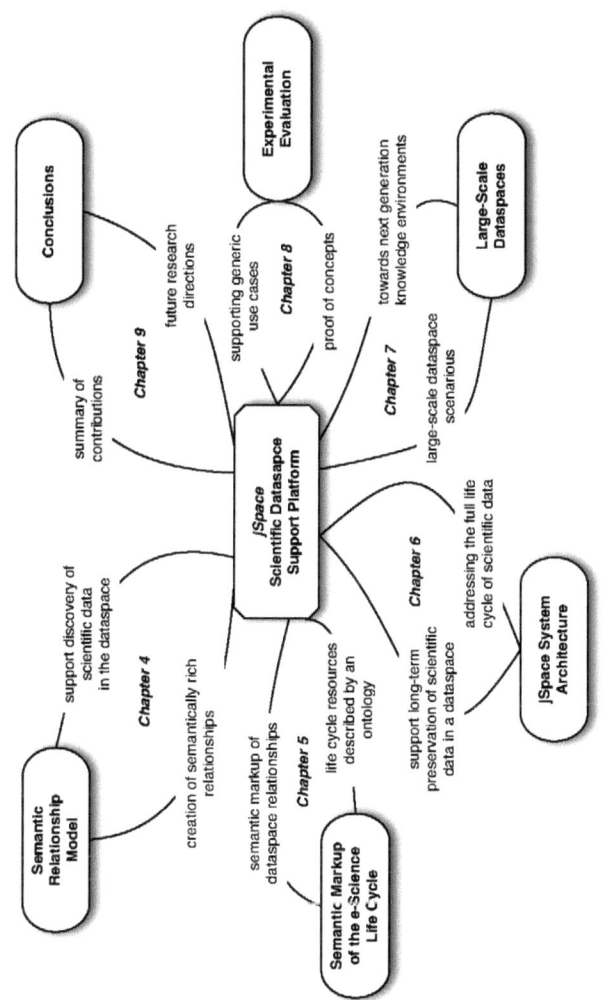

Figure 1.2: Book overview - Dataspace support platform for e-Science.

properties of that ontology. Also other existing methodologies for building an ontology are described briefly at the end of this chapter.

Chapter 6 This chapter discusses first use cases and then elaborates in great detail the architecture of the proposed dataspace-based support platform called jSpace. Also, the EPR-Framework for organizing end point references to datasets managed by the dataspace is introduced in this chapter. A reference implementation is also described within this Chapter.

Chapter 7 This chapter introduces capabilities of the proposed scientific dataspace paradigm for large-scale purposes. This includes the ability to support multiple domains and disciplines. It presents large-scale scientific dataspaces as a semantic data infrastructure that integrates multiple geographically distributed Resource Description Framework (RDF) data stores supporting SPARQL using an existing adaptive distributed SPARQL query processor. It also discusses how scalability can be achieved in the scientific dataspace paradigm. A synthetic large-scale scientific dataspace is generated and test along with exiting technologies. The approach for realizing large-scale scientific dataspaces is described in detail and tested on synthetically generated data.

Chapter 8 This chapter presents an experimental evaluation in several e-Science applications from two different research domains. It discusses for each application how the acting research groups are profiting from the described support platform and its underlying scientific dataspace. Experiences and issues from the evaluation are also discussed in this chapter.

Chapter 9 This chapter summarizes the research done. It outlines the major research contributions briefly discusses open issues and future research directions. Also research publications that have resulted from the research are listed at the end of this chapter.

Appendix A This Appendix exemplifies a life cycle resource (LCR) from a real e-Science application, in particular breath gas analysis for the detection of Molecular-Oriented Detection of Minimal Diseases. It also illustrates the classes and properties for that LCR.

Furthermore each chapter has a short introduction of the problem it addresses and concludes with a summary of the main results and achievements. If applicable, a specific related work section concerning the concepts in each Chapter is presented additionally to Chapter 3, where an in-depth analysis of available large- and small-scale data management systems is elaborated.

Chapter 2

Research Background and Context

> "... there is a lot of data that is collected but not curated or published in any systematic way."
>
> In a talk to the national Research Council in Mountain View on January 11, 2007 given by
JIM GRAY

2.1 Introduction

The term dataspace is differently considered by different research communities. In the data mining and knowledge discovery community, a dataspace is described as an infrastructure for remote data analysis and distributed data mining, where a dataspace is an example of a data web - that is, a web-based infrastructure for working with data [GM02]. The utility of such a dataspace is to reduce the time required to accomplish the data extraction, cleaning, and transforming step as well as the exploratory data analysis step of a data mining task. In the paper, Grossman and Mazucco describe a special data transport protocol for accessing data stored physically as files in distributed dataspace servers on a data web. The data within their dataspace is a distributed collection of columns. Another usage of the term dataspace is given in [IG99], where a dataspace is defined as a three dimensional physical space enhanced with connectivity to the network. Here, a dataspace is populated by classes of mobile objects producing and storing their own data. These physical objects can be queried and monitored on the basis of their properties. Spatial coordinates are the basic points of reference to navigate and query the dataspace. The idea is to provide digital information embedded in physical space for wide range applications such as efficient transportation, environmental protection, and rapid emergency response.

In [FHM05] a new abstraction for information management by describing a platform supporting dataspaces, where a dataspace contains a set of *participants* and a set of *relationships* is introduced. A participant can be any data element. The idea is to raise the abstraction level at which data is managed in order to provide a system managing different data sources, each with its own data model. The concepts are presented in a visionary way, however, their implementation in real application environments has opened new research challenges. Following that different research groups have addressed the realization of dataspace concepts for various application fields, most of them being personal information management.

In this chapter we provide background knowledge on data management, particularly in e-Science applications and introduce the idea of dataspaces. Therefore we first discuss the terms e-Science and e-Infrastructures in Section 2.2, e-Science Portals in Section 2.3 and address Service Oriented Architectures in Section 2.4. Within Section 2.5 and its subsections we then address the term *scientific data management* by splitting it into its four main research challenges. It will not address specific implementations of such solutions, which are discussed deeply as part of the related work in Chapter 3. The idea is to give the reader an overview of available solutions for data management in e-Science applications and comparing them in dimensions of a space of data management solutions.

2.2 e-Science and e-Infrastructures

Science has evolved in the past several decades from an empirical and theoretical approach to one that includes computational simulations and modeling [BGS06], commonly known as enhanced science. The term e-Science is often used to refer to highly collaborative computational science that uses distributed software infrastructures in order to support shared efforts. Technological progress in such e-Science infrastructures have enabled researchers to run complex, computational investigations that include data access, analysis, and largely automated model execution.

Cyberinfrastructures also called e-infrastructures for e-Science [HT05] promise to change the way scientists will tackle research challenges in a number of domains, including earth sciences [RSP07], medicine [The10] and life sciences [Kri04].

The e-Science [HT05, RJS03] and the e-infrastructure [Ste08, Nat07b] programs are initiatives focused on re-energizing and expanding the use of the web and related services to enable more effective research, global collaborations, better utilization of unique resources, and to help address emerging challenges in scientific research. Initial focus was on grid [FKT01a], distributed and high performance computing. Problems of workflow, provenance, middleware, and interoperability were also addressed. A 2007 NSF report added (1) data, data analysis, and visualization, (2) cyber services and virtual organizations, and (3) learning and workforce development to the goals of the e-infrastructure vision [Nat07b]. The first item recognizes that science is becoming increasingly data-driven as low-cost sensors, low-cost storage, faster networks are enabling the construction of large data archives that in turn permit discovery through data mining. The second item above from the NSF report recognizes that science is increasingly conducted by larger teams (big science), requiring researchers with specialized skills not always locally available, resulting in distributed virtual teams. Concurrently a new generation of scientists has grown up with the web and social media and are comfortable and proficient with cyber services. Finally, the third item in the NSF report recognizes that an important role for e-infrastructure is education and workforce development.

2.3 e-Science Portals

An e-science portal is a conventional web portal that sits on top of a rich collection of web-based services that allow a community of users access to shared data and application resources without exposing them to the details of grid or cloud computing [GPC+08]. Due to wireless connectivity improvements and hardware getting mobile and constantly smaller and cheaper, portal developers are facing new challenges. Enormous amounts of data will be produced at a rate never seen before in any field of human activity, requiring next generation e-science portals to cope with and making use of it. Social networking tools are being intensively used by scientists forming virtual scientific communities. This led to an evolution of digital scientific discourse [CWW+08] and other dynamics that drive virtual scientific activities such as research intelligence [She08] and workflow-using e-scientists [GDR07] in a way making it important to preserve scientific experiments on the whole, including primary data, intermediate data, derived data, the processes, and the tools and their versions used. In this context e-Science portals providing tools to enhance collaboration of scientists are gaining more and more attraction within various research domains.

On the one hand an e-Science portal can provide the user a single point of access to information, data, and tools that is available and maintained in some kind of organized and distributed scientific space. On the other hand, by having the scientists in front of the portal conducting scientific experiments, portals can also be utilized as an instrument to capture information about what the scientist is doing, why, and in which context. Once having these crucial semantics about scientific experiments organized in an efficient manner and attached to its corresponding primary and derived data, they could provide deeper insights into studies than someone could grasp from publications or technical reports.

Current leading portal platforms such as the Liferay portal platform [Inc10] are composed of a number of portlets, which can be described as self-contained interactive elements that are written to a particular standard [Yua10]. Since portlets are developed independently of the portal itself, and loosely coupled with the portal, they are apparently SOA (Service-Oriented Architecture).

2.4 Service Oriented Architectures (SOA)

The computational and data intensive applications in the modern grid, cloud, and other distributed computing areas often make use of components (services) as the building blocks of their applications within service oriented architectures (SOA) [ST05].

There are multiple definitions of SOA. The OASIS group and the Open Group have both provided formal definitions. OASIS defines SOA in the SOA Reference Model definition [LME09] as the following:

> *A paradigm for organizing and utilizing distributed capabilities that may be under the control of different ownership domains. It provides a uniform means to offer, discover, interact with and use capabilities to produce desired effects consistent with measurable preconditions and expectations.*

Great progress has been made in the last decade to utilize SOA in grid computing [RBJS03] and recently also in cloud Computing [BBG11, FA11] in order to facilitate the virtualization of heterogenous resources like data sources and computational resources.

Distributed computing from its very beginning, is in practice to serve the scientific community by solving their large and complex problems that involve resources from across organizations [FKNT02a, FKNT02b]. Amongst all these distributed technologies grid computing has played an important role in the last decade in the promotion of scientific and engineering research activities.

Cloud computing has evolved as the new next-generation technology that facilitates the creation of large-scale computing and storage services for hosting application services requiring high availability and performance.

2.5 Key Data Management Tasks in e-Science

The complex interaction in e-infrastructures, which includes people, services, applications, data, instruments, and computational resources has pointed out a strong need for data management.

Data management in e-Science addresses methodologies to provide advanced data-intensive systems and applications. This allows scientists to better determine what data exists and where it resides and thus to achieve greater and faster investigations within scientific studies addressed. The interconnection of the outputs in scientific studies with their corresponding input data and the preservation of the whole data life cycle represents important challenges in this context. By semantically enriching this data life cycle and further, by making it accessible for researchers, it not only helps to discover interesting new datasets and patterns but also enables the studies and experiments to be re-used and reproduced, which is important for a research community and in particular in cross-disciplinary science. We therefore classify the field of scientific data management into four supreme disciplines as follows:

- determining of what data exists and where it resides

- searching the data (space) for answers to specific questions

- discovering interesting new datasets and patterns

- assisted and automated publishing of primary and derived data

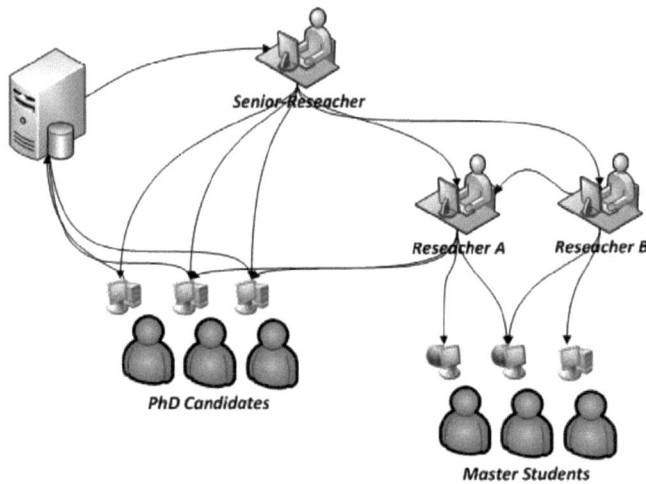

Figure 2.1: Small-scale research lab.

2.5.1 Determining of What Data Exists and Where it Resides

Small-scale research groups consisting of a senior researcher, one or two post-graduate researchers and few PhD- as well as Master-students are very common in the European and the US research landscape (Figure 2.1). Typically every member of the research group is equipped with a workstation where the scientist stores scientific data and experiments he or she is using, creating, modifying, etc. in a way he or she thinks to be appropriate. In some cases there might be a central data-host, where the results of the group are being centrally stored, this however ends up in many cases as a simple big flat directory with lots of un-owned data with dubious content.

Especially when people leave the research group, e.g. a PhD candidate completed his thesis, it is most likely the case that the only pieces of information, results, data, and knowledge left at the research lab is represented by the thesis, publications, or technical reports the scientist has written. It is hardly possible that scientific experiments conducted by a scientist who left the research group some time ago can be re-run, because it is not easy to determine what data exists and where it resides. In many research labs it is even not possible for the composer of an experiment to repeat it after some time had passed away, lets say a year. This is due to lack of efficient scientific data management mechanisms that allow scientists to automatically record what experiments are being conducted including long-term preservation of their corresponding data items.

An instance of the above mentioned research group typically contributes to one or more collaborative multi-national research projects, where meetings are organized at a regular basis. Moreover they participate in scientific communities by attending international conferences and similar meetings. Typically data and knowledge exchange among groups and individuals that participate in such meetings, is based on presentations and publications. However, this simple mechanism of data exchange does not provide enough information to enable other scientists from third parties to re-run experiments not to mention to re-use its corresponding existing data. Therefore it is of utmost importance to enable scientists easy-to-use methods to determine what data exists and where it resides. Key-challenge in this context is the semantic enrichment of data products as well as their intelligent organization within distributed space of data.

Provenance (also referred to as lineage and pedigree) has beed defined by computer scientists in different ways [BSS08, BKT01, SPG05]. However, in the context of service oriented architectures, provenance of a piece of data can be defined as the process that led to that piece of data [GLM04]. Data provenance and process indexScientific!dataspace model represent the two basic views of provenance. Data provenance is the lineage/history of a data product, whereas process provenance is the transformation history that derived this data product. Provenance has been used both in the field of database systems [BKT01, Tan08, ZCL09] as well as in the field of scientific workflows [kep11, tav11, TDG06, vis11].

In the context of scientific data management in e-Science data and process provenance can support determining of what data exists and where it resides. For instance, if the derived result set of a scientific experiment is retrieved, process provenance can lead to the primary dataset that was input to the experiment as well as to the background dataset used to analyze the input dataset producing the derived result set. Data provenance can for instance provide the information needed to determine older versions of a background dataset (e.g. an analytical method). This can be useful if a model error was detected and the scientist wants to determine all data that is affected by the error. Thus provenance represents an important feature, which should be provided in todays scientific data management systems.

2.5.2 Searching the Data (Space) for Answers to Specific Questions

Providing answers to specific questions is a major challenge faced by the scientific data management community. Advanced scientific data management solutions should be equipped with an intelligent search and query interface. The greatest system will not be accepted by the end users, if it lacks a search interface that allows to provide answers to specific questions. Query interfaces that are limited to a single query language might provide great query features. However scientists from various domains, especially from the life science domain will not start to learn a query language in order to be able to use a data management tool that helps to determine what data exists, where it resides and what purpose the data has been collected for. The widely spread keyword query represents the easiest way to search for content. It became very popular due to internet search engines.

Advanced scientific data management solutions should provide search and query features together in an integrated way. This leads to an information gathering task where multiple search phrases and query constructs are submitted to the system in several levels. In between these levels also the combination of multiple keywords and query mechanisms such as logical operators (and, or, etc.) form together specific questions. Such questions might be expressed by scientists as the following:

A "I have detected a model error and want to know which derived data products need to be recomputed."

B "I want to apply an analysis X on dataset Y. If the results already exist, I'll save hours of computation."

C "Is there any study done on the sample probe taken from probands A and B using the analytical method C?"

Through e-Science portals and advanced user interfaces scientists should be supported with the needed tools, which enable users to express search queries visually and in a simple way.

2.5.3 Discovering Interesting New Datasets and Patterns

With an increasing amount of scientific data collections, we face not only problems in terms of their efficient management - it also brings a lot of opportunities, first and foremost the possibility to re-use existing data and experiments for new studies. In conjunction to supreme discipline "determining of what data exists and where it resides" this discipline is more about to discover new datasets and patterns from existing scientific studies that about to determine what data exists. Patterns in this context are regarded as pieces of data that can be used for different purposes, such as a generic data preparation workflow or an analytical methods that executes a standard algorithm or mathematical method of any prepared dataset. Such patterns, if organized in an efficient manner can be useful for the acting scientist and will help to focus on the initial tasks.

In order to provide scientists the possibility to re-use existing data, we need first of all to semantically enrich and preserve the existing data. Well preserved and semantically rich data can only be achieved if the full life cycle of data is addressed [Lyn08]. There are various life cycle models and paradigms developed for different purposes in different domains. For example for data mining [HKP06] there is the *CRISP (CRoss Industry Standard Process for Data Mining)* model [CCK+00, She00], or for software development there is the *Rational Unified Process* [Sta05]. Independent of the domain such models always unify common steps into a clear amount of interconnected phases to be processed successively in an iterative manner.

In e-Science the steps a scientist is conducting while processing an experiment, typically need to be organized into major phases to model an e-Science life cycle paradigm. An individual iteration or a cycle of such a model can be seen as a pattern, which might be re-used if it is well-preserved and made discoverable to a scientific community. At a lower level of abstraction even single phases of an iteration might be re-used, thus also representing patterns. Data being used in a scientific experiment need to be linked to corresponding phases of an e-Science life cycle model and following also need to be preserved within a space of data. This will allow the development of discovery services as well as the utilization of available methods to provide scientists the possibility to discover interesting new datasets and patterns.

The term *e-Science life cycle* is referred to as an iterative model that models all the above mentioned steps or phases of a scientific experiment. It represents the basis of the scientific dataspace paradigm and is deeply discussed in Chapter 4.2 where also the paradigm itself is addressed.

2.5.4 Assisted and Automated Publishing of Primary and Derived Data

Once an analytical method has been applied on some identified and prepared dataset, which as a results produced a number of derived datasets, it is important to make those results with their corresponding input datasets available in some kind of a space of data for other collaborating research groups. This collaborating research groups that might be geographically distributed around the globe will find published data through search and query services offered by a scientific data(space) management system. Such services organize meta data about published data, and relationships among data of different data categories (primary, derived and background).

Data Publication in terms of scientific data management provides publishing data as datasets that allow users to request personalized subsets of the data. The requests can be submitted via an e-Science portal and the replies returned to the scientist, depending on the user's category and his access rights.

Data Publication services are likely to unify this process and make it easy for scientists to register new datasets and for users to find these datasets. Furthermore, to automatically publish derived datasets depending on the actor's settings. In this context focus is set on building semantically rich relationships among primary and derived datasets as well as among corresponding background data that were published. These relationships, managed within a space of data, allow providing answers to specific questions submitted as requests via e-Science portals. Data publication in a dataspace environment will carry this idea much further as it will be possible for users to request data from many repositories at once, and returning relevant primary and derived data as well as available background data from each of them.

2.6 Data-Management Requirements of e-Science Applications on Dataspace Systems

We discuss the requirements of e-Science applications on a dataspace by the means of the dataspace environment components depicted in Figure 2.2.

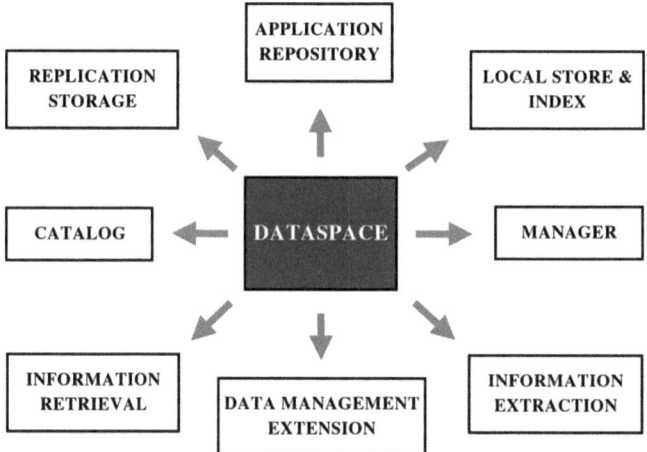

Figure 2.2: Key components of a dataspace support platform for e-Science applications.

Information Retrieval

Querying and searching are two different information retrieval methods and represent one of the main services supported by a Dataspace Management System. In general querying and searching methods should be supported by all dataspace participants independent of their data models as if applied to a single database. A well known and simple search process is the keyword search. The support of such a search method on all participants in a dataspace regardless which data model it contains is a challenging research topic. The development of keyword based search methods for relational and XML databases is faced by the data engineering community [dbx02, GSBS03, HP02]. Supporting a global query functionality allowing to formulate queries on top of all participants in a dataspace, needs intelligent methods for interpreting and translating queries into various languages. Query translation methods present a main research challenge, faced by a large body of research communities [CKS+00, KCKN04].

Information Extraction

Most frequently used data containers are relational databases, object-oriented systems, XML databases, and files. However, the world wide web has become a huge data container and thus a storehouse of knowledge. In order to allow post-processing of data obtained from the web, web information extraction techniques, extracting relevant information from semi-structured web pages should be supported. Extracted contents have to be transformed into structural information and saved locally for further processing. Non-structured web documents need to be classified first using text mining techniques, which map the parsed documents into groups organized with the help of ontologies [HQZW04]. Based on those ontologies a keyword search is possible to retrieve such documents. The third and last kind of documents that can be found on the web are structured documents, which allow easier access and integration due to the rich semantic information included in the data representation.

Data Management Extension
The Data Management Extension component offers features for enhancing low level dataspace components. A dataspace component for example could be a simple fileserver or set of web documents. As these types of data elements have no or only limited data management functions it is a task of the Dataspace Management System to provide additional data management features such as backup, recovery, and replication.

Catalog
It contains a detailed description of all participants included into the dataspace. Besides the basic information about the participant, such as owner, creation date, etc., the description should also include semantic information about the data of the participant. The user should be able to browse the Catalog to get more information about specific data sources. The Catalog can refer to a metadata repository in order to separate basic information from more detailed data descriptions.

Manager
In order to support the above mentioned features, the system needs to be managed by a central component interacting with the user. Besides user authentication, right assignment, and other services, the Manager is responsible for communication with the participants thus serving as an interface between the users and the participants of the dataspace.

Local Store and Index
This component manages the cache containing search and query results so that certain

queries can be answered without accessing the actual data source and supports the creation of query-able association between participants. Also an adequate indexing mechanism to uniquely identify each dataspace participant including their relationships need to be addressed

Replication Storage

It allows to replicate the participant data in order to increase access performance, thus high availability and recovery is supported. Also the replication of relationships needs to be addressed by a dataspace paradigm for e-Science applications.

Application Repository

Here, the users can share data analysis tools, domain specific models, evaluations, etc. that can be applied to the data available in the dataspace. The integration of analytical methods into the dataspace and the creation of relationships among datasets organized as dataspace participants that have either resulted from the usage of the analytical methods or used as input to the analytical method is therefore an important requirement to be challenged by a scientific dataspace.

2.7 Summary

Data management systems for e-Science strongly need to consider relationships that exist among primary, background, and derived data. It has become essentially for any data management system to provide information about how a data product has been derived. Today, there are well organized online libraries that organize scientific publications to a great extent. However, what is missing in this context is a way to create relations from scientific publications and technical reports that mainly describe in some sort a scientific study or experiment to (a) the primary data source used and (b) the analytical methods applied. These relationships need to be semantically enriched (e.g. more information such as why and how a specific study was applied, including contact information about the scientist responsible for caring out the study/research) to allow computer programs to query that knowledge. This challenge is referred in this book to as preservation of the life cycle of scientific data in scientific studies.

It is crucial to provide an efficient and easy way for scientists to share and publish their data including rich semantics about conducted experiment to enable their re-use.

Chapter 3

Related Work

> *"Dataspaces can be viewed as an umbrella for varied efforts in the data management community."*
>
> In: From Databases to Dataspaces, SIGMOD Record, Vol. 34, No. 4,
December 2005 by
MICHAEL FRANKLIN, ALON HALEVY AND DAVID MAIER

Since much of the research in the data management community already falls into the requirements of dataspaces, including areas such as schema mapping, data integration and model management, uniform search over multiple types of data combining structured, semistructured, and unstructured data, approximate query processing, managing and querying uncertain data and its lineage, and stream and sensor data management and processing, we can view dataspaces as an umbrella for these varied efforts. However, as we have discussed in the previous two chapters we believe that the holistic view taken by dataspaces and their supporting platforms lead themselves to a new set of research challenges.

In Section 2.6 we have identified key components of a dataspace support platform for e-Science, each representing own challenges and opening new research topics in the field of scientific data management. This chapter describes how these dataspace features were considered in the current research projects and enterprise solutions of the data management community. Thus, this chapter represents a comprehensive work to survey the state of the art in dataspace features to date. Its sections cover research projects and enterprise solutions that provide at least some of the features a dataspace systems should offer. We classify those systems into two major clusters:

1. Large-scale data management systems are considered in Section 3.1 and

2. Small-scale data management systems, including personal information management systems that provide dataspace features are described in Section 3.2.

In Section 3.3 we present a comparison matrix that indicates, which system provides which of the previously identified dataspace features. As the measure for semantic richness we have defined the utilization of the semantic web technologies. These technologies include the Resource Description Framework (RDF) [rdf04b], a variety of data interchange formats (e.g. RDF/XML, N3, Turtle, N-Triples), and notations such as RDF Schema (RDFS) [rdf04a], the Web Ontology Language (OWL) [owl04] and the SPARQL protocol and query language [PS08, C$^+$08] for semantic wed data sources, all of which are intended to provide a formal description of concepts, terms, and relationships within a given knowledge domain.

3.1 Large-Scale Data Management Systems

3.1.1 DSpace

DSpace [DSp11] is a digital repository software platform that enables organisations to:

- capture and describe digital scholarly research material using a submission workflow module, or a variety of programmatic ingest options

- distribute an organization's digital assets over the Web through a search and retrieval system

- preserve digital assets over the long term

It is typically used to provide an institutional repository for open access scholarly research, theses and learning objects, and a preservation archive. DSpace 1.0 was released by MIT Libraries and HP Labs in November 2000 as open source digital repository software under the BSD license. In 2006 a group of thirteen DSpace committers, technical experts, and other interested parties have met to review the DSpace architecture for the next release [Ock07]. Currently, by mid 2011, approximately 200 research institutions located in 35 countries have registered a live DSpace repository.

DSpace Data Model

Each DSpace site is divided into communities, which can be further divided into sub-communities reflecting the typical university structure of college/faculty, department, or research group. Communities contain collections, which are groupings of related content. A collection may appear in more than one community. Each collection is composed of items, which are the basic archival elements of the archive. Each item is owned by one collection. Additionally, an item may appear in additional collections; however every item has only one collection. Items are further subdivided into named bundles of bitstream. Bitstreams are the name suggests, streams of bits, usually ordinary computer files. According to [Fon11], most items tend to have the following named bundles in practice:

- *ORIGINAL* - the bundle with the original, deposited bitstreams

- *THUMBNAILS* - thumbnails of any image bitstreams

- *TEXT* - extracted full-text from bitstreams in ORIGINAL, for indexing

- *LICENSE* - contains the deposit license that the submitter granted the host organization; in other words, specifies the rights that the hosting organization have

- *CC_LICENSE* - contains the distribution license, if any (a Creative Commons license) associated with the item. This license specifies what end users downloading the content can do with the content

Each bitstream is associated with one *Bitstream Format*, which is a consistent way to refer to a particular file format in DSpace. Bitstream formats can be more specific than MIME types or file suffixes. For example, application/ms-word and .doc span multiple versions of the Microsoft Word application, each of which produces bitstreams with presumably different characteristics [Fon11]. The *support level* indicates how well the hosting institution is likely to be able to preserve content in the format in the future. Each item has one qualified Dublin Core [DCM11] metadata record, which can be entered by end-users as they submit content. It might also be derived from other metadata as part of an ingest process.

Items can be removed from DSpace in one of two ways: They may be "withdrawn", which means they remain in the archive but are completely hidden from view. In this case, if an end-user attempts to access the withdrawn item, they are presented with a "tombstone" that indicates the item has been removed. For whatever reason, an item may also be "expunged" if necessary, in which case all traces of it are removed from the archive. Table 3.1, which is reproduced from the DSpace system documentation in [Fon11], gives an overview of DSpace objects with concrete examples.

Object	Example
Community	Laboratory of Computer Science; Oceanographic Research Center
Collection	LCS Technical Reports; ORC Statistical Datasets
Item	A technical report; a dataset with accompanying description; a video recording of a lecture
Bundle	A group of HTML and image bitstreams making up an HTML document
Bitstream	A single HTML file; a single image file; a source code file
Bitstream Format	Microsoft Word version 6.0; JPEG encoded image format

Table 3.1: DSpace object with concrete examples [Fon11].

DSpace Metadata

DSpace organized three sorts of metadata about archived content:

- *Descriptive Metadata* - by default a qualified Dublin Core metadata schema loosely based on the Library Application Profile [DCM04] is provided, however not restricted to it. The end-user can configure multiple schemas and select metadata fields from a mix of configured schemas to describe items.

- *Administrative Metadata* - includes preservation metadata, provenance and authorization policy data. Most of this is held within DSpace's relational DBMS schema. Provenance metadata is stored in Dublin Core records.

- *Structural Metadata* - This includes information about how to present an item, or bitstreams within an item, to an end-user, and the relationships between constituent parts of the item.

Ingest Process and Workflow

The ingesting process in DSpace is illustrated in Figure 3.1. An "External SIP" is an

XML metadata document with some content files. The "Batch Item Importer" turns the external SIP into an "in progress submission" object. Depending on the policy to which the submission is targeted, a workflow process might be initiated to ensure it is suitable for inclusion in the collection. Once this steps are completed a provenance message containing the filename and checksums of the submission is added to the Dublin Core. After this the "Item Installer" imports the archived item in DSpace.

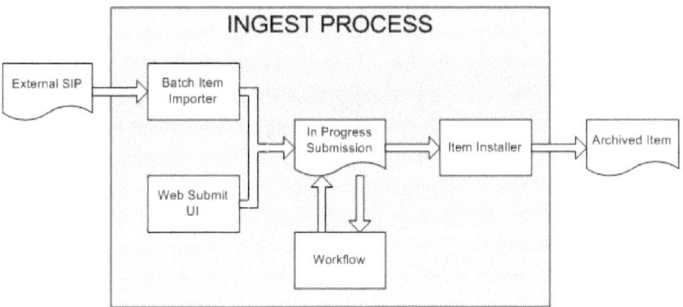

Figure 3.1: Ingest process in DSpace [Fon11].

3.1.2 Storage Resource Broker

The Storage Resource Broker (SRB) is a middleware developed by the San Diego Supercomputer Center (SDSC) [MWR05], which allows accessing heterogeneous distributed data including, filesystems, database systems and archival storage systems. It is also considered as a datagrid [MCS+06a]. SRB uses a metadata catalog service (MCAT) to provide a means to organize data in a collection-oriented view. MCAT provides a set of APIs which allows attribute-based access to data collections and items and provides an execution of distributed applications in order to establish data access at every storage site of the distributed environment. The API offers the capability to information discovery, identification of required data collection data retrieval of various distributed data sources which may be distributed across wide area networks.

SRB Architecture
Data resource access, which is managed by SRB MCAT catalog is provided by the

use of attribute names of the datasets independent from the physical file location, maintaining a location transparency. Datasets collected by SRB include descriptive as well as system metadata [RWM02]. Descriptive metadata represents the contents, whereas system metadata enables location and access control information for collected datasets. Data recorded using SRB is arranged as a hierarchy of collections and subcollections, whereas datasets arranged by the same collection can be distributed across heterogeneous storage environments.

SRB can organize data access to various archival resources such as HPSS, UniTree and ADSM, file systems such as the Unix File System, NT File System and the Mac OSX File System and databases such as Oracle, DB2, and Sybase. Furthermore, it offers a logical representation for storage system descriptions, digital file items, and datasets and supports characteristic facilities, which can be applied in digital libraries, persistent archive systems and collection management systems. SRB offers search capabilities based on user-defined metadata, which managed by MCAT. Figure 3.2 gives an high-lever overview of the architecture of SRB.

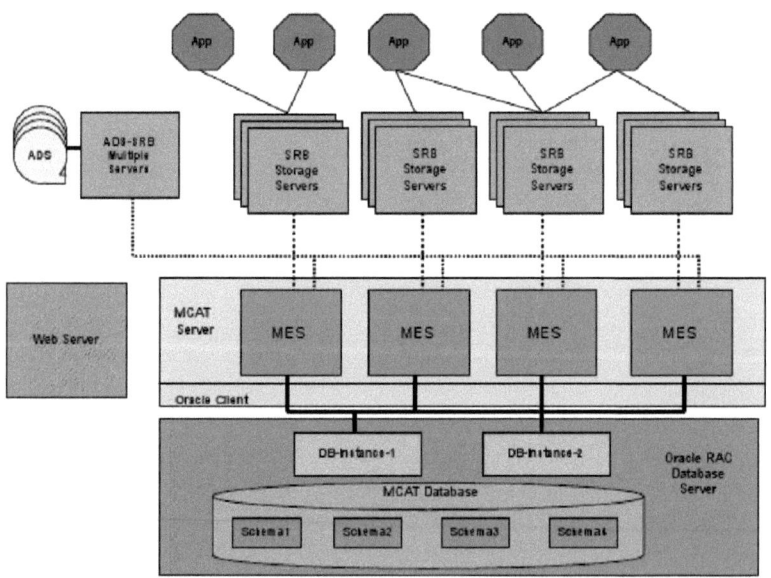

Figure 3.2: SRB architecture [MWR05].

SRB distinguishes among Physical Storage Resources (PSRs) and Logical Storage Resources (LSRs). Depending on the data source, PSRs are defined as following.

- For storage resources with file system interfaces: a PSR is the (hostname, pathname) combination, representing a certain directory path on a certain host.

- For storage resources with database system interfaces: a PSR is the (hostname, database id, table id) triple, representing a host, a database on that host, and a table within that database.

A group of declared PSRs, which for example can be a table in an Oracle database, directory path in HPSS or AIX filesystem, are joined together forming a single logical storage resource (LSR). Client APIs provide references to LSRs. A replication of a dataset, which is linked to a LSR is performed by replicating each PSR.

Access to distributed data resources is provided by a federation of SRB servers, that manage a distinct set of PSRs, and allow SRB servers to act as clients to each other. This enables a client application to access distributed data, even if there is no direct connection between application and the controlling SRB server.

The SRB Server is in constant communication with the clients receiving their requests and sending responses after they have collected the requested information on datasets provided by the MCAT service. SRB represents a federated server system, whereas every SRB server is responsible for a particular group of storage resources. The implementation of the federated SRB server described in [MCS$^+$06b] offers following advantages:

- *Location transparency* - the data can be provided by connecting from one federated SRB Server to another server using a logical attribute name or the item and data collections.

- *Improved reliability and availability* - federated servers manage the data replication being performed on various hosts and storage systems in order to provide efficient load facilities.

- *Logistical and administrative reasons* - while using one single authentication environment, the storage systems can be proceeded on distributed hosts implementing different security mechanism.

- *Fault tolerance* - if one of the storage systems is not available, the global identifier is aware of other available replicas, while automatically linking to them.

- *Integrated data access* - the data access is provided the same way locally as it is for distributed resources establishing an integrated access to distributed data environments.

- *Persistence* - the replicated data elements on different storage systems are represented by their logical attribute names providing the same data item properties and so maintain an unique access management.

The SRB Client offers an user tool that allows communication by sending user requests to SRB Servers. Main client implementations are:

- Windows GUI named InQ [Nat07a] as depicted in Figure 3.3 that offers a file-manager-like interface providing an easy way for users to manage their data stored on SRB. InQ facilitates various management operations such as traditional drag-and-drop operations for a transfer of files, a supports authentication tools managing the access, data replication, metadata management etc. Figure 3.3 shows a view of a data collection within the SRB using the InQ interface.

- A web-based Client, named MySRB [RWM02] that allows secure access and share of distributed data collections and data items stored in SRB. MySRB provided three basic facilities: (1) collection and file management, (2) metadata handling, and (3) access and display of files and metadata.

3.1.3 iRODS - integrated Rule-Oriented Data System

The integrated Rule-Oriented Data System (iRODS) [MRW05] is referred to as a second generation data Grid software [RMH+10]. It is being developed by the SDSC Storage Resource Broker team and its collaborators. iRODS further developed SRBs abstraction concept by providing a data management abstraction process named policy abstraction. iRODS provides a RULE Engine, which is responsible for rule interpretation in order to evaluate how to reply to different client requests. iRODS is open source under a BSD-type license.

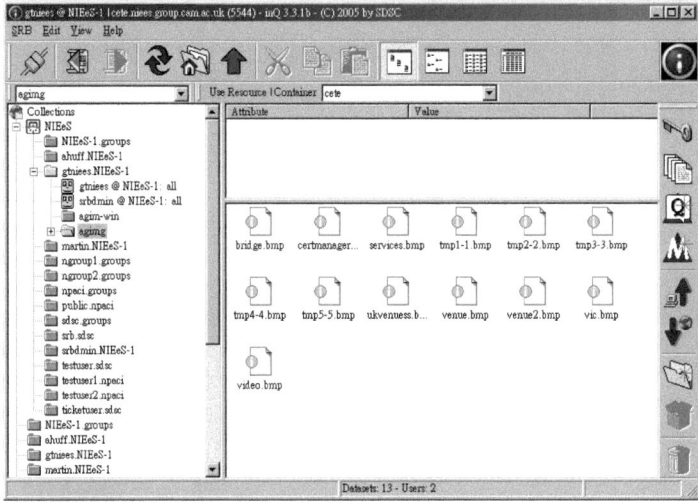

Figure 3.3: InQ SRB Client.

iRODS approach uses Rule Oriented Programming (ROP) for achieving an adaptive middleware architecture. Adaptive middleware architectures typically represent the core of a system enabling easy modifications and adaptions by users in order to accomplish their tasks without the need to perform complex code implementations. All operations that are accomplished using the iRODS system are proceeded as rules in the iRODS rule engine. These rules are initialized by application calls, while controlling performed operations.

Rule Oriented Programming
Rule-oriented programming provides user facilities for modifying and controlling operation functionality of a certain process without relaying on system or application developers. ROP provides small, well-defined operations that perform a certain task called *micro-services* [RMH+10], which are usually defined by system and application programmers. While executing rules users can change task operations by applying micro-services or by modifying already implemented code provided by existing micro-services. Different micro-services can be linked together in order to provide a higher

level facility in form of an action. Each action might be executed in various manner containing a certain number of micro-services. An action provides a particular task name, describing the executed operation, whereas micro-services indicate the corresponding task. There are two mechanisms for finding the best set of micro-services used for an action:

- *Condition* - provides permission control facilities, which can be applied on any micro-service. This mechanism introduces the so called *(action, condition, chain)-triplet* [RMH+10], which implements a rule in iRODS.

- *Priority* - responsible for controlling and testing the order of an executed rule, whereas rules with low number will be executed first.

Each time a set of micro-services is attached to a new action and afterwards performed, the iRODS rule engine calls the corresponding rule service. If there is a failure while executing micro-services, meaning that the corresponding action could not be performed, the next rule with lower number is executed.

iRODS Architecture

The architecture of the iRODs system is illustrated in Figure 3.4.

Main parts of the iRODS architecture are:

- Data Grid infrastructure - provides a client-server application and shared data sources.

- A database system - managing the data properties and operations that can be applied on them.

- A rule system - rules executing management.

The iRODS Rule Engine is implemented on each iRods server. It represents the core of the iRODS Rule System. Depending on the executed rule and its function, a set of micro-services grouped as an action is executed by the rule engine. iRODS distinguishes two kinds of rule classes:

- *System Level rules* - are server side rules responsible for system management facilities. Examples for such policies are: authentication and access control, data management operations such as representation, replication, data extraction, data replacement and distribution, automotive service logging and auditing operations.

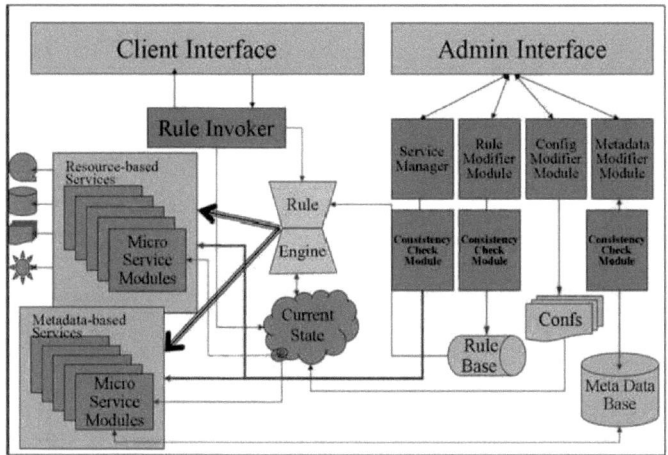

Figure 3.4: The architecture of the iRODS system [MRW05].

- *User Level rules* - are client side rules, which are executed using the *irule* command or the *rcExecMyRule* API. Users can send a request to a server asking to execute a particular set of micro-services. All data items are stored on various iRODS servers where requested operations can be performed.

The *Rule Execution Server* can queue and execute rules attached to actions, which are performed in the background controlled by the *Delayed Execution Service*. Such actions, which consists of different micro-service operations executed successively are for example checksum operations and data replication.

Features of an iRODS System

- **Virtualization -** every data collection or data source communicating with the iRODS system is represented by its logical name, which is independent from the physical location of the data source itself. The Metadata Catalog manages the data associated with the virtual representation of the logical names
- **Data Transport -** iRODS Data can be transferred among distributed storage systems in different manners. The files being moved from one system to another

can be divided into smaller files and so separately transferred (bulk method) or at once (parallel method). The system choses the method automatically depending on the size of the file.

- **Metadata Catalog -** The iRODS metadata catalog is called iCAT. It offers facilities for metadata management. It handles system and user-defined metadata, and abstract physical-to-logical name mappings. iCAT can be implemented using various database management systems.

- **The Rule Engine -** The Rule Engine implements a set of rules which are attached to executed actions that contain a set of micro-services. Any executed task triggers a rule.

- **The Execution Engine -** Micro-service are controlled by the execution engine. A set of micro-services grouped into actions can also be executed remotely. Results are returned after the action has been performed.

- **The Scheduler -** iRODS provides a scheduler, which can delay task executions. iCAT handles the schedule activity.

Since iRODS is to our best knowledge the standard component for digital preservation we have decided to use it as underlying data preservation system within the scientific dataspace support platform presented in this work. The availability of rich client applications and a Java client API for iRODS has also influenced our decision to use iRODS. However, we don't utilize the full power of iRODS in our system. We basically use iRODS to persistently store primary, background and derived datasets of scientific studies. This is further described in following chapters.

3.1.4 IBM Webshpere Information Integrator

WebSphere Information Integrator [Con05], formerly known as DB2 Information Integrator enables applications to access distributed heterogeneous data resources such as DB2 UDB, Oracle, and Sybase, and data resources which do not build upon relational data models such as text files and unstructured documents. Furthermore, it provides access to XML related sources and documents, and data being accessed using Web Service application. WebSphere Information Integrator manages metadata of corresponding data sources using a unified metadata catalog , which is provided by a federation of DB2 UDB database engines. The federated server system offers transparent object virtualization while acting as a virtual database. The system provides wrappers, which communicate with various data resources. A so called wrapper module provides various wrapper implementations for each data source, offering data access facilities used by federated servers in order to establish connections to these data sources, execute different operations and fetch desired data elements as illustrated in Figure 3.5. Each wrapper represents data using a table-like structure [ACD04].

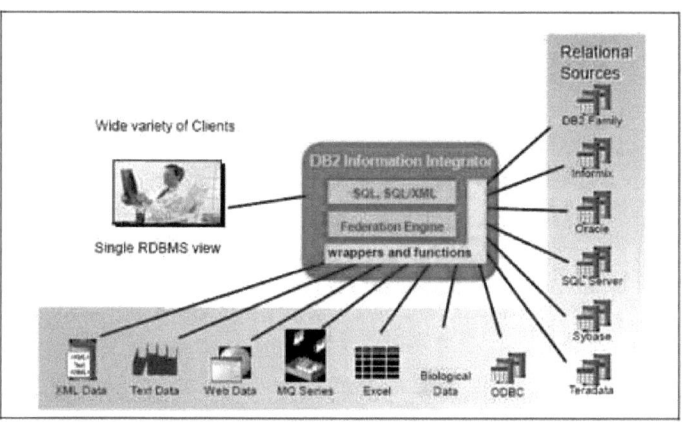

Figure 3.5: WebSphere Information Integrator data federation using wrapper [ACD04].

Overview

Federated databases act as one single database for client applications and users connecting to the database. It implements a metadata catalog identifying and managing the metadata information about data source and their properties, which is used for querying the data sources. Because the data sources are organized as relational tables providing a unified view over such data, the federated server is able to execute SQL queries as if querying a single data source. Non-relational data sources can be mapped to relational data structures allowing unified SQL querying, even if the non-relational sources do not offer SQL facilities [BAB+03]. WebSphere Information Integrator is consolidated four major components as shown in Figure 3.6:

- *Relational wrappers* - implement various wrappers for relational database access such as Sybase, Microsoft SQL Server, Oracle, ODBC, and Teradata data sources.

- *Non-relational wrappers* - implement various wrappers for mapping non-relational data sources, such as XML files, various research files from different domains such as chemistry, biology and genetics.

- *Global catalog* - handles the whole federated system metadata including data items information (operations, tables, attributes) provided by the federated system, metadata information about wrapper module implementations, logical nickname representations, and information about data sources themselves.

- *DB2 Net Search Extender* - provides search mechanism executing SQL queries across various files and documents using automatically updated index data, which is loaded into memory providing effective query results.

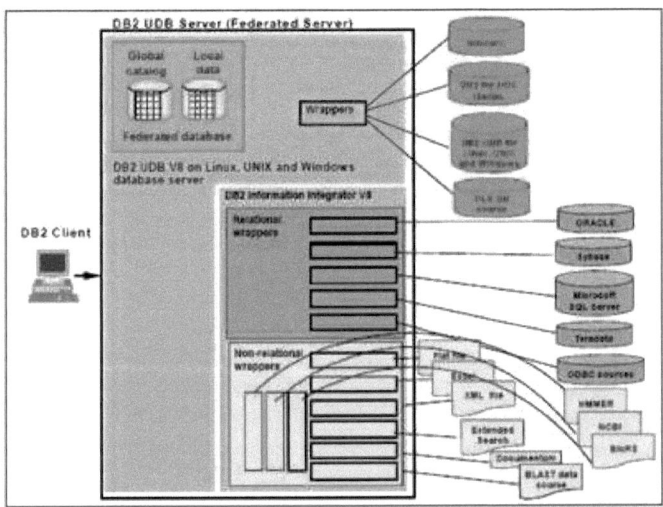

Figure 3.6: WebSphere Information Integrator components [ACD04].

The global catalog provides nickname, index, and attribute information of distributed data sources. This metadata information handled by the global catalog is used by the WebSphere query optimizer to execute SQL queries.

Functions and objects

Four of the following Information Integrator components must be defined in order to provide data access to the Federated Server:

- *Wrappers* - provide data access modules which store information about various data sources and their protocols. Additionally properties and characteristics of distributed data sources are recorded.

- *Servers* - wrappers provide data access to particular sources stored at servers, whereas each server is identified by a DLL statement, which refers to one certain data source.

- *Nicknames* - provide logical abstractions of data sources, which map the data to a local table. Each data source is identified by one unique nickname used by a server for executing SQL queries.

- *User mapping* - user access ID information on server-side is mapped to a password and data source ID used for further connections.

- *Data type mappings* - data types are mapped to DB2 data types in order to query data, whereas wrappers define the mapping facility.

- *Function mappings* - wrappers implement also special DB2 mapping facilities.

- *Global catalog* - handles the whole federated system metadata information, including data source information (attributes and operations), metadata information about wrapper module implementations, logical nickname representations, and information about data sources and mapping functions.

Federated Server

Each DB2 server having a running WebSphere Information Integrator represents a *federated server*, which can be implemented on Unix, Linux and Windows operating systems. Client applications have integrated data access across distributed data sources, which are handled as a single unified data source, having a transparent format, a location and executed operations. The WebSphere Information Integrator provides facilities for manipulation of XML sources and documents. The query results can be usual SQL statements or XML documents, which can be mapped into XML Schema. Federated Servers can be accessed through usual database or service clients, which if preformed remotely are named pushdown operations. Data source registration on the WebSphere Information Integrator is provided using following steps:

- *Registration of the wrapper module* - each wrapper is registered in the database providing data source access information.

- *Data source-server definition* - each data source needs to be declared as server of the federated system.

- *Authentication information* - registration of remote authentication facilities provided by user mappings

- *Federated system connection* - the SQL query statements should be directly executable on each data source.

- *Definition of data type mappings* - additional mapping definitions should be provided if required to be applied on particular data sources.

- *Nickname and table identification* - each data source refers to a corresponding nickname, which identifies the data sources.

There is additional nickname metadata information, named *column options*, describing data source column objects, which can provide federated servers with further information. This metadata used by wrappers indicates how the column data should be handled. Each data source contains a set of index information declared as the *index specification*. Each time a new nickname is registered, the metadata global catalog saves information about index specification of data sources adding corresponding table information about the sources.

WebSphere Information Integrator provides access to multiple data sources as listed in Table 3.2 below.

3.1.5 Chimera

Chimera [FVWZ02] is a virtual data system, which provides a workflow management tool. It mainly consists of a Virtual Data Catalog, used for derived process organization and a Virtual Data Language Interpreter (VDL), which understands user requests and

Type	Data source
Relational data source	DB2, Informix, Oracle, Teradata, Microsoft SQL Server, ODBC, OLEDB
Prepared Data	BioRS, BLAST, Documentum, Entrez, HMMER, IBM Lotus Extended Search, Microsoft Excel, flat (table-structured) filed, XML

Table 3.2: Supported data sources in WebSphere IBM Information Integrator.

is able to execute SQL statements on generated datasets. VDL is location transparent, storing the workflow related definitions in the Virtual Data Catalog. The main idea is to provide semantic information about how a dataset is derived from various data sources and which operations were performed on such data, uncovering relationships among these datasets.

The virtual data system offers different data management facilities, which can be executed on generated datasets, such as data replication, restore or redefine operations over already defined data items. Chimera virtual data catalog represents and manages all processes and operation as well as their characteristics applied on derived data. Figure 3.7 shows the architecture of Chimera. Virtual Data Language acts as an inter-

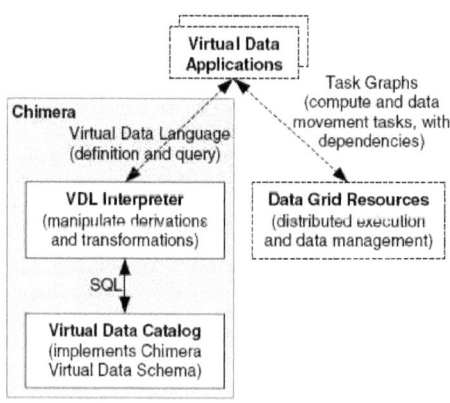

Figure 3.7: Chimera architecture [FVWZ02].

face between application calls and Chimera operations. It provides facilities for common database definitions and query declarations, which can be performed on databases. Virtual data applications can use Chimera information in conjunction with components implemented within a data Grid in order to deploy application requests. Query results can be represented in a direct graph structure specifying the virtual relations among data. The most important *entities of interest* in Chimera are:

- *Transformation* - indicates a program execution information by describing the attributes of the execution process and its properties e.g. a program name, location, version.

- *Derivation* - indicates a transformation execution information by describing the dataset information being related to performed transformations e.g. dataset name, execution time, property values.

- *Data object* - indicates an item name generated by a derivation process, representing a logical file name abstracting from an actual location of a file. Any data object is associated with a set of metadata describing the object.

The information about a derivation or transformation process can be provided by a user or generated form different access interfaces. A logical transformation is identified by its unique name, the namespace defining the range of the name, and a number of the transformation version. It might include several derivations, representing various transformation parameter values. VDL defines two data derivation operations, which are stored in the virtual data catalog, when executed by the language interpreter: (1) Transformation (TR) generates an object, and (2) Derivation (DV) generates an invocation.

The virtual data language builds upon SQL language and provides SQL query expressions over transformations and derivations by using metadata describing logical file names and transformation, derivation, as well as application names.

3.1.6 myExperiment

myExperiment [RGS07] provides a virtual research platform for workflow management in e-Science applications. It support collaborative work among scientists enabling them to exchange their knowledge more efficiently. It enables scientist to view workflows from other scientist or research groups as well as to publish their own research results in form of workflows. myExperiment is implemented as a website. It is available at *www.myexperiment.org*. The two main myExperiment components are users and contributions [GDR07]. Contributors represent workflow objects that can be organized using the myExperiment platform. Each user has access to a private section, containing a users personal information and a public section, containing information that users share with each other. There are several types of contributions as listed in the following:

- *Workflows* - represent the main objects in myExperiment. Statistic information about workflows such as view and download count is recorded.

- *Groups* - users can create and join groups, which have a title and a description. All groups are declared as public.

- *Packs* - are a set of objects or contributions.

- *Files* - various files can be saved in myExperiment.

- *Experiments* - workflows are invoked within experiments. Every experiment includes a description, a name, and a job. A job can have a different running status.

- *Site announcements* - managed by site administrators.

- *Ownership* - contributions can be shared depending on the type definition, which can be *public*, *friend* or *group*.

myExperiment offers user authentication facilities provided by OAuth, which is an open protocol to allow secure API authorization in a simple and standard method from desktop and Web applications. It is generally a protocol service, which allows users to specify and register keys and attach privileges to them.

Object resources are also known as *contributables* e.g. files, workflows and packs. myExperiment distinguishes between two different levels of object abstraction:

- *high-level* - some of the contribution metadata is not displayed and

- *low-level abstraction* - all recorded metadata can be viewed

It further defines the *Contribution Model* [Ale08] with following structural constraints:

- *Contributions* - represent objects and may have one contributable abstraction, providing following resource details: contributor id and type, date, attached permissions, and number of views and downloads.

- *Contributables* - unique abstraction name of one contribution. Only files, workflows and packs may appear as contributables.

- *Contributors* - can own many contributions, and specify permissions and policy definitions.

Contribution tables consists of *types* and *ids* while using *contribution ids* to specify relations between contributables and contributors.

myExperiment also supports resource versioning, which indicate how a particular resource was deployed over a period of time. Figure 3.8 illustrates the myExperiment website.

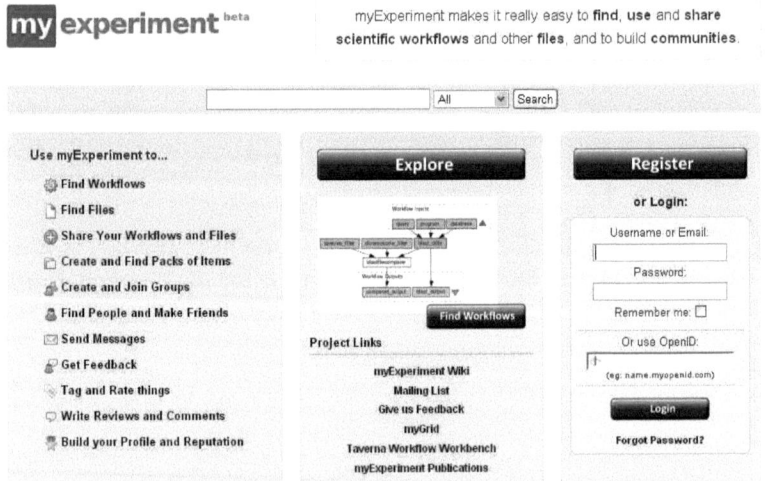

Figure 3.8: The myExperiment user interface.

3.1.7 PAYGO

PAYGO [MCD+07] is a data integration architecture inspired by the concept of dataspaces [FHM05] for achieving web-scale data integration emphasizing pay-as-you-go data management. The pay-as-you-go principle (the cloud principle as well) states that the system needs to be able to incrementally evolve its understanding of the data it encompasses as it runs. In PAYGO there are sets of schemata that are clustered into topics. Semantic mappings among sources are the core of the data integration system. Queries are posed as keywords and are routed to the relevant sources.

The PAYGO architecture evolves traditional data integration techniques to handle the scale and heterogeneity of structured Web data. Table 3.3, which was reproduced from [MCD+07] provides a comparison of the components in traditional data integration and the PAYGO architecture.

Traditional Data Integration	PAYGO Data Integration
Mediated Schema	Schema clusters
Schema mappings	Approximate mappings
Structured queries	Keyword queries with query routing
Query answering	Heterogenous result ranking

Table 3.3: Comparison of components in traditional data integration and the PAYGO architecture [MCD+07].

Instead of a mediated schema as used in traditional data integration, PAYGO has a repository of schemata that are clustered by topic. Schema mapping in PAYGO is fundamentally approximate, with a simple statement that two schemata are related to each other and belong to the same cluster in the extreme case. Unlike a traditional data integration system where schemata are mapped to a single mediated schema, PAYGO proposes that schema mappings can exist between any pair of sources. Instead of query answering, PAYGO involves ranking.

An instantiation of the PAYGO data integration architecture developed at Google is shown in Figure 3.9. A metadata repository stores all schemata and mappings that are known by the system. It also tracks the lineage of the mappings in the system such that when a mapping is changed, other mappings that depend on it are reconsidered. For schema mapping the Corpus-based schema matching technique [MBDH05] is used. The query answering component generates a structured query from the given query, routes it to the relevant sources, and then ranks the answers coming from the multiple sources.

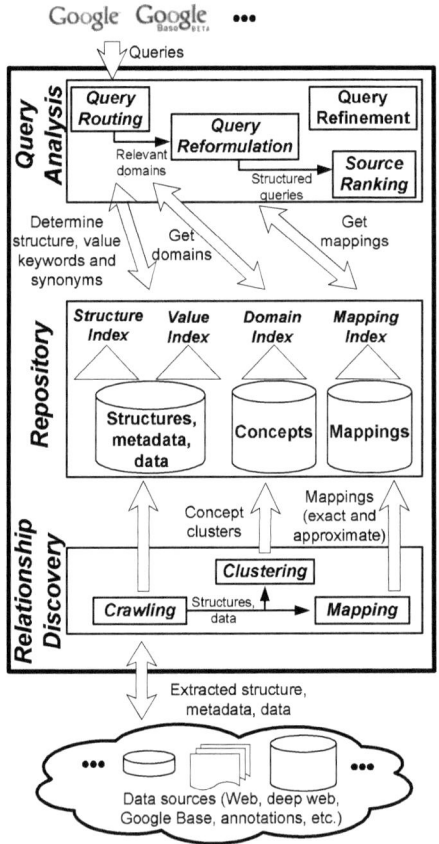

Figure 3.9: An instantiation of the PAYGO data integration architecture. [MCD[+]07]

3.1.8 Linked Data

Linked Data [HB11, BHBL09] provides a flexible publishing paradigm, which makes it easier for data consumers to discover and integrate data from large numbers of data sources. In particular, Linked Data provides:

- A unifying data model based on RDF, which has been especially designed for the use case of global data sharing.

- A standardized data access mechanism by committing itself to a specific pattern of using the HTTP protocol. It allows data sources to be accessed using generic data browsers and enables the complete dataspace to be crawled by search engines.

- Hyperlink-based data discovery. This allows hyperlinks to be set between entities in different data sources, which enables Linked Data applications to discover new data sources at run-time.

- Self-descriptive data. Linked Data eases the integration of data from different sources by relying on shared vocabularies and making the definitions of these vocabularies retrievable.

According to [HB11] a significant number of individuals and organizations have adopted Linked Data as a way to publish their data, not just placing it on the wen but using Linked Data to ground it int the Web, which results in a global dataspace that the authors call the *Web of Data* [BHBL09].

In order to connect existing data management system and business applications, Linked Data provides the addition of extra technical layer to connect these systems into the *Web of Data*. *Publishing patterns* provide the mechanisms for the integration of these systems and applications. Figure 3.10 shows the most common Linked Data publishing patters in the form of workflows, from structured data of textual content through to Linked Data published in the Web [HB11]. Basically, publishing relational data as Linked Data is realized with the use of relational database to RDF wrappers. Static input data, such as CSV files, Excel spreadsheets, XML files or database dumps are converted using RDFizing tools [rdf08] in order to be published as Linked Data. Textual document can be passed through a Linked Data entity extractor such as Calais [cal11] and Ontos [ont11], which annotate documents with the Linked Data URIs of entities references in the documents.

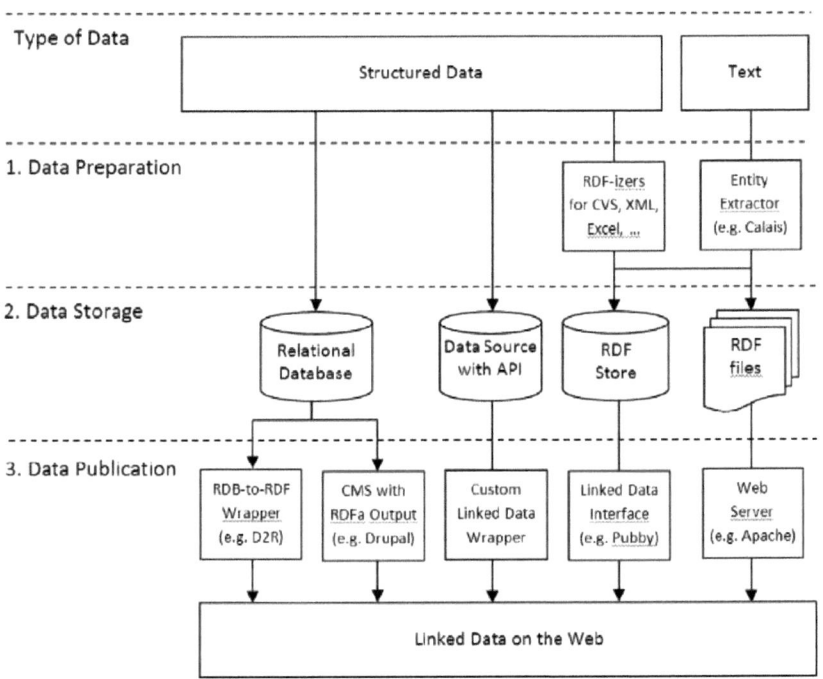

Figure 3.10: Linked Data publishing options and workflows [HB11].

3.2 Small-Scale Data Management Systems

3.2.1 SEMEX - Platform for personal information management and integration

The *SEMEX* system (short for SEMantic EXporer) [DH05, CDH+05] is a platform for personal information management and integration focusing on desktop search. It offers search-by-association, thereby taking a step towards the vision of the Personal Memex [BW45]. To enable browsing by association, Semex constructs a database of objects and associations between them. The database is created automatically from information extracted from multiple types of data sources. It provides a single logical view of the personal information of a user based on meaningful objects and associations.

SEMEX Architecture

Figure 3.11 provides an overview of the architecture of SEMEX. SEMEX has three submodules: (1) the domain management module plays the central role by providing and managing the domain model; (2) the data collection module is responsible for data extraction, integration, cleaning and indexing; and (3) the data analysis module analyzes data for search and browsing [DH05].

The system provides access to data stored in multiple applications and sources, such as the typical personal information groups like emails, address book contacts, pages in the user's Web cache, documents (e.g. Latex, Bibtex, PDF, Word, and Powerpoint) in the user's personal or shared file directory, and data in more structured sources (e.g. spreadsheets and databases). SEMEX creates a data repository of objects and associations. The repository is represented as RDF store, Jena [jen11] is used to retrieve data from the store. In order to keep the information in the repository up to date, SEMEX periodically crawls the desktop to extract instances and associations in an incremental mode.

By extracting data from multiple sources SEMEX creates instances of classes in the domain model. The domain model includes a set of predefined classes such as `Person`, `Publication`, and `Message`, and associations such as `AuthorOf`, `Cites`, `Sender`. In SEMEX personal information sources are integrated using a mediation schema over a set of personal information sources defined by a domain ontology. There are multiple modules for the extraction of associations. In order to combine all these associations, SEMEX automatically reconciles multiple references to the same real-world object. All

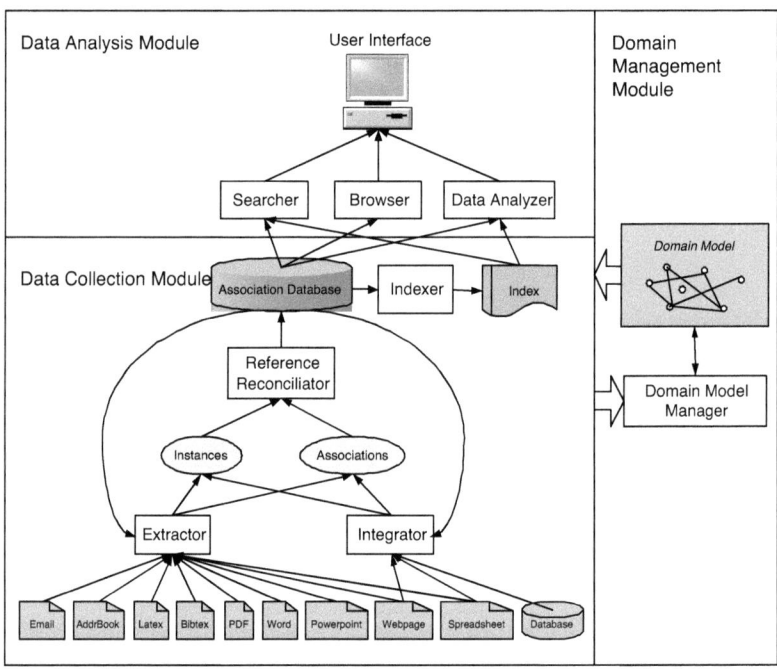

Figure 3.11: The architecture of SEMEX [DH05].

this information can be browsed and queried through the domain model. It offers an interface that combines browsing and querying options. Figure 3.12 shows a sample screenshot from browsing the SEMEX data repository. Keywords can be typed into the search box and **SEMEX** returns all the objects that are somehow associated with the keyword. It classifies the resulted objects into their classes (Person, Publication, etc.)

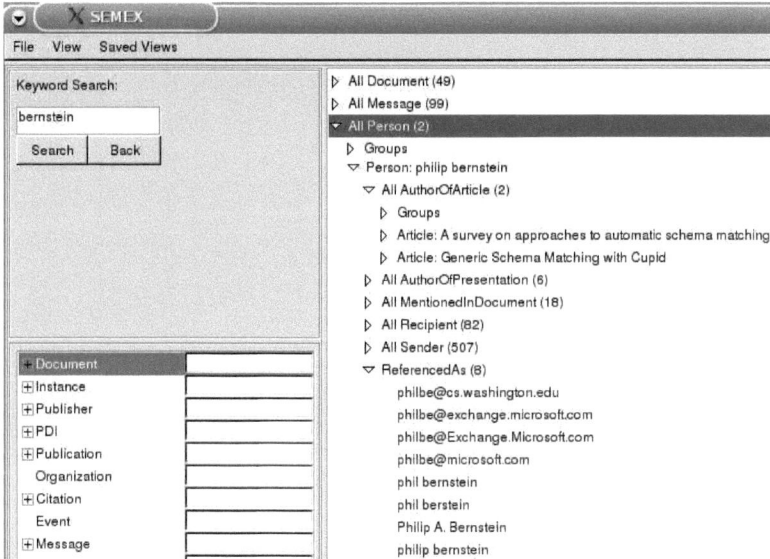

Figure 3.12: A sample screenshot of the Semex interface [CDH+05].

The data repository is further used to enable on-the-fly information integration. This is done by leveraging the logical view of personal information provided by the SEMEX system. In particular, the logical view is used as an anchor into which eternal data sources are integrated on-the-fly. It takes as an input the domain model and an external schema and generates a set of queries such that evaluating the queries on the external data source will generate a set of class and association instances of the domain model [DH05].

3.2.2 *iMeMex:* A Personal Dataspace Management System

iMeMex, which is referred to as being *a unified solution to personal information management* in [BpDG+07] was influenced by the vision of a personal information management system named *Memex* (memory extender). *iMeMex* is a software platform which handles a *personal dataspace* of an individual. Personal dataspace contains all the personal information stored by one certain user [BpDG+07].

iMeMex provides data management functionalities such as querying, updating, performing backup and recovery operations. Furthermore, *iMeMex* provides a solution to close the gap between the structure of the information inside files and the outside structure of the information provided by file and folder hierarchies. Key to this approach is to represent all available data using a single graph data model, called *iDM* [DS06].

iMeMex Architecture

The iMeMex software platform provides an own data model called *iMeMex Data Model* (iDM) and a new query language called *iMeMex Query Language* (iQL). The idea is to represent unstructured, semi-structured and structured data inside a single model. *Resource Views* represent data elements within the iDM and allow to be linked to each other in directed graph structures. *iMeMex* includes two important sublayer: *iQL Query Processor* and *Resource View Manager*. The main task of the *iQL Query Processor* is parsing iQL queries and creating concepts how to query them. iMeMex introduces a logical layer, called *Resource View Layer* that provides an abstraction from underlying substructure and data sources such as file systems, email servers, network shares, iPods, RSS feeds, etc. Figure 3.13 shows illustrates the architecture of iMeMex. The *Resource View Manager* (RVM) includes four major components: (1) Data Source Proxy, (2) Content2iDM Converters, (3) Replica&Indexes Module, (4) Synchronization Manager.

The *Data Source Proxy* is connected to various types of subsystems. It implies a set of *Data Source Plugins* that are used for data representation from different subsystem types into the form of the iDM graph structure. Currently iMeMex provides a plugin set for file systems, IMAP email servers and RSS feeds. The *Content2iDM Converter* additionally converts the content information extracted from the data source proxy component into iDM graph structure establishing further information provided by the structure of the iDM subgraphs. iMeMex offers at the moment converters for XML and LATEX.

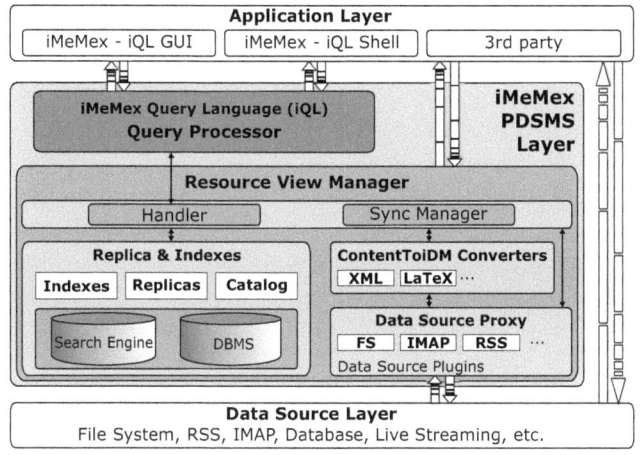

Figure 3.13: The *iMeMex* architecture [DS06].

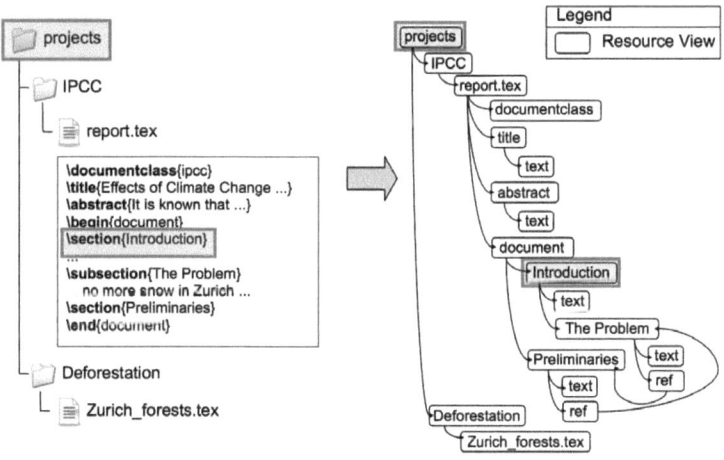

Figure 3.14: iDM represents heterogeneous personal information as a single resource view graph [Dit06].

The *Replica&Indexes Module* contains a *Resource View Catalog* All resource views are registered within that catalog. For each resource view component this module offers an option to create a replica and/or an index of the data source. A replica component is responsible for creating copies of data resources within the RVM and could be used for replication of all resource views that were extracted from remote data sources. Because of the trade-off between the distributed data that has to be queried and then shipped versus local data the iMeMex system must consider various strategies while creating replicas. The main task of the index module is to create particular data structures in order to improve the look-up times. A created index of the resource views can not retrieve the original content information of the components that were deployed while creating the index, and therefore the replication itself is not provided by the indexing task.

The *Synchronization Manager* provides a persistent update function for all registered data sources. After registration of a new data source in the RVM, the *Synchronization Manager* analyzes data content of the data source and provides information about the definition of created resource views to the *Replica&Indexes Module*. The *Synchronization Manager* scans permanently the data sources, registered by the RVM layer, checking for updates while synchronizing the catalog with the generated indexes and replicas.

iDM is used as a representation model for all kind of data including unstructured, semi-structured and structured data within a basic graph model establishing resource views that are linked to each other forming directed graph structure. Figure 3.14 illustrates how iMeMex maps heterogeneous personal data into a single resource view graph.

3.2.3 Google Desktop Search

Google desktop search is a freeware desktop search tool propagated by Google. It features a Google-like Web interface that offers an easy way to search for personal information.
The tool provides a keyword search mechanism over a variety of personal resources including emails, file directories, video and music files, photos, viewed web pages, and more by indexing the supported data types [Inc08b]. It generates file and other relevant user data copies every time a user views the data allowing the user to access the stored

information afterwards. As a result, a user can access and find needed information even after it has been deleted.

The Google Desktop tool is running a local Web server which listens to port 4664. The application handles only local request in order to provide more security [AAS07]. Figure 3.15 shows the Google desktop search interface.

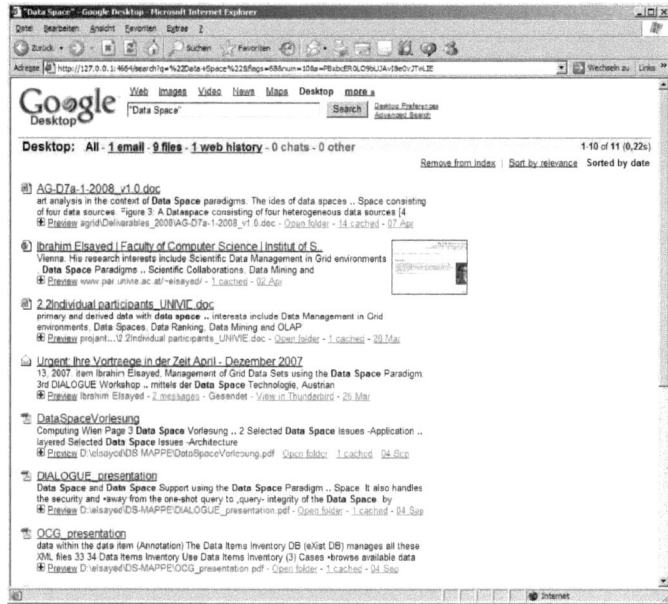

Figure 3.15: The Google Desktop interface.

3.2.4 Phlat and Windows Desktop Search

Phlat [CRDS06] is a search system for personal data providing an user interface that enables a label facility for personal data such as file directories, personal audio and video files, email, and more. A basic keyword search in conjunction with a specification of particular properties of saved personal information provide effective search results. Additionally, users can define personal information metadata, which describes the stored data more in detail and helps achieve better results of desired information.

Design Principles

The Phlat design introduces several core principles and criteria to be supported by Phlat as listed in the following:

- *Unify text entry and filtering* - a user can perform a query statement by using a filter, a keyword, or both.

- *Current search criteria has to be persistently visible* - all used filter, keywords and the order of returned search results, while performing searches, has to maintain visible for users at any time.

- *Provide rapid query iteration* - effective search results and sophisticated result updates should be provided.

- *Allow iteration based on recognition* - the applied results should provide a reuse facilities to explore the result more in detail.

- *Allow for abstraction across property values* - a user should be able to perform a unified query on various personal information independent of the underlying data types.

- *User Interface has to support both tagging and filtering* - one unified interface design should provide filter and tag facilities.

- *Integration with file system/email operations* - common data manipulation facilities such as copy/paste, drag and drop should be supported by the user interface.

Architecture

Phlat is implemented in Microsoft Visual C# and builds upon the Windows Desktop Search engine. All user personal information such as file directories, emails, audio and video files, including web-related information such as caches are indexed. Furthermore a declaration of user-defined metadata of the stored personal information enriches the index and provide more sophisticated search results.

The Phlat user interface consists of three main areas as illustrated in Figure 3.16:

The *Query Area* provides the basic information about search and query properties, indicating a status and a quality of the results. Various property filters can be attached to any query affecting the displayed results.

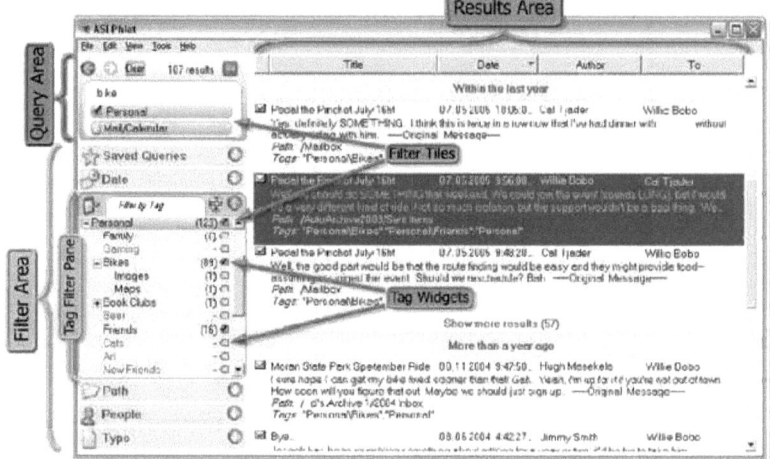

Figure 3.16: The Phlat interface [CRDS06].

The *Filter Area* consists of six filters: *Tags, Saved Queries, Path, People, Date, and Type*. Every filter displays its property value, filtering the provided query results. Filter area provides various types of filter abstractions, which can be associated with particular data elements more sophisticated search results.

The *Results Area* presents results in a table-like view, displaying properties above the actual results. Results can be ordered by each property represented by a column, consisting of the query result, the path directory of shown results, and additional tags. Users may browse through displayed search results and use them for defining new queries.

3.3 Summary

An overview of the above described large and small scale data management systems providing some dataspace features is given in Table 3.4. The described projects can be related to the work of this book. jSpace is the name of the scientific dataspace system developed as part of this work. It is discussed deeply within the next chapters. However, we briefly relate jSpace with the efforts and projects of the previously described projects.

Scale	Data management system	#
Large scale system	DSpace	1
	Storage Resource Broker (SRB)	2
	integrated Rule-Oriented Data Systems (iRODS)	3
	IBM Webshpere Information Integrator	4
	Chimera	5
	myExperiment	6
	PAYGO	7
	Linked Data	8
	jSpace	9
Small scale system	SEMEX - Platform for personal information management and integration	10
	iMeMex - Personal Dataspace Management System	11
	Google Desktop Search	12
	Phlat& Windows Desktop Search	13

Table 3.4: Large and small scale data management systems providing dataspace features.

Influenced by the vision of dataspaces introduced in [FHM05] the personal dataspace management system iMemex with an own data model, abstracting from underlying substructures of data sources, and a new query language is presented in [BpDG+07]. However, this system is limited to personal information management, handling data of an individual while not considering dataspace management facilities for large scale purposes. Another personal information management system is SEMEX [DH05, CDH+05]. It integrates personal information and accesses data sources using wrappers. The schemas of the data sources are matched and mapped automatically to the domain model. According to [HKF+09], SEMEX can be seen as as domain-specific dataspace proposal that relies on domain knowledge to match schemas to the given integration schema and reconcile references automatically

Other discussed projects like iRODS [MRW05], SRB [MWR05], and the IBM's commercial product Websphere Information Integrator [Con05] have considered some dataspace concepts such as a metadata catalog and a logical name abstraction concepts in their architecture; however key dataspace paradigms, like (a) support for creation of semantically rich relationships among participants and (b) semantic search and query capabilities based on these relationships, are not taken into consideration.

PAYGO [MCD+07] represents a large-scale, multi domain dataspace proposal that offers limited integration and provides keyword-based search facilities for the deep Web. Another approach towards evolving the Web into a global dataspace represents Linked Data [HB11]. It provides a publishing paradigm in which not only documents, but also data, can be a first class citizen of the Web, thereby enabling the extension of the Web with a global dataspace based on open standards - the *Web of Data*. DSpace [DSp11] represents a large-scale open-source solution for the preservation of digital contents, designed especially for universities and libraries but not limited to them.

A first approach towards realization of dataspaces regarding the Grid is given in [EBT06]. The Grid Physics Network Virtual Data System, formerly known as Chimera [FVWZ02], provides a virtual data system for managing and tracking different aspects of various data transformations and its results in workflow (composition of services) environments stored in a virtual data catalog, where the produced data and the steps being used to produce the data can be later retrieved for further analysis. This approach, compared to the *e-Science life cycle* data model that will be discussed in the next Chapter, is more dataset oriented managing the workflow information, while the Life Cycle data model aims on describing the entire relationship information while performing scientific studies, including information on researchers, research goal specifications, data preparation tasks, data analysis tasks, and produced results, which can be published for further discovery and experimentation.

myExperiment [GDR07] provides a virtual research platform for workflow management in e-Science applications, allowing scientist to easy the collaborative work and exchange their knowledge more efficiently. It enables scientist to view workflows from other scientist or research groups as well as publish their own research results. However, the main work here is focused on knowledge exchange in form of workflows with no regards of tracking down background data source information associated with scientific experiments. Both systems, Chimera and myExperiment are targeting to model relationships from primary and derived data through collecting provenance data of executed workflows. However, dataspace search and query features are not tightly focused.

In addition to the above mentioned systems, there are a number of research institutions around the world influenced by the vision of dataspaces working on their dataspace realization and publishing own approaches towards rising the abstraction level at which data is managed. We summarize most important additional approaches in the following very briefly. Most of them are considering dataspaces in term of personal information management. For example Yukun et al. describe in [LM08] a personal dataspace management system, named *OrientSpace*, which implements data integration and data query functions. They introduced the *CoreSpace framework*, which represent a subspace of the personal dataspace containing only objects that are frequently accessed by the owner. The data model used is based on the vertical data model, which takes a vector to describe attributes of an object (ObjectID, AttributeName, AttributeValue). Another dataspace management approach is proposed by Lei et al. in [JZY08]. It introduces the *Galaxy* data model, which is an extension of the iMeMex Data Model in order to better consider security issues, primarily access policies.

Comparison Matrix

The following table shows a comparison matrix of the above described systems and tools with regard to key-dataspace features. The systems are identified by their number given in Table 3.4.

Dataspace feature	1	2	3	4	5	6	7	8	9	10	11	12	13
Semantic Integration			x				x	x		x	x		
Advanced querying			x				x	x	x	x	x		x
Enriching keyword						x	x			x	x	x	
Property search							x	x	x	x			
Semantic relationships							x	x	x	x	x		
Browse by relationship							x	x	x	x	x		
UpdateMechanism		x	x	x	x	x				x	x	x	x
Full control of the data		x	x				x		x		x		
Automatically updates									x			x	
Schema first				x			x	x	x	x	x		
No schema		x	x		x								
Ranking query results						x	x	x			x		x
RDF								x	x	x			
OWL								x	x	x			
MetadataCatalog		x	x	x	x		x	x	x	x	x	x	x
Own data model		x		x			x	x	x	x	x	x	x
Keywordsearch		x	x	x	x	x	x	x	x	x	x	x	x
Large scale dataspaces		x	x	x	x	x	x	x					

Table continues on the next page.

Dataspace feature	1	2	3	4	5	6	7	8	9	10	11	12	13
Securityissues		x	x	x	x	x			x			x	x
Managing sub-dataspaces									x				
Role management		x	x	x	x	x	x	x	x				
Usergroups		x	x	x	x	x	x	x				x	x
Registration wizard			x						x			x	
Learning features							x						
Autonomic features				x									
Own query language		x											

Table 3.5: Dataspace features comparison matrix.

Part II

Methodology and Concepts

Chapter 4

Semantic Relationships among Dataspace Participants

> *"There is a reciprocal and iterative relationship between the world of ideas, hypotheses and mental constructs and the world of data or observations."*
>
> In: *Realising the power of data-intensive research (Draft 1.1),*
> September 2010 by
> MALCOLM ATKINSON AND DAVID DE ROURE

4.1 Introduction

In the data management community many different (data) models were developed over the past decades in order to handle the emerging semantic heterogeneity of rapidly increasing data resources and the need of interconnected usage in many scientific applications. The demand for managing multiple data sources with different data models is also rapidly expanding. Modern collaborations in science are very often based on large scale linking of databases that were not expected to be used together when they were originally developed.

Within the distributed database community, database integration approaches traditionally focus on structural heterogeneity. However, in many scientific applications, there is additionally a strong demand to solve problems of semantic heterogeneity.

Therefore the need for intelligent management systems providing access to those heterogeneous and often distributed data sources and allowing to search, query, and share them as a single information source, has never been greater.

Web and grid[1] technologies were influenced by the achievements and the progress made within the data management community. Since the late 1990's, the semantic web [BLHL01] has being introduced as the new web generation for computer-based exploitation, in front of the human-based exploitation. Therefore several languages have been defined as W3C standards for representing data (XML [xml11]), resources (RDF [rdf04b]), and knowledge (OWL [owl04]).

In parallel grid technology has traversed since the 1990's different phases of generations – from *computational grid* [Fos01] (concerning, e.g., job scheduling, system information services, life cycle management) to *data grid* [CFK+99] (concerning, e.g., distributed data access, metadata management, data replication), and recently to *semantic and knowledge-oriented grids* (this terms denote several development directions, including data mining, semantic, and knowledge grids). However, the idea of managing dataspaces rather than databases introduced by Franklin et. al in [FHM05] has only recently started to influence the web and grid technology providers. The key issue in realization of dataspaces lies in the power of the relationships framework. Semantically rich described relationships are going to be the backbone of an intelligent dataspace systems with the necessity to improve and maintain dataspace relationships.

In this chapter we discuss the development and evaluation of a scientific dataspace model for creation, representation, and maintaining of semantically enriched relationships among distributed dataspace participants. In Section 4.2 we introduce a scientific data model that we call *e-Science life cycle* supporting intelligent preservation of the complete data life cycle in e-Science applications. It represents the outcome of an elaboration study on how dataspace concepts can support e-Science applications and has lead our research to the development of the e-Science life cycle ontology on top of which we build our platform. In Section 4.3 we elaborate what data items are considered as dataspace participants in the scientific dataspace and how relationships among them can be semantically enriched. Finally, in Section 4.4 we describe related works regarding the resource space model and conclude this chapter in Section 4.5. In order to separate

---

[1]The grid is an infrastructure that enables flexible, secure, and coordinated resource (high-end computers, databases, scientific instruments, networks, etc.) sharing among dynamic collections of individuals and institutions.

the theoretical model described in this chapter, we tried to distinguish the dataspace model with the implementation of the OWL based e-Science life cycle ontology, which is discussed in Chapter refsec:ontology.

4.2 Scientific Dataspace Model

In order to elaborate how dataspace concepts can support e-Science, we have investigated what happen, or better what should ideally happen to data in e-Science applications. The result of this investigation is an iterative and hierarchical model with five main activities, represented in Figure 4.1, which we define as following:

> The e-Science life cycle - a domain independent ontology-based iterative model, tracing semantics about procedures in e-Science applications. Iterations of the model - so called e-Science life cycles - organized as instances of the e-Science life cycle ontology, are feeding a dataspace, allowing the dataspace to evolve and grow into a valuable, intelligent, and semantically rich space of scientific data [EMB08].

First we provide an overview of these activities and then in Section 4.2.1 a more detailed discussion.

At the beginning of the life cycle targeted goals are specified, followed that a data preparation step including pre-processing and integration tasks is fulfilled. Following that appropriate data analysis tasks are selected and applied on the prepared dataset of the previous step. Finally, achieved results are processed and published, which might provoke further experimentation and consequentially specification of new goals within the next iteration of the life cycle. The outcome of this is a space of primary and derived data with semantically rich relationships among each other providing (a) easy determining of what data exists and where it resides, (b) searching the dataspace for answers to specific questions, (c) discovering interesting new datasets and patterns, and (d) assisted and automated publishing of primary and derived data.

Each activity in the life cycle shown in Figure 4.1 includes a number of tasks that again can contain a couple of subtasks. For instance, the activity *Prepare Data* covers, on a lower level of abstraction, a data integration task gathering data from multiple heterogeneous data resources that are participating within an e-Infrastructure. This task consists of several steps that are organized into a workflow, which again is represented

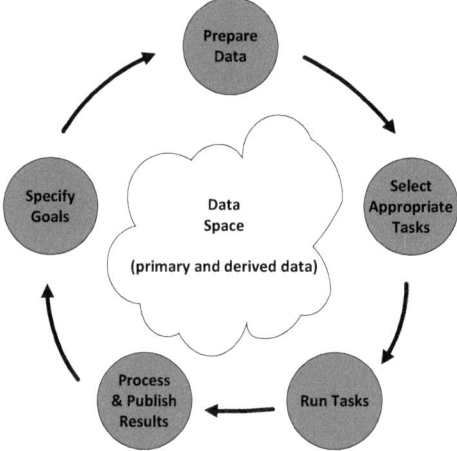

Figure 4.1: The e-Science life cycle.

at different levels of abstraction - from a graphical high level abstraction representation down to a more detailed specific workflow language representation, which is further used to enact the workflow.

4.2.1 e-Science Life Cycle Activities

1. *Specify Goals* - Scientists specify their research goals for a concrete experiment, which is one iteration of the entire life cycle. This is the starting activity in the life cycle. A textual description of the objectives, user name, corresponding user group, research domain and other optional fields like a selection of and/or references to an ontology representing the concrete domain is organized by this activity.

2. *Prepare Data* - Once the objectives for this life cycle are either specified or selected from a published life cycle that was executed in the past, the life cycle goes on with the data preparation activity. Here, it is specified which data sources are used in this life cycle in order to produce the final input dataset, by the data integration process. For example, the resource URI, name, and a reference to the

OGSA-DAI[2][KAA+05] resource file might be recorded in case OGSA-DAI is used. The final dataset as well as the input datasets are acting as participants in the dataspace and are referenced with an unique id. Additionally, the user specifies a short textual description and optionally some keywords of the produced dataset.

3. *Select Appropriate Tasks* - In this activity the data analysis tasks to be applied on the prepared dataset are selected. In e-Science applications it is mostly the case that various analytical tasks, for instance the widely used data mining techniques, are executed successively. The selected tasks, which are available as web and grid services, are organized into workflows. For each service, its name and optionally a reference to an ontology describing the service more precisely is captured. Also for the created workflow, its name, a short textual description, and a reference to the document specifying the workflow are recorded.

4. *Run Tasks* - In this activity the composed workflow will be started, monitored and executed. A report showing a brief summary of the executed services and their output is produced. The output of the analytical services used might be represented in Predictive Model Markup Language (PMML) [Dat08], which is a standard for representing statistical and data mining models. PMML documents represent derived datasets, thus they are managed as participants of the scientific dataspace and considered as resources by this activity.

5. *Process and Publish Results* - This is the most important activity in order to allow the underlying dataspace to evolve and grow into a valuable, powerful, semantically rich space of scientific data. Based on the settings of the user, one automatically publishes the results of the analysis tasks as well as all semantical information captured in the previous activities. Different publishing modes allow to restrict access to selected collaborations, user groups, or research domains.

The proposed five phases, also called e-Science activities of the life cycle model for e-Science applications can be seen as an iterative hierarchical workflow presented in its most abstract level. Each phase can be drilled down into more precisely described sub-workflows. An example can be described using the *select appropriate tasks* activity,

---

[2]OGSA-DAI is the de facto standard for data access and integration for relational and XML data as well as file resources.

which in most e-Science applications covers on a lower level of abstraction the orchestration of a number of services to be executed successively organized as workflow, as for example the NIGM-Service [EHL⁺08] of one of our sample e-Science applications described in Chapter 8.2. We can see from this, that the orchestration of tasks, services, etc. into workflows as well as their intelligent preservation has become significantly important for e-Science applications.

4.2.2 The Scientific Resource Space Model

Scientific experiments described by the e-Science life cycle are referred to as *Life Cycle Resources* (LCR). They are organized as points of a 5-dimensional space, where dimensions represent the five e-Science life cycle activities. In particular, the *Scientific Resource Space* (SRS) is defined as

$$SRS(GS, DP, TS, TE, RP),$$

whereas GS, DP, TS, TE, and RP denote the names of the dimensions of the SRS. They represent abbreviations of the five e-Science life cycle activities. Since we have developed an OWL ontology that reflects the concepts of the e-Science life cycle model described above, we give in Table 4.1 an overview of the abbreviations and their associations with OWL class names of that ontology. The ontology itself is however described in detail in Chapter 5.

	$SRS(GS, DP, TS, TE, RP)$	
	e-Science life cycle	
SRS axis name	activity name	OWL class name
GS	Specify Goals	GoalSpecification
DP	Prepare Data	DataPreparation
TS	Select Appropriate Tasks	TaskSelection
TE	Run Tasks	TaskExecution
RP	Process & Publish Results	ResultPublishing

Table 4.1: Definition of names of the *SRS axes* and their mapping to the e-Science activities and corresponding OWL class names.

A dimension of the space can be regarded as a 1-dimensional space. Table 4.2 lists the names of the e-Science life cycle activities defined and their definitions in the

Activity Name	Definition
Specify Goals	$GS = \{I_{GS1}, I_{GS2}, ..., I_{GSn}\}$
Prepare Data	$DP = \{I_{DP1}, I_{DP2}, ..., I_{DPn}\}$
Select Appropriate Tasks	$TS = \{I_{TS1}, I_{TS2}, ..., I_{TSn}\}$
Run Tasks	$TE = \{I_{TE1}, I_{TE2}, ..., I_{TEn}\}$
Process & Publish Results	$RP = \{I_{RP1}, I_{RP2}, ..., I_{RPn}\}$

Table 4.2: Dimensions of the scientific dataspace.

scientific dataspace model.

Coordinates of a dimension represent the individuals of the corresponding e-Science life cycle activity. Coordinates have a name, a set of properties and a set of individuals that are interconnected via those properties. Coordinates are defined as $I_{Xi} = \{name, P, E\}$, with $Xi \in \{GS, DP, TS, TE, RP\}$ and $i \in \{1, ..., 5\}$, where P refers to the set of properties defined for the coordinate and E refers to the set of elements that are connected to the coordinate and $name$ represents the activity name. Elements are instances of classes of the e-Science life cycle ontology. Please refer to Chapter 5 on a detailed description of the instances and classes that form together an LCR in the e-Science life cycle ontology.

Figure 4.2 illustrates *axis GS* having five coordinates. It represents the dimension *"goalSpecification"* of the multidimensional Scientific Resource Space.

Figure 4.3 illustrates a 2-dimensional *SRS* showing the *GoalSpecification* and the *DataPreparation* dimension. A point in the multidimensional *Scientific Resource Space* represents a set of *instances* of corresponding e-Science life cycle activities that are interconnected within the dataspace. Interconnected coordinates indicate that instances are participating the same e-Science life cycle experiment. An instance of a class (represented by a coordinate) can participate in multiple experiments, whereas an experiment can only have one instance on each axis. For example, there can be more than one experiment having the same goals specified, therefore using the same *GoalSpecification* instance, but there is only one instance of each e-Science life cycle activity defined in an

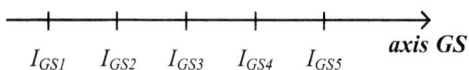

Figure 4.2: The *"goalSpecification"* dimension of the *SRS*.

iteration of the model. The point depicted in Figure 4.3 $LCR(I_{GS4}|I_{DP4})$ represents the e-Science life cycle iteration (resource) that consists of the two referenced coordinates I_{GS4} and I_{DP4}.

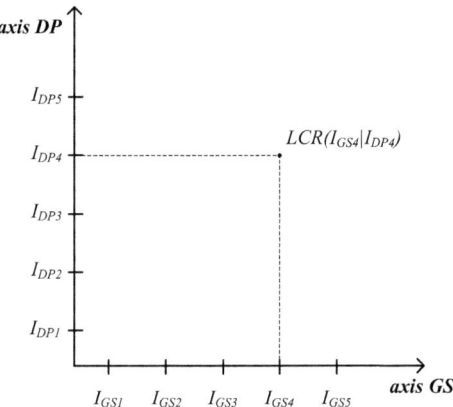

Figure 4.3: 2-dimensional scientific resource space.

Figure 4.4 illustrates a 3-dimensional space. In general a 3-dimensional *Scientific Resource Space* connects three 2-dimensional *Scientific Resource Spaces*. The illustrated example in Figure 4.4 connects the following three 2-dimensional *Scientific Resource Spaces*: $SRS(GS, DP)$, $SRS(GS, TS)$, and $SRS(TS, DP)$. Therefore each 2-dimensional SRS holds *Life Cycle Resources* defined as

$$LCR(I_{x_1m}|I_{x_2n}) = v_i \left\{ I_{x_1m} \ I_{x_2n} \right\} \text{ with } m, n \in Z_0, \ x \in SRS(), |SRS| = 2.$$

The point depicted as $LCR(I_{GS_4}|I_{DP_4}|I_{TS_4})$ in Figure 4.4 represents a *Life Cycle Resource* with three instances of the e-Science life cycle activities *"Specify Goals"*, *"Prepare Data"*, and *"Select Appropriate Tasks"*. In general, a point in a 3-dimensional *Scientific Resource Space* is defined as:

$$LCR(I_{x_1m}|I_{x_2n}|I_{x_3p}) = v_i \left\{ I_{x_1m} \ I_{x_2n} \ I_{x_3p} \right\} \text{ with } m, n, p \in Z_0, \ x \in SRS(), |SRS| = 3$$

Information about actions taken within an activity is saved as RDF graph with the individual as root element.

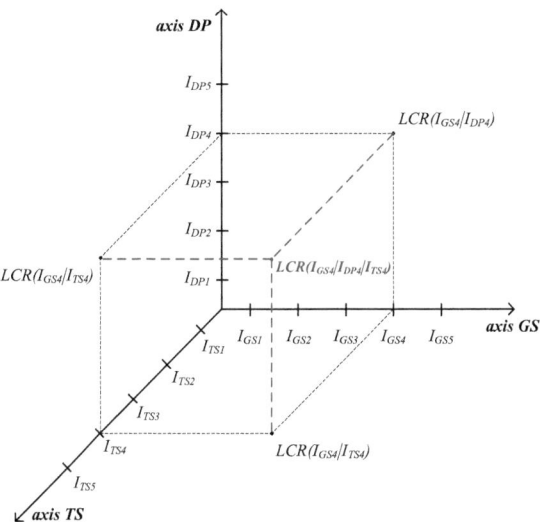

Figure 4.4: 3-dimensional scientific dataspace.

Spaces with more than three dimensions are hard to project on 3-dimensional images. One way is to split the n-dimensional cube into multiple 2-dimensional cubes and to position them accordingly. In Figure 4.5 we try to visualize the 5-dimensional life cycle resource space. We should keep in mind that the five 2-dimensional points depicted in Figure 4.5, actually form together a single point in the 5-dimensional space, therefore represent a single LCR.

A point in the multidimensional space connects coordinates (i.e. individuals of the five e-Science life cycle activities) that are participating within a LCR. A LCR can therefore be defined as a vector:

$$v_i \left\{ I_{GSj} \ I_{DPk} \ I_{TSl} \ I_{TEm} \ I_{RPn} \right\}$$

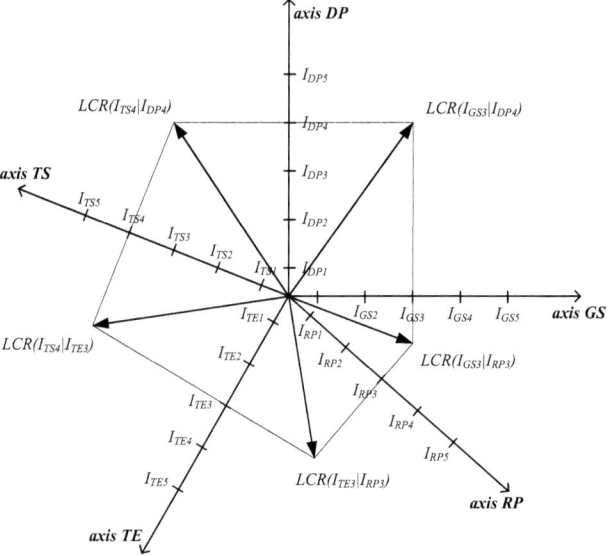

Figure 4.5: 5-dimensional scientific dataspace.

with $j, k, l, m, n \in \mathbb{N}$ representing the index of the five participating coordinates. Mathematically the 5-dimensional space is defined as a $n \times 5$ matrix as follows:

$$A = (a_{i5}) \begin{pmatrix} a_{11} & a_{12} & a_{13} & a_{14} & a_{15} \\ a_{21} & a_{22} & a_{23} & a_{24} & a_{25} \\ \vdots & \vdots & \vdots & \vdots & \vdots \\ a_{n1} & a_{n2} & a_{n3} & a_{n4} & a_{n5} \end{pmatrix}$$

Elements of the matrix are defined as a_{ij} with $i = 1, ..., m$ (the index of coordinates corresponding to a LCR) and $j = 1, ..., 5$ (the index of the e-Science life cycle activity). Each element represents an individual of an e-Science life cycle activity. The index j represents the dimension of the space i.e. the first column (elements a_{i1}) of the matrix represents the dimension *"Specify Goals"* and the last column (elements a_{i5}) represent the dimension *"Process & Publish Results"*. Thus columns represent the dimensions of the multidimensional space and rows represent points (LCR) of the space. Points in the space can also be combined of coordinates having different indexes e.g. a LCR using individual p of the dimension *"Specify Goals"* can contain instances with different index on the other dimensions. This is important when a researcher re-uses an available individual within another iteration of the e-Science life cycle. For example, when applying the same analysis method on a different dataset (that is a different instance of the *"Prepare Data"* activity). Let's assume that the three instances I_{GS3}, I_{TE3} and I_{RP3} are being re-used within a new e-Science life cycle experiment. This indicates that the acting researcher has applied a new analysis method on a new prepared dataset, but re-used the same instance of the dimension *"Specify Goals"*, *"Run Tasks"* and *"Process & Publish Results"*, thus working on the same study, executing the analytical methods on the same machine and publishing the results using the same publication modes as in his previously conducted experiments. The corresponding LCR is illustrated in Figure 4.5 and denoted as

$$LCR = v_i \left\{ I_{GS3}\ I_{DP4}\ I_{TS4}\ I_{TE3}\ I_{RP3} \right\} \text{ with } i \in \mathbb{N},\ i < n$$

n is the number of rows in the corresponding matrix and is equal to the amount of LCRs. This measure indicates the state of the scientific dataspace.

If we assume that the LCR depicted in Figure 4.5, has the highest available index in the dataspace, therefore represent its actual state, we can organize the 5-dimensional scientific dataspace in the following 4×5 matrix:

$$A_{LCR} = (I_{45}) \begin{pmatrix} I_{GS1} & I_{DP1} & I_{TS1} & I_{TE1} & I_{RP1} \\ I_{GS2} & I_{DP2} & I_{TS2} & I_{TE2} & I_{RP2} \\ I_{GS3} & I_{DP3} & I_{TS3} & I_{TE3} & I_{RP3} \\ 0 & I_{DP4} & I_{TS4} & 0 & 0 \end{pmatrix}$$

The positions I_{14}, I_{44} and I_{45} contain the value 0, which indicates that there still does not exist an individual of the dimensions 1, 4 and 5 having index 4. With an increasing number of life cycle experiments the resource space and therefore the matrix A_{LCR} is growing. However, the index is separately updated for each dimension and only when a new individual of the corresponding life cycle activity is being created.

The Scientific Resource Space Model together with the e-Science life cycle represent our basis on top of which we build our dataspace support platform, which is further described in the following sections.

4.2.3 The Environment of Dataspaces in e-Science

Figure 4.6 shows the environment of the e-Science life cycle. In particular, there is a set of participants participating to one ore more activities of the e-Science life cycle. Each activity feeds the dataspace with new participants, as for example the activity *Specify Goals* adds new domain ontologies, the activity *Prepare Data* adds new final input datasets as well as OGSA-DAI resource files, and the activity *Select Appropriate Tasks* adds new workflow description documents, while the activity *Run Tasks* adds new PMML documents describing the data mining model applied, and finally the activity *Process and Publish Results* adds new documents visualizing the achieved outputs. All these participants belong to at least one or more e-Science life cycles, expressed as instances of the ontology describing its relationship and interconnection to a great extend.

Each iteration of the life cycle will produce new instances and properties of the ontology. Based on the publishing mode, set by the scientist who accomplished the life cycle, the whole instance will automatically be published into the dataspace and thus is available to other users of a wider collaboration with respect to other research areas. We distinguish between four publication modes as listed in the following:

1. *free access* - the life cycle resource is publicly available, no access rights are defined.

2. *research domain* - the life cycle resource is restricted to members of the research domain the scientist who conducted the experiment belongs to.

3. *collaboration* - the life cycle resource is restricted to members of a collaboration defined among multiple research groups

4. *research group* - The life cycle resource is restricted to members of the research group the scientist who conducted the experiment belongs to.

Users will have access to sets of participants available in the scientific dataspace, depending on their assigned role. By this, the concept of managing sub-dataspaces is

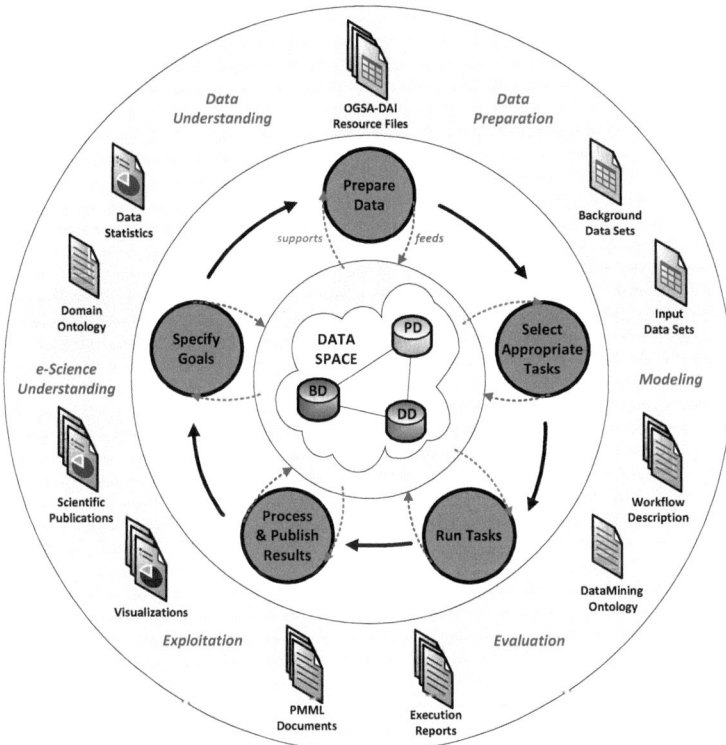

Figure 4.6: Environment of a scientific dataspace.

realized. A sub-dataspace contains a subset of participants and a subset of relationships of the overall dataspace. There can be sub-dataspaces setup for different domains, then for different research collaborations and even for single research groups. Scientific experiments that were published using the *free access* mode, will participate in the overall dataspace, thus its participants and the life cycle instances are accessible for every one having access to the scientific dataspace. In order to access data of a specific life cycle iteration, that was published using the *research group* mode, it will be necessary to be member of that specific research group, as the data will be participating only in

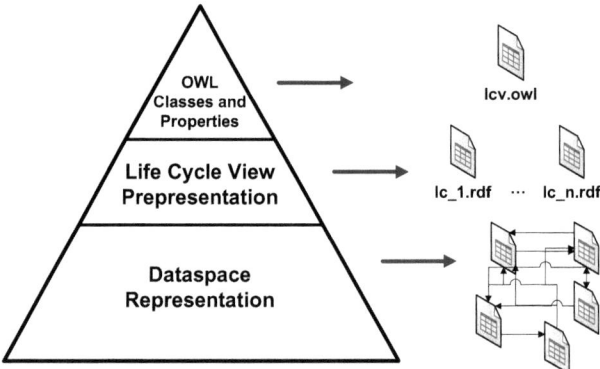

Figure 4.7: Three layers of abstraction for e-Science life cycles.

the corresponding sub-dataspace.

Once a new iteration has been accomplished using at least some activities from other life cycle instances, both the new life cycle document and the one containing activities that were re-used will get an additional relationship. We can conclude from this, that the dataspace is evolving with an increasing number of life cycles. Catalogs and repositories for ontology instances that manage these LCRs organized as RDF trees will provide search and browsing features. The development of an appropriate repository providing rich functions to insert, update and delete as well as to semantically search LCRs on a multi-institutional level is discussed in Chapter 6.

Figure 4.7 illustrates three layers of abstraction of the e-Science life cycle. On top, there are the classes and properties defined in the ontology, which models the concepts of the five e-Science life cycle activities and their interconnection, in short the e-Science life cycle. Instances of this ontology, represent specific cycles of the model for a specific e-Science application. To be precise, one instance represents a specific experiment of an e-Science application. However, we can see that with an increasing number of applied scientific experiments using the e-Science life cycle, we get an increasing number of instances of the ontology, each represented by a single RDF tree. This layer is called the life cycle view representation, as it represents different cycles of the model e.g. from different domains.

The interconnection of these large amount of diverse scientific experiments, described within instances of the ontology (as single RDF trees) represents the scientific dataspace in its most abstract view, where participants are the instances of the ontology and relationships are the connections among these files. Thus the bottom layer is called the dataspace representation.

As mentioned above, once a new life cycle is created that uses some bits of another already defined life cycle, both corresponding instances will be interconnected by the *uses-bits-of* relationship. We can see that in this high abstraction level also relationships are evolving with an increasing number of applied scientific experiments by using the life cycle model.

4.3 Relationships in the Scientific Dataspace

Scientific dataspaces will be set up to serve a special subject, which is on one hand to semantically enrich the relationship of primary and derived data in e-Science applications and on the other hand to integrate e-Science understandings into iterations of the life cycle model allowing scientists to understand the objectives of applied e-Science life cycles. Figure 4.8 illustrates what is considered as dataspace participant and relationship, respectively by breaking a typical very generic scientific experiment into its major pieces, which we organize into three categories (1) primary data, (2) background data, and (3) derived data. A typical scientific experiment consists of three types of dataspace participants:

1. an input dataset taken from a source database,

2. a set of functions (analytical methods) used to analyze the input dataset (commonly organized into a scientific workflow), and

3. the derived results, which represent the outputs of the experiment i.e. plots and histograms, reports, or publications.

Those dataspace participants are stored in corresponding data repositories of the scientific dataspace. Their interconnection is semantically rich described by dataspace relationships. They are modeled in RDF as individuals and properties of the e-Science life cycle ontology and organized in multiple RDF trees within an RDF store [KC04] supporting the the SPARQL query language for RDF [PS08, C+08]. SPARQL contains

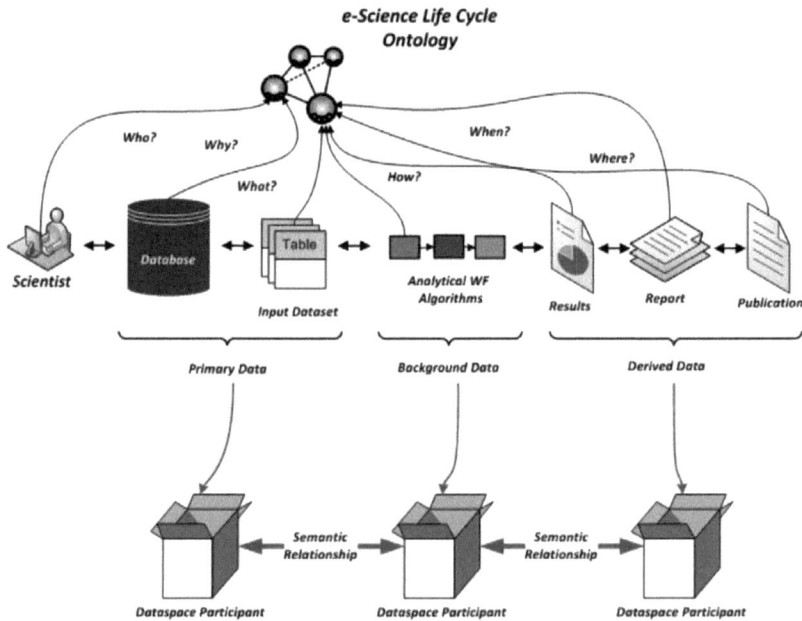

Figure 4.8: Semantic relationship in e-Science applications organized be the e-Science life cycle ontology.

capabilities for querying required and optional graph patterns along with their conjunctions and disjunctions. The results of SPARQL queries can be results sets or RDF graphs.

Experiments described by the ontology are referred to as Life Cycle Resources (LCRs). A LCR in fact represents the semantic relationship among dataspace participants. In the following section we discuss how such scientific experiments can be described by the e-Science life cycle ontology.

The scientific dataspace consists of four major kinds of interconnected databases: (1) primary databases for storing input datasets, (2) background databases for storing analytical methods used to analyze an input dataset, (3) derived databases for storing results of analyses tasks, and (4) RDF databases for storing instances of the e-Science life cycle ontology. However, depending on the underlying data preservation used to store dataspace participants for the long term, it could also be collections of datasets organized in a particular data preservation system. This is further described in Chapter 6, where we introduce the architecture of our scientific dataspace platform. Although, we use in the following the term database to refer to a collection of dataspace participants. Figure 4.9 (a) illustrates the main entities of a typical scientific experiment in the breath gas analysis application (see Section 8.3) and (b) shows their corresponding databases and how they are organized in the scientific dataspace. An important point here is the RDF-store containing relationships among primary, background and derived data items that participate in breath gas experiments in terms of individuals and properties of the e-Science life cycle ontology. The dataspace as depicted in Figure 4.9 (b) represents an instance of a breath gas analysis dataspace like it is deployed as an experimental framework for the Breath Research Institute of the Austrian Academy of Sciences. This is described more precisely in Chapter 8, where we evaluate the scientific dataspace paradigm on top of real e-Science applications. A large-scale scientific dataspace scenario with multiple geographically distributed databases is presented in Chapter 7. Our main contribution in this context is the creation of semantically rich relationships among data items of scientific experiments described in RDF.

Based on the relationships, answers to specific questions, such as the following:

A *"I have detected a model error and want to know which derived data products need to be recomputed."*

B *"I want to check if insopiration is different to expiration of breath gas dataset x. If the results already exist, I'll save hours of computation."*

C *"Is there any experiment done on the volatile organic compound isoprene on exhaled breath gas in the context of cholesterol level in blood?"*

can be answered by submitting SPARQL queries to the RDF store, which manages the relationships.

Experiments are being successively refined, by the acting researcher until the study either shows a significant result (e.g. regarding one of our two real e-Science applications this might be the definition of accurate methods for estimation of blood gas levels of certain biomarker values from breath gas samples) or ends up in a modification of the intended defined goal specification for that experiment. We are aware that we rely on active participation of members from the scientific community the dataspace is deployed

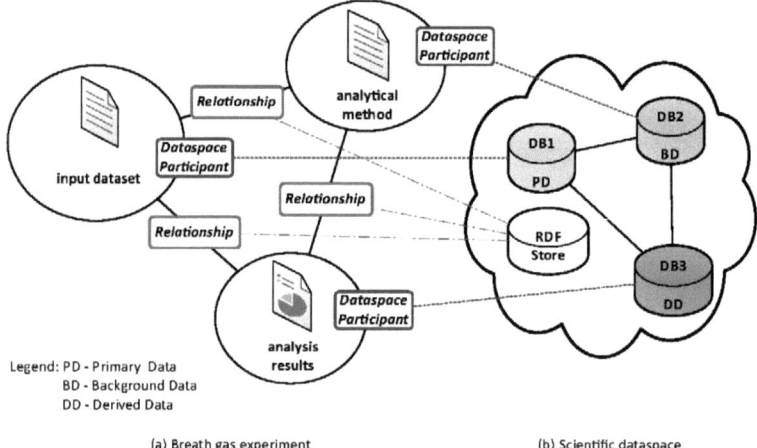

(a) Breath gas experiment   (b) Scientific dataspace

Figure 4.9: Organization of dataspace participants and their semantic relationships from a single scientific study in the scientific dataspace.

to in order to establish large scale scientific dataspaces. Therefore, we provide a simple graphical user interfaces (such as the e-Science life cycle composer composer and the e-Science life cycle Search and Query panel) that can easily be used by scientists from diverse research domains, especially by non-computer scientists, which is indeed a major requirement from any e-Science application. However, we suspect that young-researchers (Master and PhD students) will be the major users who will use the portal in terms of conducting experiments, while senior researcher will most likely interact with the portal in terms of submitting requests. Once a dataspace is deployed to a global research community we expect that it enforces building of collaborations among their participating research institutions as it supports the community in exchanging data and knowledge. This will build the basis for automation-based analysis on top of life cycle resources collected in the dataspace.

Figure 4.10 gives an overview of participants and their relationships in the scientific dataspace. The figure also shows *End Point References* (EPRs) from specific e-Science life cycle activities to dataspace participants. Basically, an EPR points to a specific dataset, that is a dataspace participant representing either a primary, a background, or a derived dataset of a scientific study. A typical study includes:

1. a single primary dataset (also referred to as the *Final Input DataSet - FIDS*[3])

2. multiple background datasets and also

3. multiple derived datasets.

Figure 4.10 illustrates in particular EPRs and the different kinds of dataspace participants to which EPRs are pointing to. The figure also shows from which e-Science life cycle activity EPRs are originating.

As depicted in the figure the activities *Prepare Data*, *Select Appropriate Tasks*, *Run Tasks* have EPRs to dataspace participants. The activity *Process&Publish Results* has an EPR to a publication, which is available in the internet e.g. hosted on the PubMed resource. The latter kind of EPR is a either a simple HTTP-URL or a digital object identifier (DOI) if available, such as the following examples, which point to a scientific publication in the breath gas analysis domain.

$$http://www.ncbi.nlm.nih.gov/pubmed/21234569 \tag{4.1}$$

$$10.1007/s00285\text{-}010\text{-}0398\text{-}9 \tag{4.2}$$

The DOI System [doi11] is as independent as possible from specific technology implementations. For web applications, the DOI name may be expressed as a HTTP URI. The method for doing so is simply to prepend the DOI with http://dx.doi.org/.

There is no need to replicate the publication into the a data repository of the scientific dataspace since todays online libraries are well organized and publications there are well preserved for the long run. It is also not needed to access the publication from within the dataspace. All that is required in this context is to provide the user the HTTP-URL and DOI, respectively where to find the publication. However, it is possible to store the publication as background dataspace participant within a dataspace repository.

---

[3]The FIDS represents the dataset that is used as input for an analysis task. For instance, in the breath gas analysis application a dataset containing raw breath gas data (e.g. breath air measurements from a mass spectrometer) is retrieved from an external data source. However this dataset is not the FIDS, because it will be further prepared for a breath gas analysis task (e.g. if only specific measurements should be analyzed). The FIDS therefore represents the final dataset that results from a data preparation task.

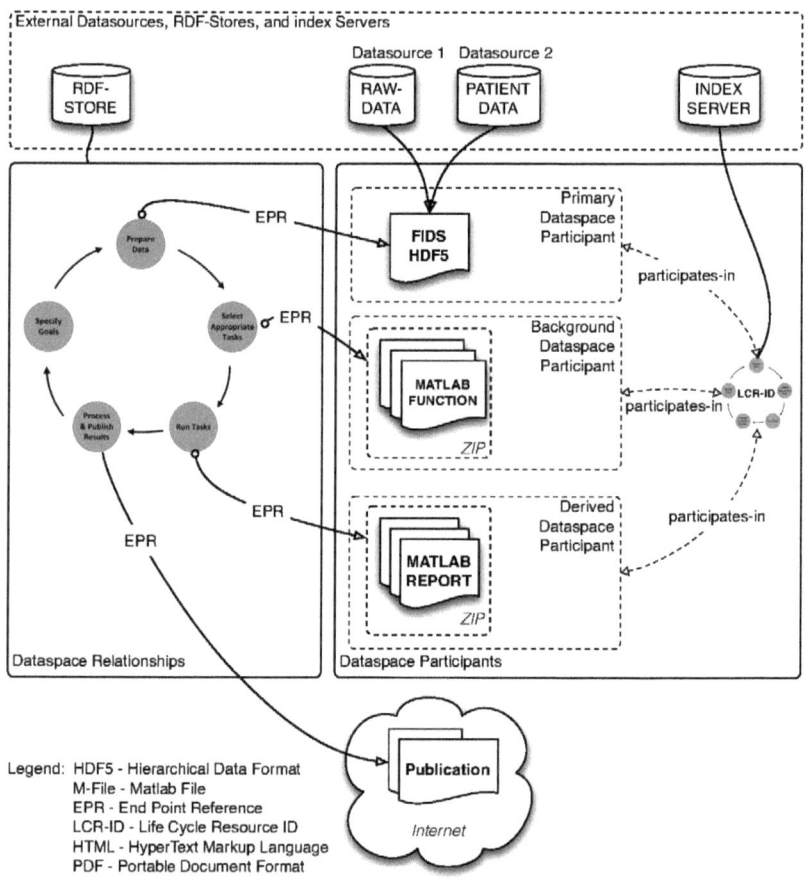

Figure 4.10: Relationships among dataspace participants in the scientific dataspace.

The other kind of queries point to datasets that are either being used in the LCR or have been generated as a result of the LCR. These datasets are considered as dataspace participants and have a certain type, which is either *primary*, *background*, or *derived*.

To sum up the above introduced multi-layer concept for creation and organization of semantic relationships among participants of a scientific dataspace we provide a overview of the abstraction layers in Figure 4.11. At first, supported by the ontology, a model independent from the various e-Science domains is set up. Then this model is applied to describe domain-specific iterations of the e-Science life cycle, which describe the relationship among data participating within the scientific dataspace, illustrated as different abstraction layers in Figure 4.11.

One iteration of the e-Science life cycle has, in short, a goal specification, a set of input data (primary data), a set of output data (derived data), a set of background data, and a set of activities describing what has been done to the input datasets in order to produce the output datasets. These datasets, illustrated as *PD*, *DD*, and *BD* in the bottom layer in Figure 4.11 are populating the scientific dataspace. They are enriched with semantic relationships among each other and described by its corresponding life cycle resource (*LCR1, LCR2, LCR3*), which are instances of the e-Science life cycle ontology. LCRs are represented as RDF Graphs and stored within a RDF store thus they can be discovered with submitting SPARQL queries to that RDF store.

4.4 Related Work

The proposed *Web Resource Space Model* [ZXS08] represents a semantic data model for specifying, storing, managing and locating web resources by appropriate classifying of resources. It enables users or applications to operate on web resources by an SQL-like query language. A web resource space is defined as a multi-dimensional classification space where dimensions are discrete. It consists of a name and a set of axis, denoted as $RS(X_1, X_2, ..., X_n)$. Each *axis* X_1 represents a classification method. X_i is partitioned by a set of coordinates denoted as $X_1 = <C_i1, C_i2, ..., C_im>$. A point in the space, determined by one *coordinate* at every axis, represents a set of resources of the same category.

A *coordinate* C represents a set of resources, denoted as $R(C)$. Resources represented by axis X_i are the union of all the resources represented by its *coordinate*: $R(X_i) = R(C_i1) \cup R(C_i2) \cup ... \cup R(C_in)$. The semantics of a *coordinate* is represented by name, basic datatype, and a set of concepts. The semantics of a *coordinate* is regulated by the semantics of its *axis*. A *coordinate* regulates a set of points. An *axisname* represents higher classification level that its coordinates. A resource space regulates a

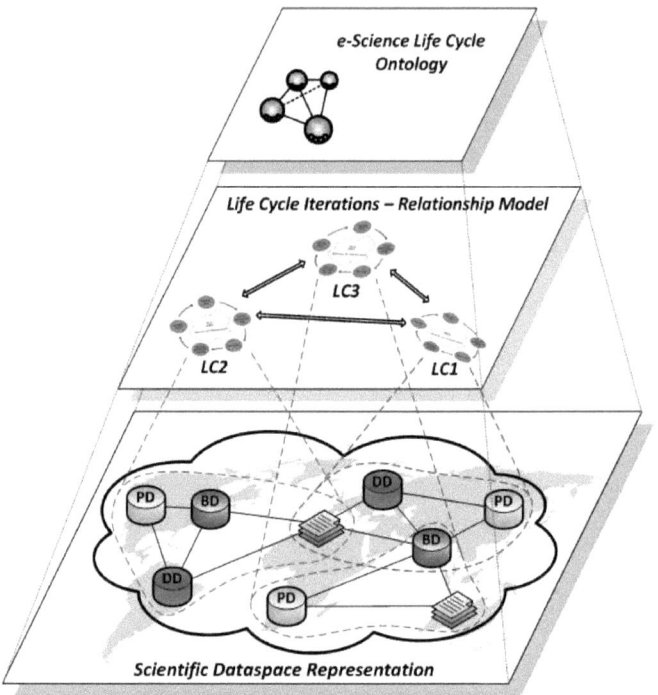

Figure 4.11: Abstraction layers of scientific dataspaces *(PD - Primary Data, DD - Derived Data, BD - Background Data)*.

set of axes and the refined classification relationship. A resource is determined by locating the point it belongs to and by selecting from the resource set according to its name and content description.

The semantics of *axis* and *coordinate* can be formally defined or informally defined. For example, the semantics of a *coordinate* can be defined by a set of concepts, which regulate the semantics of the resources it may contain.

The *Web Resource Space Model* is designed for managing web resources, such as web pages, photos, geographical information, or bio-information that is available on the web. It represents exactly the opposite approach to our scientific dataspace paradigm. While in the Web Resources Space Model data is kept in its original storage solution, we face the challenge to automatically enrich the data with semantics and to preserve it into a storage solution, which fits best for the research community the dataspace system is deployed for.

Obviously, there are major design considerations that distinguish both approaches, however some concepts from the Web Resource Space Model have influenced us in designing the *Scientific Resource Space Model*, which implements the e-Science life cycle introduced in Chapter 4.2.

4.5 Summary

In this chapter we have introduced the scientific dataspace model along with the e-Science life cycle, which models the major procedures of conducting an e-Science experiment. These procedures are modeled in five phases, which we name the *e-Science life cycle activities*. They classify at a high level of abstraction the activities a scientist is carrying out when performing a scientific experiment. Individuals of the life cycle model represent descriptions of conducted experiments and thus aim at understanding (1) what for a specific experiment was applied, (2) which data resources were accessed, (3) what transformations on these data resources were applied, (4) what analysis were performed, and finally (5) what results where achieved. We introduced our internal representation of iterations of the e-Science life cycle as Life Cycle Resources (LCR). LCRs are organized in the scientific resource space model as points of a 5-dimensional space, where dimensions represent the five e-Science life cycle activities. We then have described the environment of a scientific dataspace, by showing the all datasets and that are present in the data life cycle of the conduction of an e-Science experiment. Finally, we have derived from the dataspace environment what kind of relationships exists among identified datasets and analyzed how we can semantically enrich them using an ontology. An End Point Reference (EPR) concept, that provides a mechanism to systematically reference to datasets from e-Science experiments and studies has also been introduced. The web resource space model was described as related work closing this chapter.

Chapter 5

The e-Science Life Cycle Ontology

> *"We have to do better at producing tools to support the whole research cycle."*
>
> In a talk to the national Research Council in Mountain View on January 11, 2007 given by
> JIM GRAY

5.1 Introduction

In this section we introduce a new ontology called e-Science life cycle ontology, which we use as a semantic model for the creation, organization, representation and maintenance of semantically rich relationships in Life Cycle Resources (LCRs) using the scientific dataspace model described in Section 4.2. The model involves essential concepts of the scientific dataspace paradigm. Thanks to its domain independent applicability it can easily be used in any e-Science application. These concepts are organized in the e-Science life cycle ontology. It provides the basis for presenting generic scientific studies as LCRs with well defined relationships among their participating datasets. On the other hand the e-Science life cycle ontology supports the scientific dataspace paradigm with primitives that can specify concrete relationships among primary, background, and derived data of these LCRs.

The e-Science life cycle ontology can be seen as the heart of the underlying dataspace-based support platform. It is used to share common understanding of the structure of scientific studies among a research community. For example, suppose several different research centers conduct breath gas analysis studies. If these research centers share and publish the same underlying ontology of concepts for conducting breath gas studies, then software programs can extract and aggregate knowledge from these different research centers. The aggregated information can then be used to answer user queries or as input data to other applications (e.g. automation-based breath gas analysis). Figure 5.1 gives an overview of the main concepts of the e-Science life cycle ontology. Principally, ontologies are used for communication (between machines and/or humans),

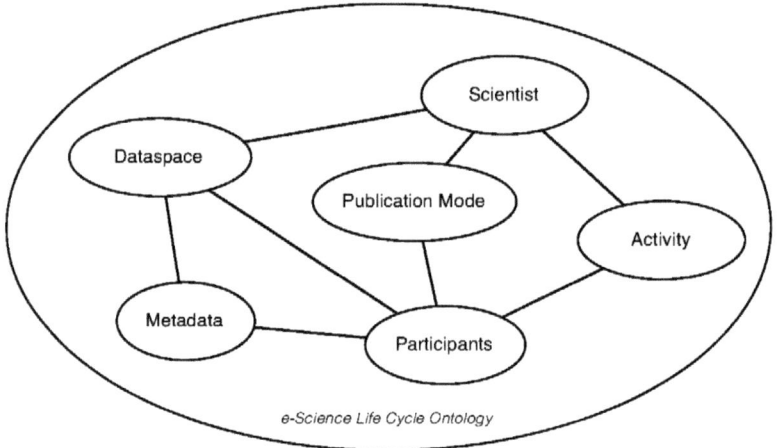

Figure 5.1: Main concepts of the e-science life cycle ontology.

automated reasoning, and representation and re-use of knowledge [CHST04]. To enable re-use of domain knowledge consolidated within scientific studies exposed as LCRs was one of the driving forces behind the development of the e-Science life cycle ontology. In this context domain knowledge is represented in semantic descriptions about scientific studies. In particular, activities of the e-Science life cycle such as the data preparation activity (providing descriptions about the input dataset used) or the select appropriate task activity (providing descriptions about the analytical methods applied to an input dataset) provide rich semantics about a conducted scientific study. With the help of the e-Science life cycle ontology we can describe scientific experiments according to the specification and implement a software program (e.g. a web service) that guides the scientist through the experiment conduction independent of the e-Science application domain. It is further possible to analyze domain knowledge since a declarative specification of the process of conducting studies is available with the e-Science life cycle ontology.

However, the ontology itself is not the goal in itself. It is rather a definition of a set of concepts and their relations for other software programs to use. In the research carried out and described in this book the ontology represents the concepts to model the entire life cycle in a scientific study. By this we provide with the e-Science life cycle ontology a framework for the management of semantically enriched relationships among datasets that participate in the data life cycle of the conduction of a scientific study. The software program that uses the ontology and its built knowledge base is represented by the software components of the scientific dataspace support platform.

5.2 Applied Methodology

As the first step in building the e-Science life cycle ontology we have selected a methodology supporting phases of the development process. Typically such a development process is organized in several phases. For the e-Science life cycle ontology development process we have selected the On-To-Knowledge methodology [SAB+03], as the most appropriate methodology because it provides the most accurate description of each phase through which an ontology passes during its lifetime. Other related methodologies for developing an ontology are described within the related work section of this chapter in Section 5.6.

The phases of the On-To-Knowledge methodology [SES02, SAB+03] are illustrated in Figure 5.2. The On-To-Knowledge approach consists of five phases and starts with a feasibility study to identify the concepts involved and to focus the domain for its application. During the kick-off phase, the requirement specification for the application is acquired. This includes knowledge sources (e.g. domain experts identified during the feasibility study). Through an analysis of that knowledge sources, a first basic ontology is developed containing most relevant concepts and relationships. It is modeled on a conceptual level. During the next phase, the refinement, knowledge is elicited with domain experts, which enlarges the ontology with more fine-grained concepts and relations. The approach ends up with a formalization phase, where the refined ontology is transferred into a formal representation language, such as OWL.

This ontology further serves as a base for developing a prototype application to evaluate the ontology in the next phase (the evaluation). It might be necessary to perform several refinement-evaluation cycles before all requirements are met. To reflect changes to the ontology being developed, a maintenance and evolution phase is considered in the On-To-Knowledge approach.

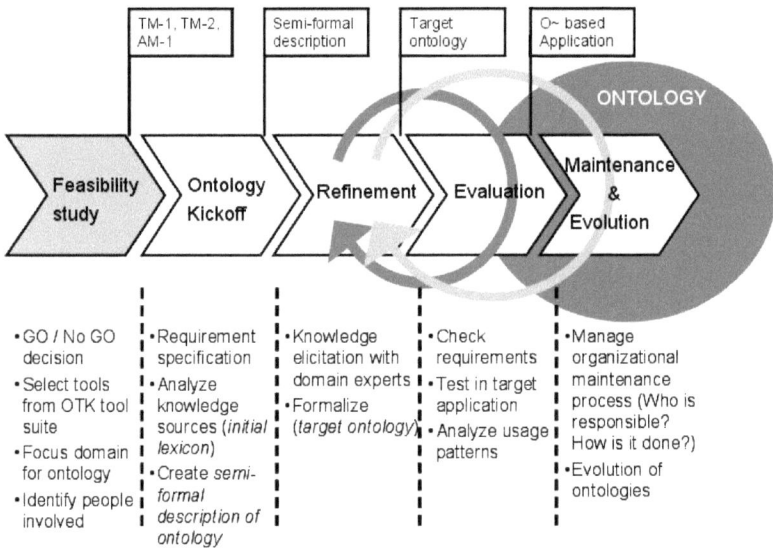

Figure 5.2: Methodology for On-To-Knowledge [SAB+03].

The most important issue building the e-Science life cycle ontology was to capture and uncover the e-Science life cycle knowledge by identifying the key concepts and relationships described in the previous chapter. The identification of general abstract terms related to defined life cycle concepts such as the participants including primary data, background data, and derived data, then life cycle activities, research domain and researcher, was an initial point in defining the classes and their relations to each other as main ontology concepts. The more specific concepts describing for example the life cycle activities more in detail such as data preparation activity, which background data it uses, and what kind of output data it produces, were identified next. Required semantic relationships between identified concepts were declared providing a higher complexity level while appropriate notation indicating the relation role between classes was identified.

There was great emphasis on defining authentication concepts based on a publication mode of a particular life cycle provided by a scientist who executed the corresponding life cycle. While going more into detail defining specific ontology concepts, a certain rework was occasionally required in order to guarantee the consistency of the ontology. Finally, ontology use case scenarios and applications were applied to identify further classes and relations providing more knowledge about the ontology. The ontology was created using Protégé Ontology Editor and Knowledge Acquisition System [Sta10].

5.3 e-Science Life Cycle Ontology Development

In this section we are going to illustrate and describe how we applied the On-To-knowledge methodology processes [SAB+03] in the development of the e-Science Life Cycle Ontology.

5.3.1 Feasibility study

In this phase we have collected metadata about real scientific study in cooperation with scientists from the application domain. This allowed us to understand the semantics of the data and relationships involved in the process of conducting a scientific study in a specific application domain. Furthermore it allowed us to investigate the general concepts and to elaborate the process describing the model and application usage. We illustrate identified people who are involved in the e-Science life cycle ontology and show a usage scenario in Figure 5.3.

Typically, senior scientists will interact with the ontology in terms of submitting search and query requests (e.g asking for LCRs from a specific person, organization, or research field) while PhD, and master students are continuously feeding the semantic repository with new individuals describing their scientific studies. On the other hand there is an ontology engineer, who is responsible for maintaining the ontology and for the evaluation in case changes were applied to the ontology. We also identified a domain expert as involved person, who provides an ontology for his research domain with a defined vocabulary of terms used in the application domain the e-Science life

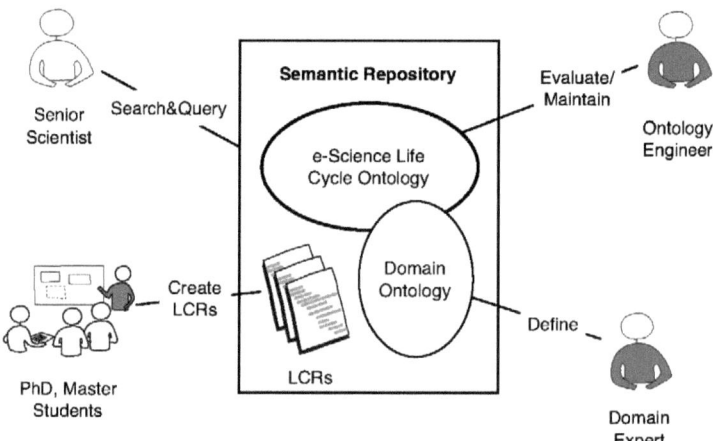

Figure 5.3: Identified people involved in the e-Science life cycle ontology.

cycle ontology and its underlying dataspace support platform is deployed to. This usage of a domain ontology in conjunction with the e-Science life cycle ontology is considered optional, since there are still many research domains, without a domain ontology that defines their common vocabulary.

The next section presents the basic concepts and their taxonomies, which are covered by the e-Science life cycle ontology as identified with collected metadata about a real scientific study during the feasibility study.

5.3.2 Kickoff

In this phase we specified all requirements for the e-Science life cycle ontology targeting the main concepts such as the participants, activity outputs, main activity tasks, more detailed domain and goal identification, ontology design models with respect to data sources involved, use cases and user role definitions, including the concepts and relationships identification. As knowledge source we mainly used the previously collected metadata about real scientific studies from the Non-Invasive Blood Glucose Measurement application[1], which have to be reflected by classes and properties in the ontology. Additionally the scientific dataspace model introduced in Section 4.2 and the environment of scientific dataspaces elaborated in Section 4.2.3 served as knowledge source to specify the dataspace-related requirements for the ontology (e.g. the need to model different types of dataspace participants). Last but not least senior researchers from both evaluating e-Science applications (see Chapter 8) have provided valuable inputs for specifying the requirements, based on which we created a semi formal description of the ontology.

The life cycle of conducting a scientific study comprises various steps, each step focusing on a different aspect or task. Therefore, a major concept in the e-Science life cycle ontology represents the e-Science life cycle activity. At the highest level the ontology covers all five activities of the e-Science life cycle. Figure 5.4 illustrates the concept taxonomy of life cycle activity.

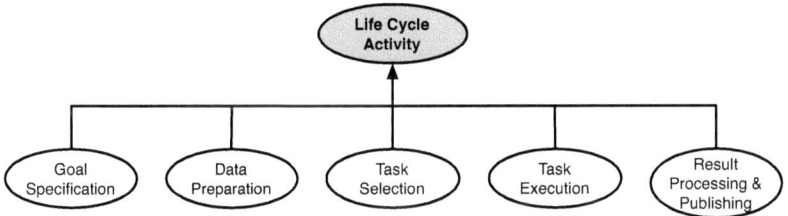

Figure 5.4: Lice cycle activity concept taxonomy.

Each activity has one or multiple references to either a primary, a background, or to a derived dataset, which is considered as dataspace participant in the ontology. There are different types of background and derived datasets that can be produced or accessed during the process of conducting a scientific study. We have considered some in the e-Science life cycle ontology that were relevant in our two e-Science applications. However, depending on an application domain, there might be additional domain specific kinds of such datasets. The concept taxonomy of this types of dataspace participants and its corresponding subtypes are shown in Figure 5.5. Data Mining ontology as shown in the figure represent a typical background dataset, however they investigation is out of scope of this work.

---

[1]This application is described in Chapter 8 in Section 8.2.

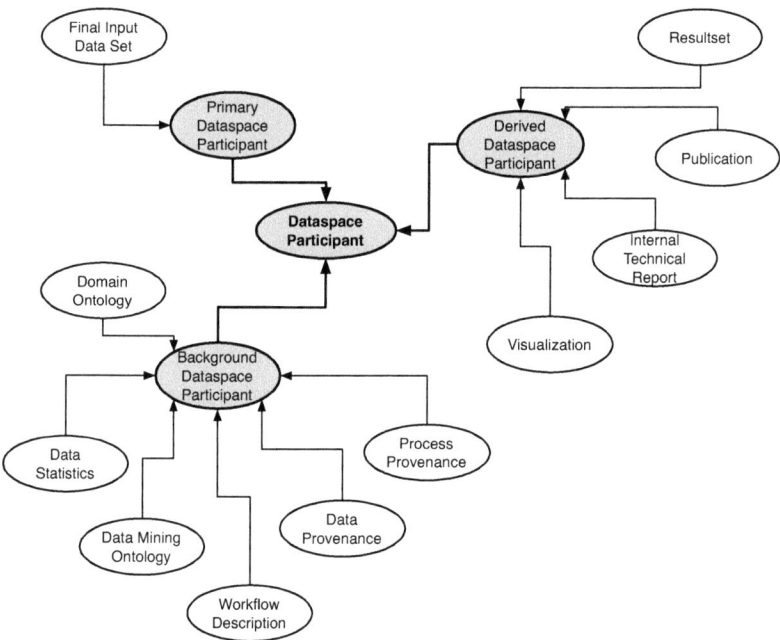

Figure 5.5: Dataspace participant concept taxonomy.

Another key concept defined in this phase is the publication mode concept. Since, it is important for a scientist who accomplished a study to share it with different kind of people, research teams, or groups, we have modeled several publication modes that can be attached to a specific LCR. The publication mode concept taxonomy is shown in Figure 5.6.

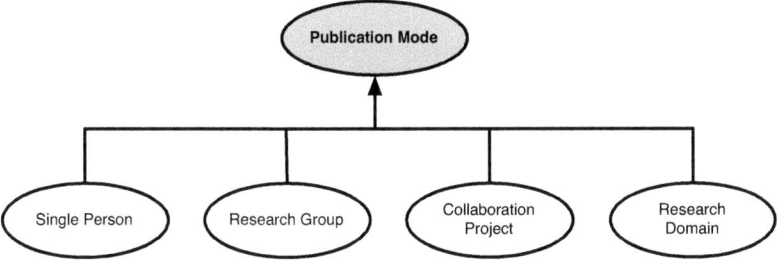

Figure 5.6: Publication mode concept taxonomy.

Since it was a major requirement to keep the e-Science life cycle ontology domain independent we have not provided much more concept taxonomies. However, we have used as much as possible a generic approach to model the concepts of the e-Science life cycle more precisely e.g. using the attribute triple <Concept, Attribute Name, Attribute Value>. This allows to specify domain-independently the attributes that are needed in a specific application domain. For instance, in the breath gas analysis domain it is necessary to model, which mass spectrometer was used to generate raw data prepared in the final input datasetindexFinal input dataset. Therefore an attribute Mass Spectrometer Type can be defined as individual of the generic concept Attribute Name, which can be connected to any concept defined in the ontology. This generic concept of describing domain-specific attributes is shown in Figure 5.7.

5.3.3 Refinement

In this phase we have modeled and formalized the abstract concepts and relationships specified in previous processes. In order to formalize the presented conceptual model we transformed it into a standard ontology language. We have decided to use the Web Ontology Language (OWL) [W3C04] because of the expressivity of the DL language, which is underpinning OWL and the ability to perform reasoning over the ontology.

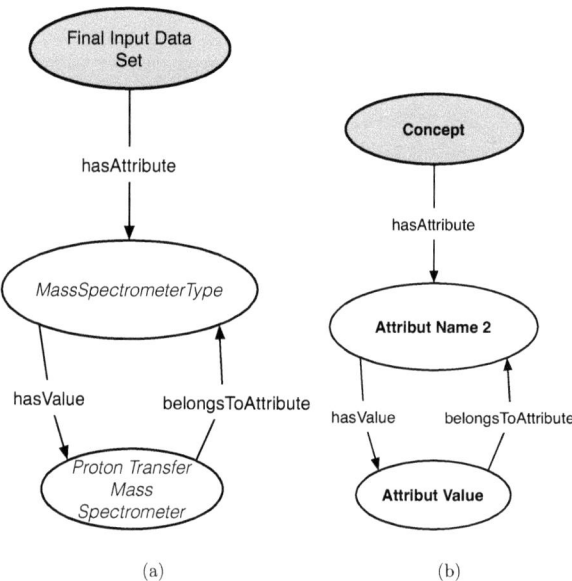

Figure 5.7: Generic metadata concept and example.

This assures that the ontology can be built in a logically consistent form in which the structure implied by the descriptions is complete. Moreover, this enabled us to take advantage of the reasoning at development time. The e-Science life cycle ontology has been modeled using the Protégé Ontology Editor [Sta10] supported by the Pellet reasoner [pel11], which enables to check consistency of a developing ontology.

Every OWL class, defined by a user, is a subclass of a predefined class *owl:Thing* and therefore each individual is member of this class. *LifeCycle* class represents a central OWL class related with five main activities as shown in Figure 5.8. We de-

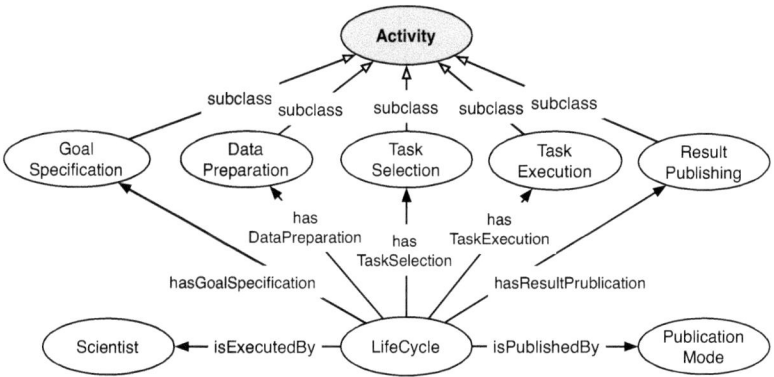

Figure 5.8: e-Science life cycle - activity relations.

fine a class *LifeCycle* as a subclass of the predefined class *owl:Thing*. A constraint *owl:maxCardinality* defines a value, which specifies the number of property values individuals of a class may contain at most, in this case a *LifeCycle* may contain at most one value of each of the declared properties: *hasGoalSpecification, hasDataPreparation, hasTaskExecution, hasTaskSelection, hasResultPublishing*, which refer to the five main life cycle activities. Furthermore, we specify that the class *LifeCycle* may only be executed by *scientist*, and that each lifeCycle is published by a particular publication mode. Figure 5.9 gives a more detailed illustration of a publication mode. Life cycles may be published in the dataspace and thus is available to other users of a wider collaboration with respect to other research areas. We distinguish between five publication modes: (1) *Person*, represented by a class *Person*, meaning that only selected persons may view the published results, (2) *research domain*, represented by a

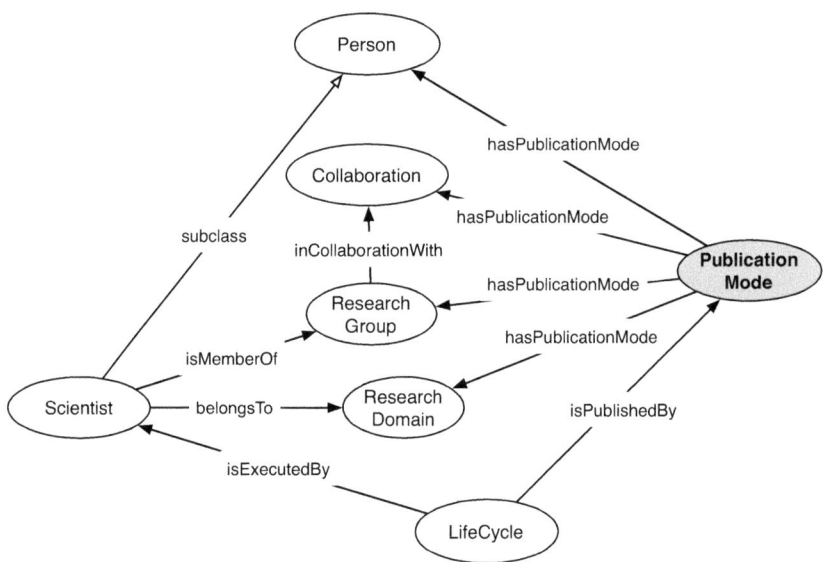

Figure 5.9: e-Science life cycle - publication mode.

ResearchDomain class, while restricting the results to certain domains, (3) *Collaboration*, represented by a *Collaboration* class with restrictions to particular collaborations, and (4) *Research group*, restricting the published life cycles to some particular research groups, represented by the *Research Group* class. Figure 5.9 provides further relationships indicating that a class *scientist* is derived from the class *Person* while being member of some research groups and belonging to certain research domains.

Each activity feeds the dataspace with new participants, which are categorized into tree different participant subgroups: background data, primary data and derived data. The concepts identifying the different participant subgroups are illustrated in Figure 5.10, and defined as subclasses of the class *Participant*. All these participants belong to at least one or more e-Science life cycles.

The scientific dataspace itself is modeled as set of data sources - the so called dataspace participants - and relationships describing their interconnections. A participant of the scientific dataspace paradigm described in this work is a dataset that either represents input data to a scientific experiment, or it represents the analytical method being used within that experiment, or it is a dataset that has emerged during execution of an experiment. We therefore classify four types of participants: (a) primary data participants - the input dataset, (b) background data participants i.e. an analytical method (web service, Matlab script, etc.), (c) derived data participants - emerged datasets, and (d) other data participants. Appropriate DBMSs for storing these three types of datasets need to be set up by a dataspace administrator when deploying the dataspace for a specific scientific community. The decision what DBMS to select depends on the schemas of the corresponding datasets, to be used by the scientific community, to whom the dataspace is deployed for. Figure 5.10 shows how the dataspace is modeled in the e-Science life cycle ontology.

For instance in the breath gas research domain primary data consists of the breath gas measurements, calculated by different types of mass spectrometers and integrated with corresponding laboratory values of the probands. This data is managed as relational data by a MySQL DBMS. Datasets taken from this datasource, for analysis within a scientific breath gas experiment are considered as *final input datasets*indexFinal input dataset. A final input dataset represents a primary participant. This dataset is replicated into a "primary" database, which is specifically set up for managing primary data participants in order that data used within a scientific experiment can be accessed even when the original data and its structure have been moved, changed or access

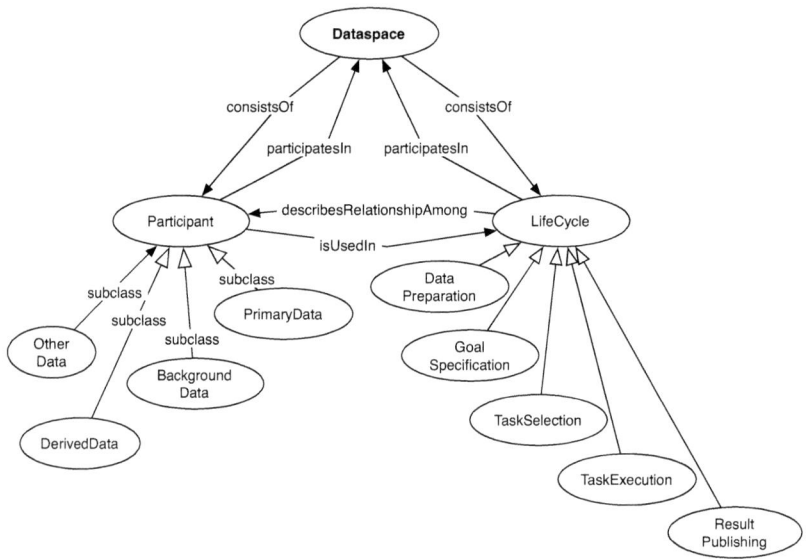

Figure 5.10: OWL classes and properties regarding the dataspace participants and relationships of the scientific dataspace implementation.

rights to its datasource have been modified. This replication process contributes to serve long-term data preservation within the scientific dataspace. It has effect only on primary datasets, as other datasets are emerging during execution of the experiment, therefore can be saved directly into their corresponding DBMS. Background data participants typically represent the analytical methods (mainly Matlab scripts) being used in breath gas analysis experiments. Their outcomes (histograms embedded in XML or HTML documents describing them) represent derived data sources. The brath gas analysis application, its datasets and their usage within a real-world breath gas study are described in Section 8.3.

Depending on the e-Science application, also other kind of data sources can participate. For instance the breath gas analysis scientific community has established a "volatomics" data base, which records basic metadata of finished (already published) studies of exhaled breath. This data source is regarded as data source with type "other" and can refer to a set of life cycle resources that correspond to a study.

Each participant is described by some metadata. This is captured by the OWL class *metaData*, which is a generic class for describing instances according to user-defined or application oriented attributes and their values. An instance of the class *metaData* typically has the form of a triple *'instanceID, attribute, value'*. For example, a short textual description of a participant would look like *'participant073', 'description', 'breath gas analysis measurements taken from 20 probands at sleep laboratory 1'*, which means that the instance *'participant073'* of the OWL class participant has a metadata attribute *'description'* whose value is *'breath gas analysis measurements taken from 20 probands at sleep laboratory 1'*. With this data description concept it is possible to describe nearly any metadata about nearly any instance of the e-Science life cycle ontology. Thus, scientists can independently describe participants according to their needs. Figure 5.11 illustrates how dataspace participants are described by the *metaData* and corresponding OWL classes.

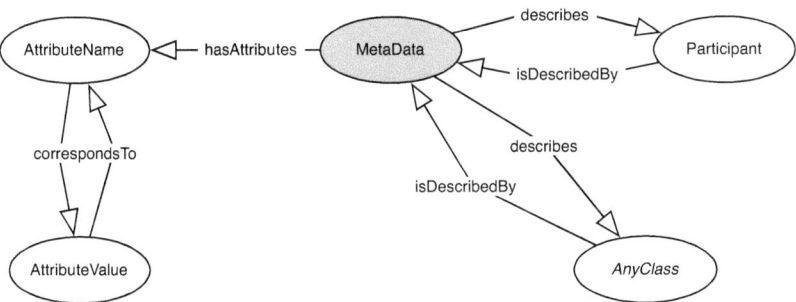

Figure 5.11: Data description concept in the e-Science life cycle ontology.

Relationships among the above described types of dataspace participants are semantically rich described by the instances and properties defined in a life cycle resource. The relationships are managed by the RDF store. Any data source of type "primary", "background", or "derived" within the dataspace is participating within at least one life cycle resource, which describes their interconnection to a great extent. Relationships among participants within the scientific dataspace model how datasets (primary, background, or derived participant) were used in scientific experiments. That means, whenever a dataspace participant is retrieved by some kind of supported search&query mechanisms, the requesting user will automatically receive additional information about

- which experiments the participant is involved in,

- what the purposes of these corresponding experiments were,

- which other participants are also involved in these experiments, therefore are interconnected to the received participants,

- who the creator of the participant is, which research group he corresponds to and how to contact him.

This information is meant to be the semantically rich relationship among participants of the scientific dataspace described by the classes and properties of the e-Science life cycle ontology.

The implemented solution to store links in the e-Science life cycle ontology is illustrated in Figure 5.12. A link to a dataspace participant is considered as an End Point Reference (EPR) in the e-Science life cycle according to the EPR-Framework as introduced in Section 4.3 in the previous chapter. Therefore links among dataspace participants are represented by its EPRs defined by instances and properties of the e-Science life cycle ontology. This means that multiple dataspace participants that are referenced with EPRs by a specific *Life Cycle Resource* (LCR) are interconnected and thus have a relationship. This relationship is defined by the EPR class of the e-Science life cycle ontology and semantically enriched by instances and properties of its corresponding LCR. Figure 5.12 shows the classes and properties of the e-Science life cycle ontology that are related to managing EPRs.

A concrete example is given in Figure 5.13. There we illustrate a possible RDF tree with instances and properties from the ontology that represent an EPR to a primary dataset, which is stored in an iRODS server. In the e-Science life cycle ontology we provide an ERP class that is connected to two other classes, *EPR-Type* and *EPR-Value* with properties defined among them as illustrated in Figure 5.13. The type stores as a literal what type of EPR it is (e.g. iRODS). The EPR-Value class stores as a literal the URI that is pointing to the dataspace participant. Using iRODS this could be e.g. the path to the dataset stored within the iRODS server.

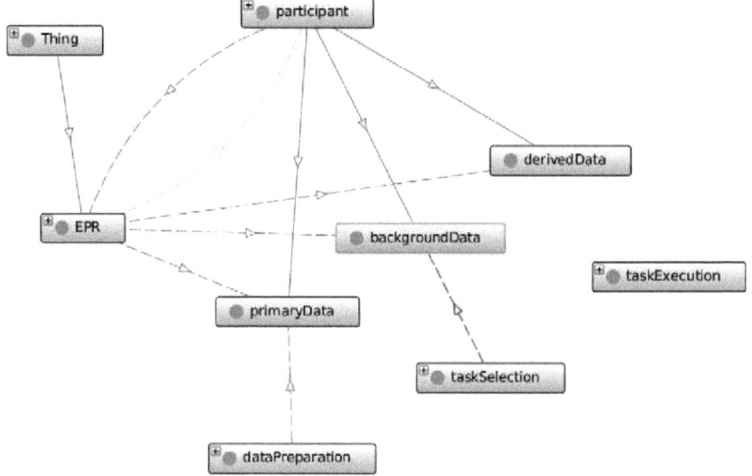

Figure 5.12: OWL classes and properties of the e-Science life cycle ontology regarding EPRs.

5.3.4 Evaluation

The consultation with scientists from our driving research applications[2] have led to more fine-grained concepts and relations as described above. In this phase we demonstrate the usage of the implemented ontology. The e-Science life cycle ontology is evaluated in the context of two real e-Science applications. Several life cycle resources were created using simple forms, where domain experts from both applications have provided detailed information about conducted studies of their research domain. We manually created individuals of the OWL classes defined in the ontology with the data collected from real scientific studies. In this evaluation phase the Protégé individual editor was used to create individuals, which form several LCRs. The SPARQL query language is used to extract the ontology knowledge using the build-in SPARQL query panel of Protégé. A real LCRs is presented in Appendix A. We defined some test queries that address

---

[2]Non-Invasive Blood Glucose Measurement and Breath Gas Analysis see Chapter 8

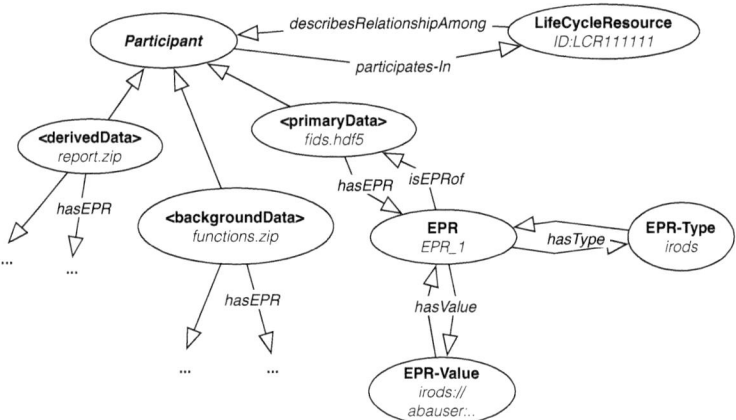

Figure 5.13: e-Science life cycle ontology instances and properties of a concrete example of an EPR.

the kind of requests we expect researchers would like to submit to the ontology.

A query submitted, will receive not only the matching data but also data of its interconnected e-Science activities allowing a user to explore the query results more in detail, discovering e.g. which analytical methods were applied on a particular input dataset, the end point reference to its derived resultset and its corresponding publications. In the following we illustrate some concrete SPARQL query examples that have been used in this evaluation phase:

SPARQL Query Example 1
Let's assume a user would like to list all LCRs having NIGM[3] workflows selected as appropriate task within the activity *Select appropriate Task* and the scientists they were executed by. A concrete SPARQL query might look as follows:

```
PREFIX owl: <http://localhost/LifeCycleOntology.owl#>
```

---

[3] Non-Invasive Blood Glucose Measurement (NIGM) represents our first real e-Science application on top of which the dataspace support platform is evaluated. This application is described in detail in Section 8.2

```
SELECT ?LifeCycle ?TaskSelection ?Scientist ?WorkflowName
WHERE {
            ?LifeCycle owl:hasTaskSelection ?TaskSelection.
            ?LifeCycle owl:isExecutedBy ?Scientist.
            ?TaskSelection owl:hasWorkflow ?Workflow.
            ?Workflow owl:workflowName ?WorkflowName.
            FILTER regex(?WorkflowName, "nigm", "i")
}
```

A list of results is displayed in Figure 5.14.

lifeCycle	taskSelection	scientist	workflowName
NIGM_CADGrid_002	taskSelection_NIGM_2	CADGrid-researcher2	NIGM exp
NIGM_CADGrid_004	taskSelection_NIGM_2	CADGrid-researcher1	NIGM exp
NIGM_CADGrid_001	taskSelection_NIGM	CADGrid-researcher3	NIGM

Figure 5.14: SPARQL query example 1 results in Protégé.

The *select* statement consists of *?LifeCycle ?TaskSelection ?Scientist ?WorkflowName* data variables that are returned in the query result. The SPARQL results are represented in a table form, whereas every row represents one query answer and each variable used in the select statement represents a column in the result table. We match all workflow names containing the case-sensitive expression *NIGM*, indicated by *"i"*.

SPARQL Query Example 2

Furthermore, let's say a scientist wants to apply a NIGM-analysis on acupuncture point HE GU[4]. If the results already exist, he or she could save hours of computation. We might specify a following query to provide a answer to this particular question:

```
PREFIX owl: <http://localhost/LifeCycleOntology.owl#>

SELECT ?LifeCycle ?GoalSpecification  ?Keywords ?Visualisation
WHERE {
```

[4]This is an acupuncture point on the Large Intestine Meridian according to Traditional Chinese Medicine

```
            ?LifeCycle owl:hasGoalSpecification ?GoalSpecification.
            ?GoalSpecification owl:hasDescriptionData ?DescriptionData.
            ?LifeCycle owl:hasTaskExecution ?TaskExecution.
            ?Visualisation owl:isVisualisationOf ?TaskExecution.
            ?DescriptionData owl:keywords ?Keywords.
            FILTER regex(?Keywords, "meridian\index{Meridian} HE GU", "i")
}
```

The results of the above specified query are displayed in Figure 5.15:

lifeCycle	goalSpecification	keywords	visualisation
NIGM_CADGrid_004	goalSpecification_NIGM	Meridian HE GU	EXMP_visualisation
NIGM_CADGrid_001	goalSpecification_NIGM	Meridian HE GU	NIGM_visualisation

Figure 5.15: SPARQL query example 2 results in Protégé.

As we can see a user has found some already published visualizations on *meridian HE GU*, which can be now explored more in detail by further exploring its corresponding LCR.

SPARQL Query Example 3

Suppose we need to know which datasets were used while performing a particular LCR executed by a scientist called *Mayer*, and which research groups he is member of. A corresponding SPARQL statement may look as follows:

```
PREFIX owl: <http://localhost/LifeCycleOntology.owl#>

SELECT ?lLifeCycle ?DataSet  ?Scientist ?LastName ?ResearchGroup
WHERE {
            ?LifeCycle owl:isExecutedBy ?Scientist.
            ?DataSet owl:isDataSetOf ?DataPreparation.
            ?Scientist owl:isMemberOf ?ResearchGroup.
            ?LifeCycle owl:hasTaskExecution ?TaskExecution.
            ?Scientist owl:lastName ?LastName.
            FILTER regex(?LastName, "mayer", "i")
}
```

The results of the above defined query are displayed in Figure 5.16:

lifeCycle	dataSet	scientist	lastName	researchGroup
◆ NIGM_CADGrid_001	◆ dataSet_001	◆ CADGrid-researcher3	mayer	◆ CADGrid-buct.edu.cn
◆ NIGM_CADGrid_001	◆ dataSet_002	◆ CADGrid-researcher3	mayer	◆ CADGrid-buct.edu.cn
◆ NIGM_CADGrid_001	◆ dataSet_003	◆ CADGrid-researcher3	mayer	◆ CADGrid-buct.edu.cn

Figure 5.16: SPARQL query example 3 results in Protégé.

As shown in the figure, the query results provide information about particular datasets executed by a certain scientist. Additionally, we display a scientist's unique id, last name and the scientist's research group. Having found the needed information, a user can e.g. further explore what analysis task was applied on a discovered dataset, the concrete workflow, the workflow report, the results and its corresponding visualizations.

SPARQL Query Example 4

Let's assume we have found some interesting results published in a dataspace but have no access to the published data so as to explore the details of the executed life cycles. We can search for the publication mode of published results in order to receive an access permission:

```
PREFIX owl: <http://localhost/LifeCycleOntology.owl#>

SELECT ?LifeCycle ?Scientist ?Visualisation ?PublicationMode
WHERE {
          ?LifeCycle owl:isExecutedBy ?Scientist.
          ?TaskExecution owl:hasVisualisation ?Visualisation.
          ?LifeCycle owl:isPublishedBy ?PublicationMode.
          ?Visualisation owl:visualisationName ?VisualisationName.
          FILTER regex(?VisualisationName, "nigm", "i")
}
```

The results of the above defined query are displayed in Figure 5.17:

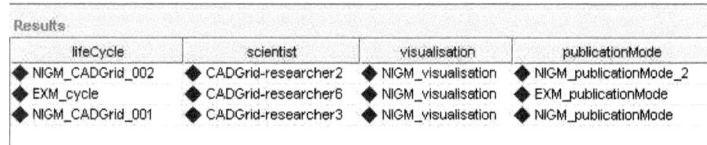

Figure 5.17: SPARQL query example 3 results in Protégé.

Knowing the particular life cycle iteration information and the corresponding publication mode, a user can either ask for permission or become a member of the particular research group, the life cycle is restricted to, in order to receive access to needed results, which act as participants in a scientific dataspace.

5.3.5 Maintenance and Evolution

In this phase we describe how the e-Science life cycle ontology is maintained. Since the scientific research methodology is not static; it changes and is assumed to be changed (evolution), so does the specification for the e-Science life cycle ontology change. To reflect these changes, the e-Science life cycle ontology must be maintained frequently, as are other software components of the underlying dataspace support platform .

One point that should be mentioned in this context is that maintenance of ontologies in general is a primarily organizational process [SAB+03]. Ontologies require strict rules for their update-delete-insert processes. It is therefore essential to thoroughly test possible effects to the application before applied changes to the ontology can be switched-over to a new version of the ontology. As shown in Figure 5.2, the On-To-Knowledge methodology foresees an iterative process within the last three phases in order to provide well defined and evaluated ontologies prior to their deployment in real world applications. We strictly follow this approach, since it has beed verified to be effective in various ontology using applications.

5.3.6 Life Cycle Ontology Properties

Object properties are relationships among concepts defined by the ontology. Logical characteristics of relationships (e.g. functional, transitive, symmetric, reflexive) as well as their domain and range restrictions are fundamental concepts of OWL, that help to provide a well defined specification for the e-Science life cycle. Other OWL concepts such as bounded lists, property restrictions, cardinality constraints guarantee that the process of conducting a scientific study is followed according to the specification defined by the e-Science life cycle ontology.

A declaration of a object or data type property alone, does not imply which individuals are related to each other. By the use of *range* and *domain* statements we can define which classes are related to each other. A restriction domain indicates that the subject of such declared property has to belong to related instance of a class.

For example, a property domain of *execute* is restricted to individuals of the class *scientist*. A *range* statement indicates that the objects of the property range have to belong to an instance of the defined class, which means that the property range is restricted to individuals of the class *lifeCycle*. Let us look at a definition of the *hasDescriptionData* object property. It also includes defined inverse properties *describes*, which interchanges a direction of a range and domain relation of the *hasDescriptionData* property. We use an *owl:unionOf* statement to create an union of individuals of the classes listed inside the statement, restricting the property only to individuals of these classes. The property range is restricted to individuals of a class *descriptionData*.

In the next example we declare a *hasGoalSpecification* object property defining that individuals of a class *lifeCycle* belong to instances of a class *goalSpecification*. Furthermore we declare a *owl:FunctionalProperty* as a subclass of *rdf:property*. This property definition may contain one value for each object at most, which means that one particular life cycle instance may include only one individual of a class *goalSpecification*. The following tables summarize all defined object and data properties and their restrictions defined in the e-Science life cycle ontology. Object properties are resented in Table 5.1 and data properties in Table 5.2.

Object Property	Range	Domain	inverse Property
hasPrimaryData	dataResource	dataSet	usedToGenerate
belongsToDomain	researchDomain	scientist	isDomainOf
hasCollaborativeGroup	ResearchGroup	Collaboration	inCollaborationWith
hasDataPreparation	DataPreparation	LifeCycle	
hasDataSet	DataSet	DataPreparation	isDataSetOf
execute	Scientist	LifeCycle	isExecutedBy
hasGoalSpecification	GoalSpecification	LifeCycle	
hasMembers	Scientist	ResearchGroup	isMemberOf
Table continues on the next page.			

Object Property	Range	Domain	inverse Property
hasReferenceTo	DomainOntology	GoalSpecification	
hasReportFile	ReportFile	TaskExecution	isReportFileOf
hasResultPublishing	ResultPublishing	LifeCycle	
hasServiceOntology	ServiceOntology	Service	isServiceOntologyOf
hasTaskExecution	TaskExecution	LifeCycle	
hasTaskSelection	TaskSelection	LifeCycle	
hasVisualisation	Visualisation	ResultPublishing	isVisualisationOf
hasVisualisation	Visualisation	TaskExecution	isVisualisationOf
hasWorkflow	Workflow	TaskSelection	isWorkflowOf
hasWorkflowDocument	WorkflowDokument	TaskSelection	isWorkflowDocumentOf
isPublishedBy	PublicationMode	LifeCycle	isPublicationModeOf
isUsedFor	Workflow	Service	usesService
isResourceFileOf	DataPreparation	ResourceFile	
usedToGenerate	DataSet	DataResource	
hasEPR	Participant	LifeCycle	isEPRof

Table 5.1: Excerpt of object properties.

Data Type Property	Domain	Range
firstName	Person	&xsd;string
lastName	Person	&xsd;string
age	Person	&xsd;integer
homepage	Scientist	&xsd;string
birthDate	Person	&xsd;date
country	Person	&xsd;string
state	Person	&xsd;string
phone	Scientist	&xsd;string
email	Scientist	&xsd;string
title	Scientist	&xsd;string
keywords	DescriptionData	&xsd;string
description	DescriptionData	&xsd;string

Table continues on the next page.

Data Type Property	Domain	Range
name	DescriptionData	&xsd;string
reportURL	ReportFile	&xsd;anyURI
resourceURI	DataResource	&xsd;anyURI
serviceOntologyReference	ServiceOntology	&xsd;anyURI
visualisationReference	Visualisation	&xsd;anyURI
visualisationType	Visualisation	&xsd;anyURI
resourceFileDescription	ResourceFile	&xsd;string
resourceFileReference	ResourceFile	&xsd;anyURI
workflowReference	Workflow	&xsd;anyURI
workflowName	Workflow	&xsd;string

Table 5.2: Data type properties.

5.4 Reasoning the e-Science life cycle ontology

Knowledge described by an ontology is sharable, understandable to machines, and supports the enrichment of data sources and relationships at the semantic level. However, in order to get the most out of an existing ontology and its defined individuals the usage of a reasoner is essential. A reasoner is an important component for working with OWL ontologies. If possible all querying of the e-Science life cycle ontology should be done using a reasoner. This is because knowledge in the ontology might not be explicit and a reasoner is required to deduce implicit knowledge so that the correct query results can be obtained. Pellet [pel11] is an open-source OWL reasoner that provides standard reasoning services for OWL ontologies. The Jena Semantic Web Framework for Java [jen11] provides an in-process interface to the Pellet reasoner that is used in conjunction with the search component of the dataspace support platform.

The following inference problems are often considered in practice according to the W3C Recommendation of OWL 2 Direct Semantics [W3C10].

- Ontology Consistency
- Ontology Entailment

- Ontology Equivalence
- Ontology Equisatisfiability
- Class Expression Satisfiability
- Class Expression Subsumption
- Instance Checking
- Boolean Conjunctive Query Answering

In the following we provide some reasoning examples in order to explore some of the effects of applying reasoning in the e-Science life cycle ontology. There is a number of inferences that can be made, both about the classes defined in the ontology (for example discovering that class definitions are inconsistent), and about the instances of the ontology (for example discovering that a particular instance is inferred to be a member of a particular class).

Ontology consistency is a mandatory first step before any other reasoning service can be done, since any consequence can be inferred from inconsistency. The consistency of a set of axioms should be checked and it should be verified if the input axioms do not contain contradictions. Below is an inconsistency example regarding a LRC of the e-Science life cycle ontology. Let's define the following 6 axioms.

(1) lifeCycle hasGoalSpecification max 1
(2) LCR234 type lifeCycle
(3) GS478 type goalSpecification
(4) GS452 type goalSpecification
(5) LCR234 hasGoalSpecification GS478
(6) LCR234 hasGoalSpecification GS452

In (1) we put a cardinality restriction to the property *hasGoalSpecification* with the OWL class *lifeCyce* specifying that an instance of the class *lifeCyce* can have only one *hasGoalSpecification* property assigned. In (2) we define a new instance of that class *lifeCyce*, which is LCR243. In (3) and (4) we define two new instances of the class *goalSpecification*. In (5) the instance GS478 of the class *goalSpecification* is connect to LCR243 and in (6) a second instance of the class *goalSpecification* (GS452) is connected to the same lifeCycle instance, which would mean that a specific LCR has in fact two different goals defined. This, however does not make any sense in regard of the e-Science life cycle, plus it is not consistent with the cardinality restriction defined in (1). A reasoner would therefore declare the ontology as inconsistent.

Using the semantics defined in the following 8 input axioms, we exemplify inferences about the e-Science life cycle ontology and individuals as listed below.

```
Input axioms:
(1) executes inverseOf isExecutedBy
(2) activity equivalentTo (goalSpecification or dataPreparation)
(3) goalSpecification disjointWith dataPreparation
(4) LCR234 isExecutedBy scientist1
(5) DP67 type dataPreparation
(6) LCR234 hasDataPreparation DP67
(7) hasDataPreparation inverseOf belongsTo
(8) LCR313 hasDataPreparation DP67

Some inferences:
scientist1 executes LCR234 (1,4)
DP67 type activity (2,5)
dataPreparation subClassOf activity (2)
DP67 type not goalSpecification (3,5)
DP67 belongsTo LCR234 and LCR313 (6,7,8)
```

Another example described in words in this context would be e.g. if we query for let us say all LCRs of a given person. Since the ontology distinguishes between a scientists and students (both inheriting from the class person) we would not get all results if the SPARQL query does not explicitly specify that it is a scientists. However, this is not always possible since in some cases the requesting user might not know it. Applying a reasoner in preface to the query execution, enables us to provide a better result set.

5.5 Scope of the e-Science life cycle ontology

An ontology in general is a collection of concepts and their relations to one another established by a community that wants to use a common semantic for sharing knowledge, information or data. The e-Science life cycle ontology aims at proving a common language for sharing or exchanging scientific studies independent of any application domain. However, depending on the application domain there might be domain ontologies such as the Cell Type Ontology [BRA05] etc. to be used in conjunction with the e-Science life cycle ontology.

EXPO [SK06] represents an ontology for scientific experiments that contain over 200 concepts about experimental methods. It is available in OWL-DL and it was last modified in 2006[5]. It provides a structure to describe common concepts of scientific experimentation as experimental goals, experimental methods and actions, types of experiments, rules for experimental design, etc. Expo can be seen as part of a general ontology of science that should formalize scientific tasks, methods, techniques, etc. It represents a well-defined ontology with a large amount of definitions that allow to describe scientific experiments up to a high level of detail. However, the developers of EXPO doesn't take much into account that the process of describing a scientific experiment is definitely seen by acting scientists as something undesired. The developers of EXPO argue that "convenient tools will need to be developed to enable practicing scientists to annotate their own experiments ... We envisage such tools will, for example, ask the user to describe the domain of the experiment, if the experiment involved any hypotheses, what experimental results support or reject hypotheses, etc." So far EXPO has not been evaluated in real e-Science applications.

Based on our experiences during the development and evaluation of the e-Science life cycle ontology we believe that it is hard to get researchers to accept that they have to fill out a large number of forms during the process of executing an experiment. We think that this acceptance is crucial for the success and broad usage of an ontology. It is therefore a challenge to find the balance between providing well-defined semantics about scientific experiments and requesting information from the acting scientists. As much as possible should of course happen automatically, however there are some information that cannot be captured unless from the acting person. For example, if we have a research portal attached to the application domain, where the scientific experiments are conducted, then information about the responsible person (e.g. his affiliation, email, etc.) can automatically be captured. However, it is still not possible to get information such as the intended goals of a specific experiment.

In the e-Science life cycle ontology we have therefore tried to keep the number of experiment descriptions that have to be provided by the acting scientists very small

---

[5]http://sourceforge.net/projects/expo/files/

and on the same time we tried to get as much as possible from its semantics.

Another related work regarding the e-Science life cycle ontology is *The Ontology for Biomedical Investigations* (OBI) [OBI11]. The Ontology for Biomedical Investigations project is developing an integrated ontology for the description of biological and clinical investigations. The current release of the ontology is from July 2011, which indicates that the project is active in contrast to the Expo ontology, where the latest release goes back to 2006. The latest complete version of the ontology is available online[6]. The ontology includes a set of universal terms, that are applicable across various biological domains, and domain-specific terms relevant only to a given domain. It is being built under the Basic Formal Ontology (BFO) [BFO11], which is focused on the task of providing a genuine upper ontology, which can be used in support of domain ontologies developed for scientific research. OBI support the annotation of biomedical investigations, regardless of the particular field of study. Therefore many ontologies and external resources are imported into OBI, some of them are depicted in Figure 5.18. The problem that comes with importing many external resources is that reasoning becomes slower and the ontology is harder to navigate.

What makes the e-Science Lifecycle Ontology unique in contrast to the above described related ontologies is that it models not only the process of conducting scientific experiments, but it also provides a framework for the preservation of the experiments including their data (primary, background, and derived datasets). This is challenged by the EPR-Framework, which allows to define references (End Point References) to real datasets stored in a data preservation system. Figure 5.18 illustrates the environment of the e-Science life cycle ontology, by showing an upper and lower ontology that will be used in conjunction with the e-Science life cycle ontology. The figure also shows additional related ontologies including their upper and lower ontologies. These ontologies include EXPO and OBI. They are related in the way that they also consider in some way in their concepts the process of conducting an experiment. However, we would like to note that they are not part of the e-Science Lifecycle Ontology, rather they are co-existing ontologies differently approaching to describe and annotate scientific experiments.

An upper ontology is a model of the common objects that are generally applicable across a wide range of domain ontologies. It employs a core glossary that contains, the terms, and associated object descriptions, as they are used in various, relevant domain

---

[6]http://purl.obolibrary.org/obo/obi.owl

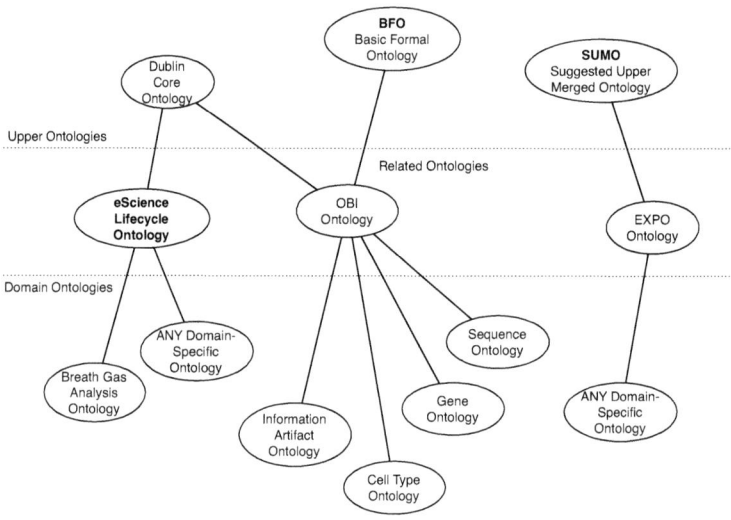

Figure 5.18: Environment of the e-Science lifecycle ontology.

sets. There are several standardized upper ontologies available for use, including Dublin Core [DCM11], Basic Formal Ontology (BFO) [BFO11], and Suggested Upper Merged Ontology (SUMO) [SUM11]. A list of available domain and upper ontologies describing concepts of particular research domains is provided at the Semantic Web Wiki[7]. In the e-Science life cycle ontology we use the Dublin Core Metadata terms together with other standards that are used within OWL such as RDF, RDFS, and XSD. Figure 5.19 shows all the ontology prefixes that we have used in this context. At the moment we don't use any domain specific vocabularies and standards such as the Unified Medical Language System (UMLS) [UML11], which is popular in the biomedical domain. However, we believe that we might also utilize such external vocabularies in the future, in particular after gaining experience and feedback from real usage of the e-Science life cycle ontology within applications of breath research. The ontology prefixes are listed in Figure 5.19.

---

[7]http://semanticweb.org/wiki/Ontology

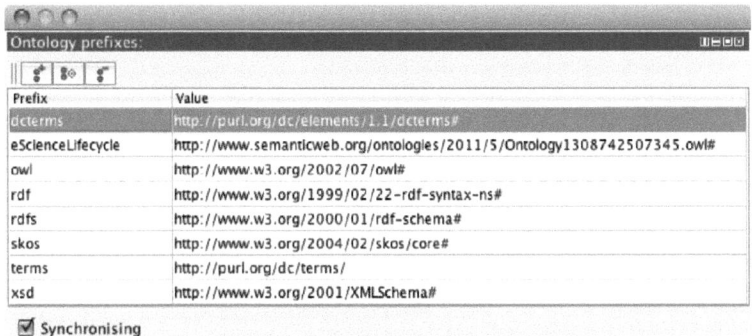

Figure 5.19: Ontology prefixes.

5.6 Alternative Approaches to develop an Ontology

The goal of this section is to present the main methodologies for ontology creation. A methodology is defined by IEEE [IEE08] as *a comprehensive, integrated series of techniques or methods creating a general system theory of how a class of through-intensive work ought be performed* [GPFLC04]. The ontology development process deals with identifying the most crucial activities which are performed while creating ontologies. There are three main Types of activities [GPFLC04]:

- *Ontology management activities* - task identification, arrangement, and execution time is managed by this activity including control and quality facilities for performed tasks.

- *Ontology development oriented activities* - describes the most important issues considering ontology development such as the ontology environment, referring to how and where the ontology will be used, the ontology specification, conceptualization, formalization and implementation, addressing the main development steps, and finally the ontology application.

- *Ontology support activities* - include a knowledge discovery, evaluation and documentation process while building ontologies.

In the following we present some of the most important methodologies for building ontologies.

5.6.1 Unschold and King's method

In 1995 Unschold and King introduced in [Usc96] the first method for creating ontologies. The main process includes four building steps, which are:

1. *Purpose identification* - specification of the relevant application domain terms, goals, ontology purpose and user identification.

2. *Ontology building process* - key concepts identification and term relationships of the specified domain, textual descriptions and definitions of classes and relationships are provided. We distinguish here between three different concept strategies in order to build an ontology:

    - *the bottom-up strategy* - first the specific concepts such as a *dataSet* or *workflowDocument* are identified and then a more general abstraction is modeled grouping the concepts for example into *derivedData* participants of a dataspace. As a result we receive more detailed concepts while increasing a inconsistency risk and requiring more rework.

    - *the top-down strategy* - first an abstract concept is modeled and then a specification of this model. This results in a less consistent model, requiring greater rework and more effort.

    - *the middle-out strategy* - this approach specifies the core concepts and basic classes which for example are represented through different participant categories such as *backgroundData*, *primaryData* and *derivedData*, Then, we specify the concepts on the top such as *participant* and concepts on the bottom such as *workflowDocument* representing a particular derived data output document.

3. *Evaluation* - the ontology is evaluated using appropriate application environments.

4. *Documentation* - the notation, concepts and their relationships should be documented.

5.6.2 Grueninger and Fox's Methodology

In 1995 Grueninger and Fox proposed in [GF95] a formal building an evaluation concept for designing ontologies. The core methodology processes are:

1. *scenario identification* - the ontology development is application scenario related, providing solutions and a formal knowledge model of the classes and relationships which will be used while building ontology;

2. *informal competency question elaboration* - represent the informal questions, expressed in natural language, that should be answered using the implemented ontology;

3. *terminology specification* - using the extracted content and knowledge of a ontology, one can identify the terminology indicating the concepts and their relations;

4. *formal specification of competency questions using formal terminology* - the informal questions, expressed in natural language, are formally represented;

5. *axioms specification using first order logic* - term definition of a ontology using axioms; and

6. *completeness theorem specification* - condition definition providing the complete answers to the competency questions.

5.6.3 Methontology

Methontology was introduced in 1997 in [GPFLC04] by the Ontology Group at Universidad Politecnia de Madrid, allowing building knowledge level ontologies. The core task processes while creating ontologies using Methonology are:

1. *glossary of terms specification* - term definition of the relevant domain of interest is specified, including concepts, instances, properties representing the relationships among the concepts, textual descriptions, synonyms, etc;

2. *concept taxonomy specification* - after the terms are identified, a concept taxonomy is specified providing a hierarchy model definition. Each of the in *Unschold and King's method* introduced strategies (top-down, bottom-up, middle-out) can be applied here;

3. *ad hoc binary relation diagram specification* - the relationships among concepts are defined specifying the domains and ranges of each relation;

4. *the concept dictionary specification* - property and relationship specification describing the previous generated taxonomy concepts, including all domain related concepts, their instances and relationships;

5. *detailed specification of the ad hoc binary relations* - detailed description of the concept dictionary in form of a relation table representing the Object Properties;

6. *detailed attribute specification* - all attributes specified in the concept dictionary are described in detail, including the name, the value types, domain and ranges, representing the Data Type Properties;

7. *detailed class attribute definition* - all class attributes specified in the concept dictionary are described related to the class they belong to;

8. *detailed constants definition* - each constant specified in the term glossary is described;

9. *formal axiom definition* - formal axiom table, including the logical expressions, description, name, corresponding concepts and attributes, is generated;

10. *rule definition* - ontology rule definition, including the name, description, expression describing the rule, concepts and relations; and

11. *instance definition* - instance specification, including the name, the concept the instance belong to and the attribute values.

5.7 Summary

The e-Science life cycle is the heart of our scientific dataspace paradigm. The e-Science life cycle ontology addresses the precise description of scientific experiments by taking advantage of the well-defined semantics of the Resource Description Framework (RDF) [rdf04b] and the expressive formal logic-based OWL language [owl04]. The ontology is used to trace semantics about procedures in e-Science applications.

To systematically design and build the ontology, we carefully selected a methodology to help us during the process of the ontology implementation. The methodology supports the development in organizing the ontology primitives and specifying their basic characteristics in details. We started with understanding the principal terms and concepts used in the e-Science life cycle and then we followed the recommended phases of the On-To-Knowledge methodology.

The profound knowledge about iterations of the e-Science life cycle, consolidated within instances of the ontology represents a relationship model for scientific dataspaces, because it provides (a) creation, (b) representation, and (c) searching of semantically rich relationships among dataspace participants. Realization of a scientific dataspace paradigm will highly contribute to the development of data preservation frameworks for e-Science.

With the help of the e-Science life cycle ontology, it is possible for scientists to describe, execute and share their e-Science experiments with others. Furthermore, it is feasible to search for published instances of the life cycle or even for instances of single activities of the life cycle. In such a way, a scientist could search for all published goal specifications corresponding to his research domain, by searching for a given domain name. The dataspace will then provide not only the published instances of the activity, but also the complete instance of the e-Science life cycle, including the inputs of other activities and its corresponding results. In addition, it will provide similar life cycle iterations from the repository by using the semantically rich relationships described by the ontology. With this in mind, it will be easier for research groups to engage collaboration, provide knowledge transfers within collaborations and among different research groups with respect to different research areas.

In conclusion, the e-Science life cycle is likely to unify the process of publishing primary, derived, and background datasets as well as their interconnection and make it easy for scientists to register and describe new e-Science experiments and for users to find, explore and understand these applied experiments. Examples of concrete life cycle resources are provided in Chapter 8 and in Appendix A as part of the experimental evaluation in two different real-world e-Science applications.

Chapter 6

A Dataspace-Based Support Platform jSpace

> *"A preservation environment manages communication from the past while communicating with the future."*
>
> ――――――――――――――――――――――――――――――――
> In: Towards a theory of digital preservation, The International
> Journal of Digital Curation. Vol 3, No 1, 2008 by
> REAGAN MOORE

6.1 Introduction

A lot has been written lately about the need to store and archive important data from scientific studies and complete experiments (including primary, derived, and background data) to meet today's mandates of various government regulations. With more and more data being stored electronically, how does a research organization keep this information safe and accessible for years to come when? There has not been any one digital storage technology used to meet the challenge of "forever" data preservation [Har03]. This chapter discusses generic use cases in Section 6.2 and in Section 6.3 the architecture of such a support platform, which we named *jSpace*. jSpace provides tools that form together a dataspace-based support platform, where the preservation of dataspace participants and semantic enrichment of dataspace relationships are realized. A reference implementation is described in Section 6.4 and finally in Section 6.5 this chapter is concluded. jSpace is build on top of the e-Science life cycle described in the previous chapter. This model addresses the precise description of scientific experiments by taking advantage of the well-defined semantics of the Resource Description Framework (RDF) and the expressive formal logic-based OWL language. jSpace allows to construct semantic data about experiments at a high abstraction level, which hides from the scientist most of the underlying complexity involved in the process, such as working directly with RDF or writing SPARQL queries. If used in conjunction with a modern preservation system, such as iRODS [RMH+10], jSpace can furthermore support the preservation of dataspace participants and relationships to be available in the long run.

6.2 Generic Use Cases

We apply a use-case driven, object-oriented process, using the UML as a notation for its models. Therefore we first describe the use cases supported by the system, before we discuss architectural components that have been selected to best achieve the use cases. The use case diagram depicted in Figure 6.1 gives an overview of the use cases implemented by jSpace.

6.2.1 Search&Query Dataspace

Search&Query Dataspace provides scientists to interact with the dataspace in terms of submitting Search&Query requests. dataspace systems in general are supposed to support a simple keyword-based search and a more powerful query interface [HFM06]. We should keep in mind that Search&Query scientific dataspaces is of exploratory nature, therefore an iterative process, which can be described as follows.

At first, a Search&Query request is submitted via the Search&Query interface to the system. Such a request can be expressed in many different formats (a single keyword or a set of keywords or a SPARQL query - for advanced users). Then a SPARQL query is generated (if the request in not already expressed in SPARQL) and submitted to the RDF store, which executes the query. The results are represented as RDF data and are returned to the requesting client where they are displayed. The result

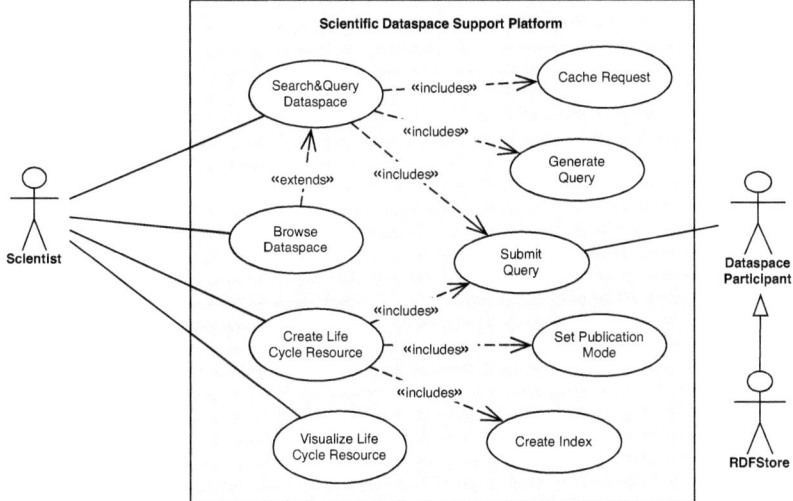

Figure 6.1: Overview of the use cases of the system.

set in this first iteration of the Search&Query process contains all available life cycle resources the requester has access to and that match the query he submitted (e.g. those life cycle resources that contain the keywords he entered). Users might reduce the number of matched life cycle resources by applying filters. In a further iteration of the Search&Query process the user submits queries to retrieve data items that were used in the life cycle resources he has explored. Such data items include primary (e.g. an input dataset such as breath gas measurement samples), background (e.g. analytical methods such as a Matlab [1] script or a scientific workflow document), and derived data (e.g. visualized results such as histograms from the analysis task). This kind of data is retrieved by submitting structured queries to the corresponding participant of the scientific dataspace. Depending on the type of the data source it can be SQL, XQuery, or any other query language supported by the underlying data source.

Based on the e-Science life cycle, search and query services can be provided for all participants of the scientific dataspace. Hence, it is possible to forward a keyword query

---

[1] Matlab is a numerical computing environment and programming language

to all participants, which has the aim to identify relevant datasets. However, each query submitted to the scientific dataspace, will receive not only the matching data but also data of its followed e-science activities. For instance, considering a data mining project it will be possible to receive what mining task were applied to a discovered or prepared dataset, the concrete workflow, the workflow report, the results presented in PMML and its corresponding visualizations.

6.2.2 Browse Dataspace

Browse Dataspace is a task of type "Search&Query Dataspace" but specializes the way how the user is exploring the dataspace. It is actually a Search&Query activity (the same subtasks, *Generate Query*, and *Submit Query* are included), but has a few extra processes that go above and beyond the usual Search&Query activity. These extra processes are e.g. visual presentation of the dataspace, no filters except the publication modes are applied to the query, which is submitted to the RDF store. In other words, the browse function generates a let's say "`select*from dataspace`" considering the access rights of the requesting user. Note that only semantic description (i.e. dataspace relationships expressed as individuals and properties of the e-Science life cycle ontology) are returned to the user and not the entire dataspace with all participants. Browse Dataspace can only be utilized by human actors, whereas Search&Query Dataspace is also of use for applications.

6.2.3 Create Life Cycle Resource

Create Life Cycle Resource represents the use case where a scientist enters information about the scientific experiment he or she is currently conducting. This process creates a new life cycle resource and includes the following steps. First a local copy of the e-Science life cycle ontology is loaded into memory of the local machine by the *Life Cycle Composer* and a Jena-based ontology graph model is created. Then, individuals of classes of the ontology are created as instructed by the scientist. That means that the classes of each e-Science life cycle activity are being instantiated in this step. Setting a publication mode is also done by creating individuals of the corresponding classes on the e-Science life cycle ontology. For each individual a new index is being requested and included into the individual. In particular for each activity of a Life Cycle Resource a unique ID is being generated. Once a new LCR is accomplished an unique ID will be attached to each of the five e-Science life cycle activities of that LCR. These IDs form together a key to uniquely identify the LCR. Such a key might look like the following:

$$\text{oeaw-aa:4.1.3:5:9:12:23:24} \tag{6.1}$$

The first item of the key (oeaw-aa[2] in the example above) indicates the organization to which the dataspace instance[3] is deployed and the second (after the semicolon) indicates the version of the ontology. That follows (after the second semicolon) the ids of the corresponding e-Science life cycle activities. Activity ids are separated by a colon. The first item of the key refers to the activity *Specify Goals*, the second to *Prepare Data* and so forth. This index concept is flexible with changes to the ontology. For instance if an new version of the ontology is developed and let us assume an activity is added to the e-Science life cycle, then an additional id will be added to the key. Important in this context is to specify the correct order of activities (e.g. data preparation should/must be after goal specification). The indexes are managed by the *Dataspace Indexer* and the indexing mechanism is described more precisely in Section 6.3.4.

Finally, a SPARQL/Update[4] query is generated and submitted to the RDF store by the Search&Query processor. This will add the new instance of the e-Science life cycle into the RDF store to be discoverable and therefore re-useable by other scientists.

6.2.4 Visualize Life Cycle Resource

Visualize Life Cycle Resource represents the use case where a single life cycle resource is being visualized in order to visually provide an overview of its interconnected dataspace participants that correspond to the life cycle resource. Also the semantic information stored within each e-Science life cycle activity will be visually presented to the user within this use case.

---

[2]oeaw-aa is the identification code of the Breath Research Institute of the Austrian Academy of Sciences, to which a scientific dataspace is deployed as experimental framework in the context of our evaluation study, described in Section 8.3.

[3]Multiple interconnected instances of the dataspace support platform build up a large-scale dataspace. This is introduced and described in detail within Chapter 7.

[4]SPARQL/Update is an update language for RDF graphs. It uses a syntax derived from SPARQL. Update operations are performed on a collection of graphs in a Graph Store. Operations are provided to change existing RDF graphs as well as create and remove graphs with the Graph Store. http://jena.hpl.hp.com/~afs/SPARQL-Update.html

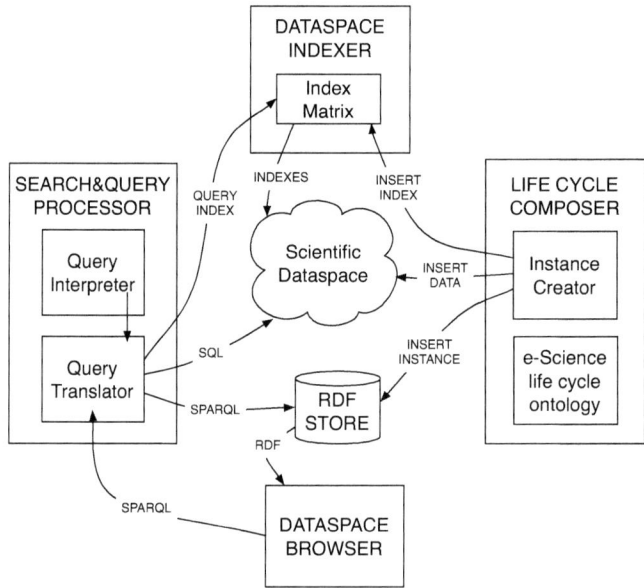

Figure 6.2: Holistic view of the system architecture [EB10].

6.3 jSpace System Architecture

This section provides a high level overview of the technical architecture for the dataspace-based support platform jSpace. It outlines the technologies used to provide a system for broad collaboration and participation in a distributed network for scientific experiments and studies in various application domains. In facilitating interoperability through standards, jSpace helps its users to enhance scientific expertise, promote professional collaboration, and raise the level of their output. The architectural components that have been selected to best achieve the use cases presented in the previous section are presented as main entities of the architecture in Figure 6.2.

They are in particular the *Life Cycle Composer* - for creation of e-Science life cycle resources, the *RDF store* - for storing those resources, the *Life Cycle Visualizer* for visualizing them, the *Dataspace Indexer* - for indexing the participants and relationships, the *Search&Query Processor* for allowing scientists to find those life cycle resources, and the *Dataspace Browser* for exploration of the dataspace. These, with each other cooperating software programs represent the environment in which the *Scientific Dataspace* is able to grow and evolve into a space of well preserved scientific data. They also provide the organization and retrieval of scientific data within the dataspace.

6.3.1 Search&Query Processor

Searching and querying a dataspace in general is not like querying a database. In a dataspace we need to drift away from the one-shot query to query-by-navigation. Users will have to pose several queries, which results in an *Information Gathering Task* (IGT). IGT was introduced by Halevy et al. in [HFM06] as one of the major principles of a dataspace system.

In jSpace this task is implemented as an iterative process of submitting different types of queries. Figure 6.3 illustrates two iterations of the IGT of a concrete example in the breath gas analysis application domain. The information a scientist is gathering in the first iteration, illustrated in Figure 6.3 (a) represent semantics about applied e-Science experiments, like what were the research goals, what dataset was used, what analytical methods, etc. Due to the fact that dataspace participants as well as their relationships are precisely described by instances of the classes of the e-Science life cycle ontology, therefore organized as RDF resources, the *Search&Query Processor* is built on top of the SPARQL query language [PS08] and its processor, which has been accepted as a W3C recommendation for querying RDF resources.

Queries posed in the first iteration of the IGT are therefore submitted to the RDF store, which organizes all available instances of the ontology. This query is expressed as SPARQL query constructs and it will lead the scientist to those resources he or she might be interested in. After the scientist has identified those resources (scientific experiments) that he or she is interested in, he or she might continue his IGT with a second iteration. The information that can be gathered within this second iteration, illustrated in Figure 6.3 (b) represents the datasets itself that are used within previously identified resources. Such datasets are for example the input dataset used, or the dataset derived from selected scientific experiments. In order to apply such kind of deeper searching and querying a more sophisticated query is submitted in the second iteration of IGT to the scientific dataspace in particular to the corresponding DBMS

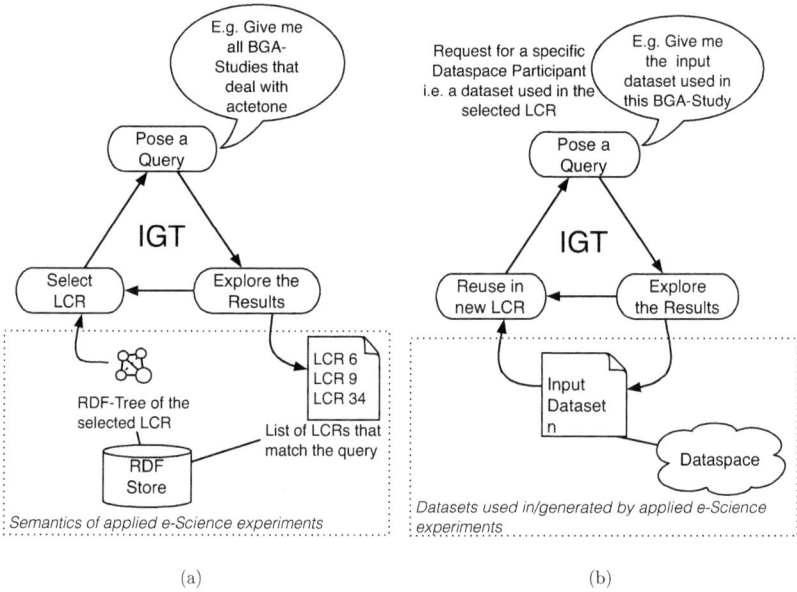

Figure 6.3: IGT of a concrete example in the breath gas analysis application domain.

that participates in the dataspace. Depending on the data preservation system used to store the datasets of scientific studies it can be expressed in a different query language. In our reference implementation that is discussed in Section 6.4, we have successfully been using the Jargon Java Library [jar11] to access and query for a dataset stored in an iRODS server that we have set up for our prototypical implementation.

The *Search&Query Processor* consists of a *Query Interpreter* and a *Query Translator*. The query interpreter receives a request, which can be expressed in either as SPARQL-Query or as a keyword or set of keywords. The request is forwarded to the *Query Translator*, who generates a SPARQL query (if not yet already expressed in SPARQL) out of the keywords. This SPARQL query is then submitted to the RDF store. Figure 6.4 provides an UML activity diagram of the above described iterative information gathering task, which implements the previously introduced use case '*Search&Query Dataspace*" in jSpace. The diagram is organized into swimlanes showing

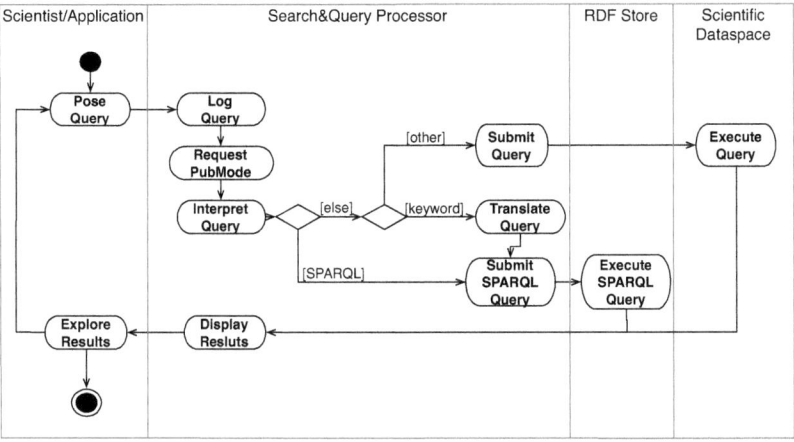

Figure 6.4: UML activity diagram of the IGT implemented in jSpace.

the responsibility for actions. Each activity is briefly described in Table 6.2.

Activity	Guard Condition	Description
Pose Query		The scientist or an application poses a query. This query can be expressed in different formats as described in Section 6.3.1
Log Query		The query is logged within the system log. In particular, type, timestamp, user, and role are logged with the query.
Request PubMode		The Search&Query Processor requests the publication mode and maps it to the user role.
Interpret Query		The query is parsed and interpreted.
	SPARQL	If it is a SPARQL query, no transformation is needed, therefore can be directly submitted to the RDF store.
	keyword	Keyword-based queries are forwarded to the Query Translator.

Table continues on the next page.

Activity	Guard Condition	Description
	other	Other indicate that the requester is already in a further iteration of the information gathering task. Such requests are submitted to the data sources in the scientific dataspace to retrieve a particular dataspace participant (dataset that participates in a previously selected LCR)
Translate Query		Keyword requests are translated into a SPARQL query, including the publication mode and user role of the requester.
Submit SPARQL Query		The SPARQL query is submitted to the RDF store.
Execute SPARQL Query		The RDF store executes the SPARQL query.
Submit Query		The SQL Query is submitted to a specific datasource in the dataspace.
Execute Query		The datasource executed the SQL Query.
Display Results		The results are displayed.
Explore Results		The requester explores the results and optionally continues the information gathering task by posing another query, therefore starting a new Search&Query Iteration.

Table 6.1: Description of the activities and guard conditions in the use case "*Search&Query Dataspace*".

6.3.2 RDF Store

The RDF store manages the e-Science life cycle resources. A life cycle resource consists of a couple of instances of the OWL classes and their properties defined in the e-Science life cycle ontology. These instances, consolidated within a life cycle resource (LCR) describe on a semantically high level a scientific experiment. Life cycle resources are expressed in RDF. Once a new LCR is composed via the *Life Cycle Composer* by a scientist, a new life cycle resource is created, indexed and added to the RDF store.

6.3.3 e-Science Life Cycle Composer

The e-Science life cycle composer enables a scientist to describe his scientific experiments. It guides him through the five e-Science life cycle activities, creates new instances of them, and attaches them to a new life cycle resource. It communicates with the indexing engine, which provides unique indexes for new instances of e-Science life cycle activities and adds the new indexes into its index structure, the *index matrix*. This indexing mechanism is described more precisely in Section 6.3.4.

In real world scenarios it might often be the case that instances of an e-Science life cycle are being reused. For example, the instance of the e-Science life cycle activity *"Specify Goal"* will be used several times in many iterations of an e-Science life cycle, because the specified goals don't change during investigations on the same study, whereas the activity *"Select Tasks"* or *"Run Tasks"* might change in almost every e-Science life cycle.

To further explain this, let's assume a breath gas analysis scientist is working on a study, which has the goal to provide a manuscript describing behavior of the volatile organic compounds (VOCs) acetone, acetonitrile, and isoprene in exhaled breath. In order to fulfill the above introduced study the researcher first (in the first iteration of the life cycle) takes a look at the expired and inspired concentration (measured in ppb) of the three VOCs in the breath gas samples. Then, in a second iteration he investigates the concentrations by splitting the samples into male and female samples and finally, in a third iteration of the life cycle, the researcher examines the relation of breath isoprene in the context of smoker, non-smoker, and ex-smoker. In all these three iterations of the e-Science life cycle the specified goal does not change as they correspond to the same study conducted by a single researcher.

Now, to ease the researcher during conducting the above experiments, the e-Science life cycle composer allows to simply re-use already defined life cycle instances, thus it is not necessary to always describe all five e-Science life cycle activities, which of course would be a sticking point of the system.

The e-Science life cycle composer can be seen as the feeding interface to the scientific dataspace. It is the appropriate and easy to use way to enter semantically rich information about how the participating data items in the dataspace are related and interconnected together. Strong requirement here is to provide a simple and clear interface that can easily be used by scientists from diverse research domains, especially for non-computer scientists. The definition of guidelines to be followed by Master and

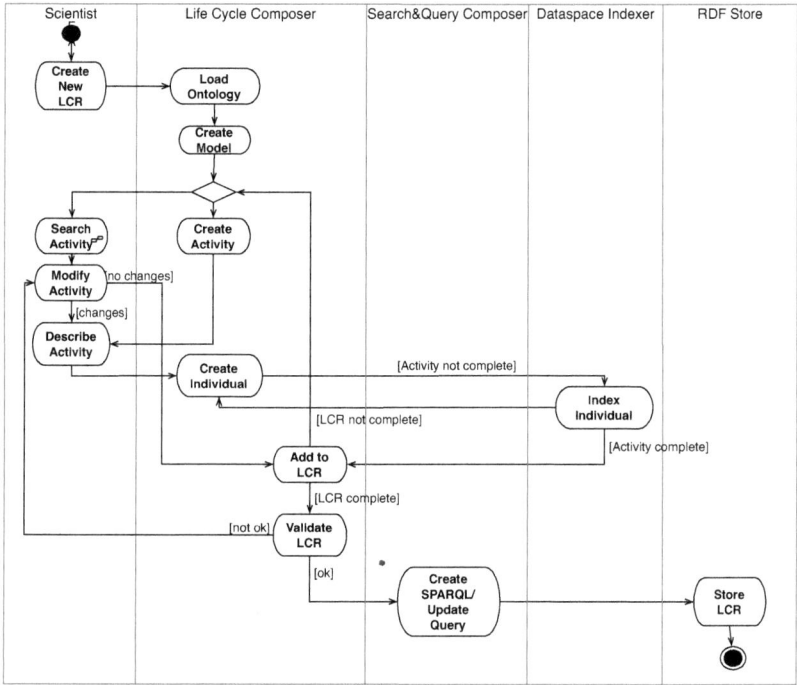

Figure 6.5: Activity diagram attached to the use case *"Create Life Cycle Resource"*.

PhD students when conducting a scientific study represents an essential task which, if applied forcefully can lead to evolution of the dataspace into a semantically rich large-scale scientific data space.

Once an iteration of the life cycle is complete the user can set a publication mode to the created life cycle resource, which restricts access to the resource.

The above described example is illustrated as activities in the UML activity diagram in Figure 6.5. The diagram shows how the use case *Create Life Cycle Resource* is implemented in jSpace. The diagram is organized into swimlanes showing the responsibility for actions. Each activity is also briefly described in Table 6.2.

Activity	Guard Condition	Description
Create New LCR		Creates an empty life cycle resource.
Load Ontology		Loads the e-Science life cycle ontology.
Create Model		Creates the Jena ontology model.
Create Activity		Creates an empty e-Science life cycle activity.
Describe Activity		The process of entering information about the conducted experiment.
Create Individual		Creates individuals of corresponding classes of the e-Science life cycle ontology.
Index Individual		Generates an index for the created individual.
	Activity complete	The activity is complete if all mandatory individuals were created.
	Activity not complete	The iteration continues until the activity is complete.
Add to LCR		Adds the activity to the RDF-graph that represents the life cycle resource.
	LCR complete	If the life cycle resource is complete, which means the all five e-Science life cycle activities were created and described accordingly, the life cycle resource will be validated.
	LCR not complete	In this case the Scientist continues with either creating a new activity or by searching and applying available activities in order to complete the life cycle.
Search Activity		Searches for existing e-Science life cycle activities can then be re-used. This is a sub-activity, which invokes the activity graph illustrated in Figure 6.4. The activity graph nested in it is executed and the sub-activity is not exited until the final state of the nested graph is reached. The results are displayed into the Life Cycle Composer.
Modify Activity		For the purpose of applying changes to re-used activities. Also, if the life cycle resource was not valid

Table continues on the next page.

Activity	Guard Condition	Description
	no changes	Indicates that no changes were applied to a selected e-Science life cycle activity, therefore can be re-used (added to the life cycle resource) without creating a new index.
	changes	The e-Science life cycle activity will be changed therefore a new index will be created. This activity could either be a selected one from the search results or a newly created that need to be changed because validation was not ok.
Validate LCR		Checks consistence of the created life cycle resource (RDF-graph.)
	ok	If the created life cycle resource is valid it will be saved in the RDF store.
	not ok	If the life cycle resource is not valid, then it is necessary to modify corresponding activities. This iteration continues until the created life cycle resource is valid.
Create SPARQL/Update Query		Creates a SPARQL/Update query, which inserts the life cycle resource into the RDF store
Store LCR		Stores the life cycle resource in the RDF store.

Table 6.2: Description of the activities and guard conditions in the use case "*Create Life Cycle Resource*".

6.3.4 Dataspace Indexer

The purpose of the Dataspace Indexer (DI) is to organize life cycle resources, including their subscription. DI implements a storage and indexing mechanism for the Scientific Resources Space model described in Section 4.2.2. Life cycle resources are represented as points of a 5-dimensional space, where dimensions represent the five e-Science life cycle activities. Coordinates of a dimension represent the instances of the corresponding activity. A distinct set of instances with one coordinate on each axis is represented by a point in the space, therefore forms a life cycle resource.

The Dataspace Indexer organizes representations of the life cycle resources in a flat table. Each row in the table represents a life cycle resource. The first column stores the index of the life cycle resource. In the other columns the indexes of instances of the five e-Science life cycle activities are stored. The first life cycle resource created will have index 1 in all five corresponding individuals of the e-Science life cycle activities. Starting from the second life cycle resource the index assigned to a previous life cycle activity might occur again. This is for the purpose that an instance might be reused within another life cycle resource. Individuals of the second life cycle are therefore subscribed with either index 2 or index 1. The third row in Table 6.3 allows an index up to 3, because here again individuals are attached to either a new index 3 or in case of re-use to the corresponding index of the re-used individual, which is in the current state of the dataspace either 1 or 2. However, in order to generalize this indexing mechanism let's say I_x are the indexes I of a life cycle activity $x \in \{GS, DP, TS, TE, RP\}$. Then I_x can be defined as the interval

$$[1, n] := \{i \in \mathbb{N} | 1 \leq i \leq n\}$$

where n is the total number of life cycle resources available in the dataspace. For example, I_{GS} represents the indexes over the life cycle activity "Goal Specification". Individuals of that life cycle activity, are therefore indexed by elements of the interval $[1, n]$. Each individual corresponds to a life cycle resource (LCR). Thus, we define

$$i_{LCR_y(x)}$$

as the index i of of an individual of a life cycle activity $x \in \{GS, DP, TS, TE, RP\}$ that corresponds to the life cycle resource y. If the total number of LCRs n is equal to the index i of the individual of an life cycle activity x corresponding to LCR n, which means:

$$n = i_{LCR_n(x)}$$

we can derive that individuals of the corresponding life cycle activity x were not re-used within the dataspace. In case that

$$n > i_{LCR_n(x)}$$

LCR	GS	DP	TS	TE	RP
1	1	1	1	1	1
2	$i \in \{1,2\}$	$i \in \{1,2\}$	$i \in \{1,2\}$	$i \in \{1,2\}$	$i \in \{1,2\}$
3	$i \in \{1,2,3\}$	$i \in \{1,2,3\}$	$i \in \{1,2,3\}$	$i \in \{1,2,3\}$	$i \in \{1,2,3\}$
⋮	⋮	⋮	⋮	⋮	⋮
k	$i \in \{1,2,...,k\}$	$i \in \{1,2,...,k\}$	$i \in \{1,2,...,k\}$	$i \in \{1,2,...,k\}$	$i \in \{1,2,...,k\}$
⋮	⋮	⋮	⋮	⋮	⋮
n	$i \in \{1,..,k,..,n\}$	$i \in \{1,..,k,..,n\}$	$i \in \{1,..,k,..,n\}$	$i \in \{1,..,k,..,n\}$	$i \in \{1,..,k,..,n\}$

Table 6.3: Flat table storing indexes of individuals of the e-Science life cycle activities.

we know that individuals have been reused by the scientist in other life cycle resources. Then the difference between n and i indicates the total amount of re-used individuals for the corresponding life cycle activity x.

Additionally, we organize two metadata attributes (*DS-P* and *ONT-V* together with the indexes in the flat table of the DI. DS-P (dataspace platform) provides important information about where (at which location/dataspace platform) as specific LCR was conducted, in case we deal with a multi-institutional dataspace infrastructure[5]. ONT-V indicates the version of the ontology. Table 6.4 is an extract of a index table from the DI showing a view concrete example of keys organized by the DI. This index concept is flexible with changes to the ontology. For instance if an new version of the ontology is developed and lets assume an activity is added to the e-Science life cycle, then an additional ID will be added to the key. Important in this context is to specify the correct order of activities (e.g. data preparation should/must be after goal specification). Having the version number of the ontology in the index schema, it will be possible to map it always to the right activity and LCR, respectively.

Having the indexes organized by the DI in the above described manner, it allows us to quickly evaluate the state of the dataspace in terms of calculating specific measures such as (total number of unique LCRs, number of reran LCRs, etc). Also questions like - *What activity was re-used most?* - can simply be answered without the need to access any RDF store. The examination of dataspace measures allows to monitor system usage and thus helps improving the system.

---

[5]Such a scenario is discussed in terms of large-scale scientific dataspaces in Chapter 7

LCR	DS-P	ONT-V	GS	DP	TS	TE	RP
⋮	⋮	⋮	⋮	⋮	⋮	⋮	⋮
311	uibk	1.1	157	263	25	311	311
312	uibk	1.1	157	264	25	312	312
313	uibk	1.1	158	264	25	313	313
⋮	⋮	⋮	⋮	⋮	⋮	⋮	⋮
356	uibk	1.1	162	307	28	356	356
366	uibk	1.1	162	307	28	366	366

Table 6.4: Example flat table storing LCR indexes.

6.3.5 e-Science Life Cycle Visualizer

The dataspace browser represents a useful tool for exploring multiple life cycle resources. It provides an overview when a large number of life cycle resources are returned from querying the dataspace. However, in the case a single life cycle resource is selected or returned it is more appropriate to visualize it showing more details and thus providing the scientists an easy way to learn about the scientific study the life cycle resource is corresponding to. The e-Science Life Cycle Visualizer visualizes single iterations of the e-Science life cycle. It receives a life cycle resource and visualizes it, by illustrating the properties set in each life cycle activity. This also includes metadata about the life cycle resource and the defined publication modes. This tool represents an additional and optional tool, which is independent of the core architecture. Anyhow, it represents a useful tool, which might be helpful, when users want to get better insights into single life cycle resources during exploration of the dataspace.

6.3.6 Dataspace Browser

The dataspace browser is a tool that allows the user to navigate trough the e-Science life cycle resources available in the dataspace in a visual way. It is implemented as a portlet for easy integration into a community portal. It submits requests to the *Query Processor*. These requests are SPARQL queries attached with the role of the requesting user. The most important issues here is to consider the role of the user, as based on it, the user will see more or less e-Science life cycle resources. For instance the scientific dataspace may contain life cycle resources to which the publication mode *Researcher* was assigned. Such life cycle resources should be only accessible for the researcher who created the resource. Therefore, the request from the *Dataspace Browser* will include the role of the user. The *Query Interpreter* interprets this request, which means that the appropriate publication modes to which the user has access are extracted from the user role. The *Query Translator* then considers these publication modes in the SPARQL query that is submitted to the RDF store. The response represents RDF-data and is used as input for the dataspace browser.

There are a number of tools available that visualizes RDF data. Depending on the scientific application needs, an appropriate tool can be integrated to the web portal of the community the scientific dataspace is deployed to. Welkin [MC04] has been used in one of our e-Science applications to provide a visual interface for browsing the dataspace and in particular its life cycle resources. Figure 6.6 shows the GUI of Welkin with a test dataset loaded. It currently visualizes real data from the Breath Gas Analysis application (see Chapter 8.3).

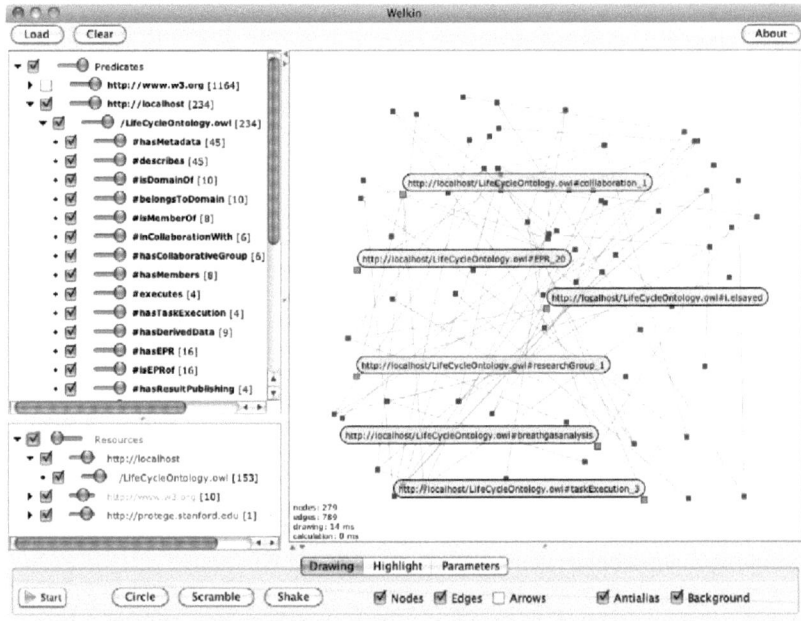

Figure 6.6: The Welkin RDF Visualizer [MC04] visualizing three life cycle resources.

The dataset loaded into Welkin consists in this example of three particular life cycle resources, each representing individuals and properties of the e-Science life cycle ontology from a concrete real breath gas analysis study. Such a dataset represent a typical result set retrieved from querying the dataspace in the first iteration of the search and query process. Scientists might use Welkin to further browse the results set, until they found the resources they are interested in and therefore want to further investigate by loading its primary, background, and derived data. Alternatively they might explore the result set as a textual list. By double click on a node more information about the resource is shown in the GUI as depicted in Figure 6.6.

6.4 Reference Implementation

A prototype of jSpace has been implemented and tested with small research groups within our e-Science applications. More details about this applications are provided in Chapter 8. Guidelines defining mandatory descriptions for experiments were elaborated in cooperation with scientists from the applications. This prototype is based on the Jena framework with MySQL databases to provide persistent RDF data storage. We used the persistent ontology model provided in the Jena framework in order to create and store LCRs according to the concepts defined in the e-Science Life Cycle ontology. A dataspace client has a local copy of the ontology, which is used by the *RDF Store Connection Manager* to create a local ontology model. This model is then used to create new instances and properties according to the ontology. In this prototype we have used the iRODS system as underlying data preservation system to store datasets of conducted e-Science experiments. The iRODS Integrated Rule-Oriented Data System [RMH+10] can be used as a data repository for storing participants of the scientific dataspace. The main advantage of using iRODS as data repository is that dataspace participants can be identified using an Uniform Resource Identifier (URI). An URI is usually described as a string of characters used to identify a name or a resource on the internet. It provides a simple and extensible means for identifying a resource. This identification mechanism enables interaction with representations of the resources over a network using specific protocols. Schemes specifying a concrete syntax and associated protocols define each URI. The java URI interface provides constructors for creating URI instances from their components or by parsing their string forms, methods for accessing the various components of an instance, and methods for normalizing, resolving, and relativizing URI instances. iRODS uses the URI schema to provide access to its files. In the following we introduce iRODS EPRs. These are EPRs that point to dataspace participants stored in a iRODS dataspace repository.

In iRODS each file that is managed within an iRODS server can be accessed through its URI. Therefore the accessing user has to provide his username and password, which is included in the iRODS URI to authenticate himself and to allow iRODS to proof wether the requestor has the necessary access rights for the requested dataset. The iRODS URI schema is described below.

$$irods://username:password@host:port/path \tag{6.2}$$

This is a good way to instantiate a file object, because the URI contains all the necessary login information. Password can be included in the URI or (more safely) sent separately. In our approach only the path will be saved within instances of the e-Science life cycle ontology. Username and password are not available outside of the dataspace support platform. A standard iRODS user is used within the platform to communicate with the iRODS server. The other necessary information to construct the iRODS URI such as host and port will be save locally within a properties file.

The iRODS EPR therefore is consolidated using the iRODS URI Schema. An example of an iRODS URI is given below.

$$irods://rods:rods@localhost:1247/home/rods/tesfile \tag{6.3}$$

Of course not the complete URI as shown above will be stored in the LCR, because then the iRODS user and password could be used to access other dataspace participants to which the user has no access rights.

In the case a user wants to attach additional documents (e.g. publications) to a LCRs, an iRODS EPR will be saved in the RDF tree of the corresponding LCR. The publication is then considered as background dataspace participant. This might be useful, when the acting scientist who accomplishes an experiment want to attach multiple publications or even other not published documents such as technical reports to the LCR.

During the implementation our focus was however put on the semantic markup layer as illustrated in Figure 6.7. There are multiple data preservation systems that provide efficient mechanisms to manage datasets and files. The jSpace architecture is flexible

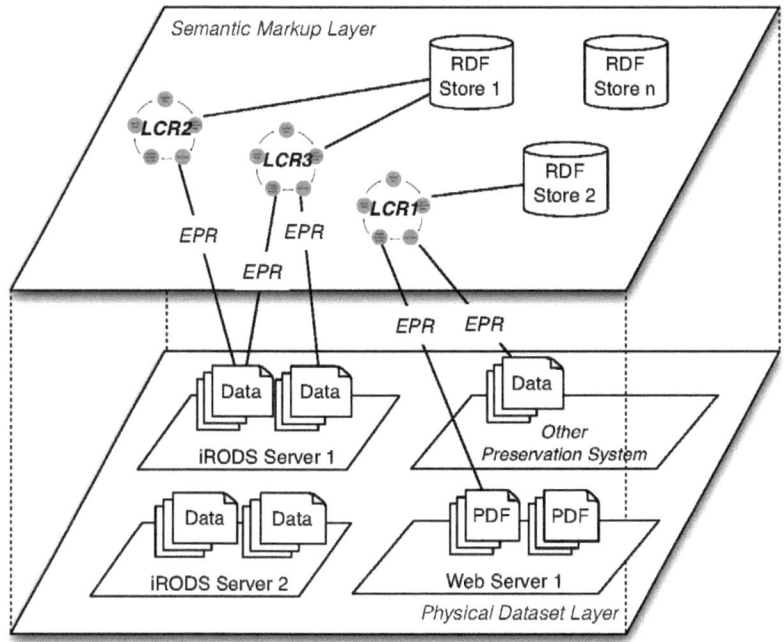

Figure 6.7: Semantic markup and physical dataset layer of the scientific dataspace support platform.

to the usage of any underlying data preservation system. It therefore depends on the application domain to choose an appropriate system for the dataspace participants layer shown in Figure 6.7. Important criteria for the selection of such a system is the ability to identify a specific dataset in the preservation system using a kind of End Point Reference (EPR). In the iRODS this is realized using the iRODS URI Schema, where all information needed to access a concrete dataset in an iRODS server is defined.

The e-Science life cycle composer, a tool implemented in Java provides an easy

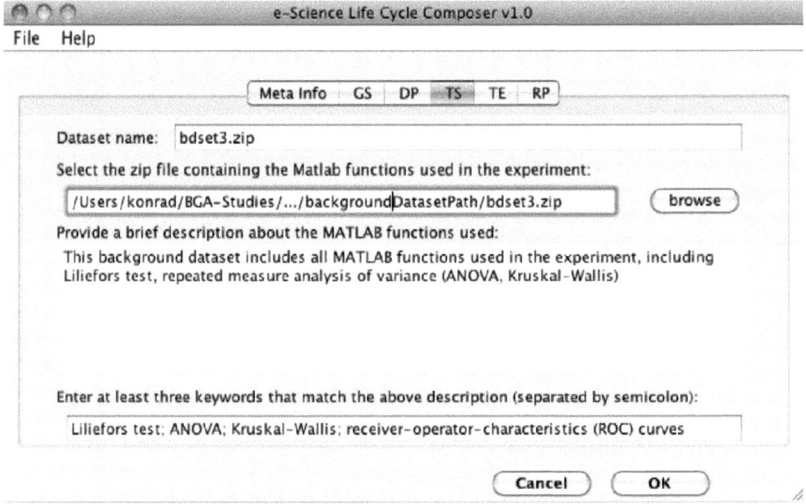

Figure 6.8: The e-Science life cycle composer GUI.

graphical user interface to researchers allowing to describe and publish scientific experiments. It organizes text fields for pre-defined descriptions of scientific experiments in five tabs according to their activity. For instance the *TaskSelection* activity, shown in the e-Science Life Cycle Composer GUI in Figure 6.8, requires to fill in a brief textual description and some corresponding keywords and to upload an archive file of the analytical methods being used in the experiment. The acting research group in the example shown in Figure 6.8 mainly uses Matlab for their calculations. A typical background dataset therefore is the collection of Matlab functions used in an experiment compressed as zip archive. Once an experiment has been finished, it can be published into the scientific dataspace by a single click on the OK button of the GUI. The information entered is used to create a new LCR, which then is saved in the corresponding RDF store. Connection details about local and global RDF store as well as about the corresponding data preservation system (is in this case settings of the server deploying iRODS) are stored in a configuration file. Using the Jargon Java API the e-Science life cycle composer communicates with the iRODS server, which is dedicated to host dataspace participants and stores the uploaded datasets into the iRODS directory. Besides, a LCR is created and stored in the local and global RDF store, depending on the publication mode set by the user. The LCR is consolidated as instances and properties of the e-Science life cycle ontology.

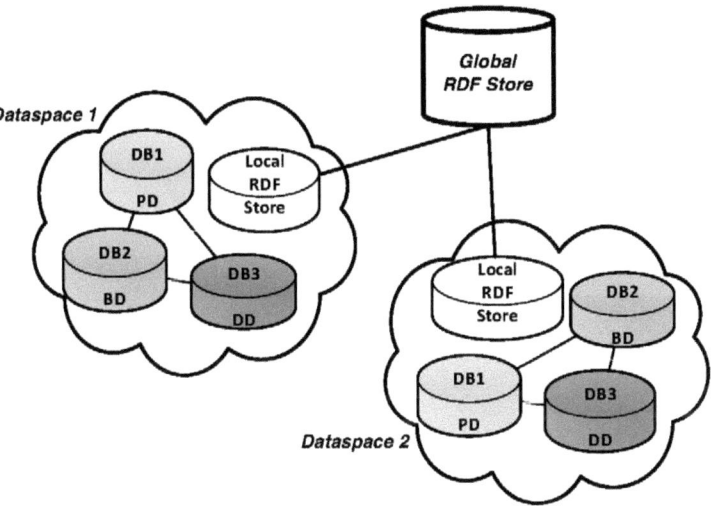

Figure 6.9: Global centralized RDF store connecting two scientific dataspace instances.

This prototype of jSpace implements the data warehouse alike approach in order to provide efficient access to scientific experiments that were conducted at different research centers. Figure 6.9 illustrates this approach, showing two scientific dataspace instances that are connected to a global centralized RDF store. Local stores should guarantee high performance for scientists working on the local site. Scientific studies being conducted at any research lab that participates in a dataspace environment are stored in local stores as long as access should be limited to researchers of the local organization. Once researchers want to share their experiments with other external collaborators or make them public to the scientific community, its corresponding LCRs will be stored in a central global store, which is shared with other dataspace instances.

We simulate a second dataspace instance. The *Connection Manager* handles a

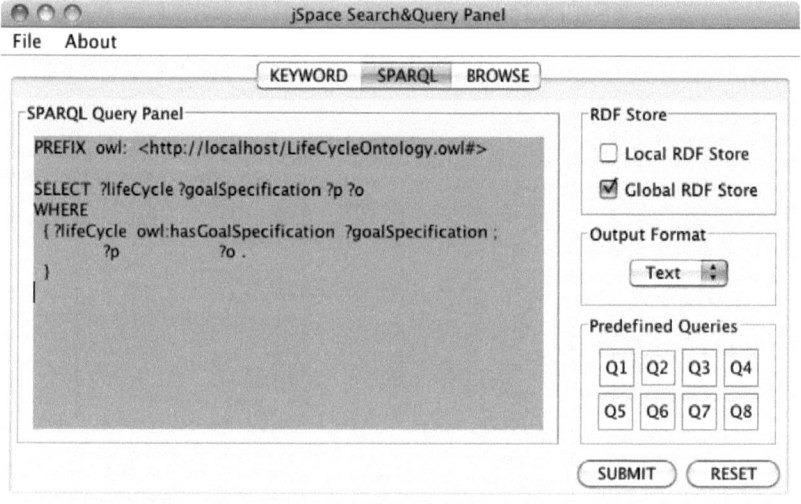

Figure 6.10: The jSpace Search and Query Panel showing the *SPARQL-tab*.

connection to a global and one to a local RDF store. Every dataspace instance has their own local RDF store to organize metadata of experiments that should be available only for the local organization. A *Publication/Update Manager* commits new LCRs to the global store. On the physical dataset layer each dataspace instance deploys at least a single iRODS Server, where datasets used in an experiment are stored.

The jSpace Search and Query Panel is a tool that enables the user to submit search and query requests to the scientific dataspace. The RDF store is queried, which means that dataspace relationships are queried using this prototype. This is the first iteration of the search and query process described earlier. In the second iteration also the datasets of conducted experiments (dataspace participants) are queried. The Search and Query Panel is implemented as Java GUI with three tabs, the *KEYWORD-tab*, the *SPARQL-tab*, and the *BROWSE-tab*. A Screenshot showing the *SPARQL-tab* is given in Figure 6.10.

It allows to submit SPARQL queries to either the local RDF store or a global store if available. The local RDF store represents the RDF store of the local scientific dataspace instance. Querying the global store means that the query is submitted also to the other RDF stores from other dataspace instances that are participating in a large-scale scientific dataspace. This means that a large-scale scientific dataspace consists of multiple local scientific dataspace instances and therefore result in a distributed collection of RDF stores. Since the structure and the layout of all RDF stores is based on the same e-Science Life-Cycle Ontology, it can easily be queried using the adaptive distributed SPARQL query processor, SPARQL-ADERIS [LKMT10a], which is integrated into jSpace. The integration of jSpace and SPARQL-ADERIS, which results in a distributed semantic data infrastructure is described earlier in this chapter. The Query results are integrated and shown to the user in the *BROWSE-tab*. The output format can be selected. Text, JSON, RDF, and XML can be generated. Predefined SPARQL queries are available by clicking on the buttons *Q1* to *Q8*. The configuration of the local and global RDF stores such as databases connections, etc. can be changed using the menu entry under File/Config.

In the *KEYWORD-tab* the user simply types in one ore more keywords, selects whether he wants to query the local or the global RDF store and the output format. Optionally he can define a search filter (this in not yet fully implemented). By clicking on the *SUBMIT*-button a SPARQL query with the keywords as *FILTER regex* expression is generated and shown in the *SPARQL-tab*. The *BROWSE-tab* currently simply shows the results of the query in the format chosen by the user.

6.5 Summary

Currently, three breath gas research teams from one of our driving e-Science application produce at an average 48 breath gas experiments in three different studies in a single week. The total size of a LCR of a typical breath gas experiment including its primary, derived, and background datasets amounts to approximately 7 MB. The average number of triples that correspond to a single LCR is 170 with an average size of 150 KB stored in Jena's SDB triple layout. From this we can estimate the total size of the scientific dataspace after six month with a single research lab involved to roughly 8.7 GB with about 8160 triples in the local RDF store (approx. 50K triples in three years). In regard to the Berlin SPARQL benchmark [BS09], which states that the overall runtime for executing 50 query mixes on a 250K triples Jena SDB test dataset is short above one minute, we can be confident that the presented solution provides reasonable performance. Based on this high-level estimation jSpace might need to scale up not before three years of deployment. However having multiple organizations or even various related e-Science application domains involved, it might be much earlier.

Scalability can be achieved by interconnecting multiple dataspace instances, which leads to a large-scale scientific data space infrastructure. Such a scenario is discussed in Chapter 7.

The e-Science life cycle has been applied as relationship model for the scientific dataspace. Jena SDB Version 1.3.1 with MySQL Version 5.0.67 as underlying relational DBMS is used to implement multiple local and one global RDF stores. For the search and query interface we provided Joseki SPARQL Server Version 3.4 as HTTP interface. A number of most important queries, such as {*Get me all experiments with VOC 'keyword'*}, and {*Get me all experiments from researcher 'name' where specified goal includes 'keyword'*}, or {*Get me all experiments with ANY keyword equals 'keyword' and input dataset 'datasetName' is used*} were predefined in SPARQL to enable the breath gas researcher to easy interact with the SPARQL query interface.

We are aware that we rely on active participation of members from the scientific community in order to establish a large scale scientific dataspace for breath gas analysis. Therefore we provide a simple interface that can easily be used by scientists from diverse research domains, especially for non-computer scientists, which was a major requirement from our driving application. However, we suspect that young-researchers (Master and PhD students) will be the major user group of the e-Science life cycle composer, while senior researcher will most likely interact with the system in terms of submitting requests.

The jSpace architecture provided in this chapter is based on top of exiting libraries and software components such as the Jargon java API for storage and retrieval of dataspace participants within an iRODS server. Also, the java framework for building semantic web applications, called Jena and the SPARQL-ADERIS library for adaptive distributed query processing on top of multiple RDF stores have been integrated into the jSpace architecture. They all form in conjunction with the jSpace Java API the fundament of the scientific dataspace support platform on top of which multiple application can be build. The main contribution in this context therefore represents the jSpace Java API, that provides all needed methods to construct semantic data about experiments, which hides from the scientists most of the underlying complexity involved in the process. Within a reference implementation we have utilized the jSpace API in the context of two implemented Java tools: (a) the e-Science Life Cycle Composer to create and store scientific experiments into the dataspace and (b) the jSpace Search&Query Panel to retrieve existing scientific experiments from the dataspace.

Chapter 7

Realizing Large-Scale Scientific Dataspaces

> "What is needed is a data environment that supports multiple domains, multiple disciplines and enables secure but verified access to research data."
>
> Scientific Computing World, Issue 116, February/March 2011
> CHRIS MOLLOY (VC for corporate development at IDBS)

7.1 Introduction

In many scientific applications we can find multiple databases that are interlinked in some way. Scientists typically access a dataset, analyze it using some analytical methods or scientific workflows and finally process and store their results locally. However, many data-intensive e-Science applications face the issues of an inability to integrate data across multiple domains and therefore a failure to get out the most value of the large and increasing amount of data they are producing.

During our investigations we came to the conclusion that an appropriate solution to this issue can either be a) to address and extend current data management systems and develop methods to provide better interactions among each other by the means of standard interfaces or, b) to start with the creation of semantically rich described relationships among those existing databases. Since the first approach is likely to be a long-term challenge that might result in a never-ending story, we have chosen to investigate the latter approach. It can best be established if the complete life cycle of data in e-Science applications is addressed. Therefore we started a bottom up approach to develop a scientific dataspace paradigm.

A typical small-scale research group, which is very common in the European and the US research landscape has been introduced in Chapter 2 in Section 2.5. There, we described the problems scientists face due to the lack of efficient scientific data management mechanisms. It is hardly possible to re-run a scientific experiment after the responsible scientists has left the research group, to recall the only one of the described problems. Our response to that was described in the previous chapters in detail. We have developed the e-Science life cycle ontology and on top of it the scientific dataspace support platform to support members of a research group e.g. in determining what data exists and where it resides. So far we have been considering that the dataspace is deployed for a single research group. However, in this chapter we introduce large-scale dataspaces, that is a collection of multiple interconnected existing dataspace instances.

We provide a large-scale scientific dataspace architecture overview in Figure 7.1. It illustrates a scenario with three geographically distributed dataspace instances at participating research groups. The research groups are collaborating in terms of collaborative science, e.g. scientific studies are being exchanged, and conducted in cooperation very frequently. At each research center an instance of the dataspace support platform jSpace and its underlying infrastructure is deployed. It provides local users who are employed at the corresponding research group to preserve semantically enriched scientific studies including all related data (primary, background, and derived data). This results in a distributed data environment for the research community that is interested in the scientific studies conducted in multiple cooperating research groups. The large-scale scientific dataspace is therefore consolidated of multiple interconnected dataspace instances, each deployed for a single research group. It can be accessed from a web portal or using the jSpace API from within an application.

In this chapter we consider large distributed collections of scientific studies and introduce capabilities of our scientific dataspace paradigm for above mentioned large-scale purposes. This includes also the ability to support multiple research domains and disciplines. We present large-scale scientific dataspaces as a semantic data infrastructure that integrates multiple geographically distributed Resource Description Framework

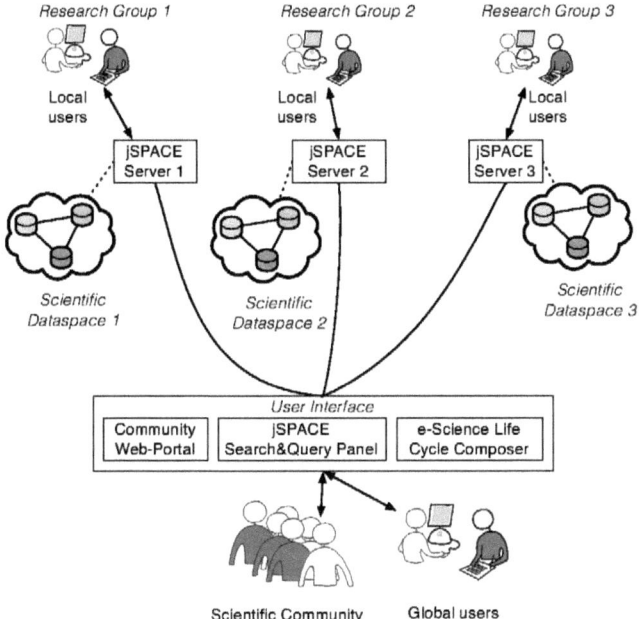

Figure 7.1: Large-scale scientific dataspace architecture overview.

(RDF) [KC04] data stores supporting SPARQL [PS08, C+08] using an adaptive distributed SPARQL query processor [LKMT10a, LKMT10b]. The semantic data infrastructure represents a large-scale scientific dataspace with multiple scientific dataspace instances connected.

The rest of this chapter is organized as follows. First we discuss in Section 7.2 how scalability can be achieved in the scientific dataspace paradigm we presented. Then we discuss in Section 7.3 the large-scale semantic data infrastructure implementing a horizontal scalability approach, and in Section 7.4 we present a synthetic large-scale dataspace that is generated to evaluate the scientific dataspace support platform. In Section 7.6 we provide a performance evaluation and in Section 7.7 we briefly discuss alternative solutions for distributed SPARQL query processing, which is a core part of large-scale scientific dataspaces. Finally we conclude this chapter in Section 7.8.

7.2 Scalability in Scientific Dataspaces

Vertical scalability in the scientific dataspace is the ability to increase the capacity of an existing dataspace platform - for example, adding new storage power to an existing RDF store to provide storage space for more LCRs or migrating to a server with larger hard disk drives to provide storage space for more datasets from scientific studies. On the other hand, *horizontal scalability* is the ability to connect multiple dataspace entities so that they work as a single logical unit, a large-scale dataspace. Since vertical scalability is in this context not relevant our focus is on horizontal scalability. Extending the storage space of an existing server can easily be applied if necessary. In the following we address horizontal scalability issues for the scientific dataspace.

As already mentioned earlier, we have considered in our scientific dataspace paradigm databases or other data storage and preservation systems that host (a) accessed datasets, (b) analytical methods or scientific workflows used, and (c) derived results as dataspace participants interconnected by dataspace relationships. On the one hand we consider on a lower level of abstraction the contents of this databases itself as *dataspace-participants*, i.e. the final input datasetindexFinal input dataset or a single analysis function (e.g. a Matlab-file) used within a specific scientific experiment. On the other hand we consider on a higher abstraction level complete dataspace instances as participants of a large-scale dataspace connecting multiple dataspace instances that might be from different domains and disciplines. Therefore, there are different levels of abstraction regarding the contents of the scientific dataspace. They are illustrated in Figure 7.2 on top of a concrete example from the breath gas analysis application domain. In the lowest abstraction level, participants of the scientific dataspace represent concrete datasets that were used within an experiment. They form together a Life Cycle Resource (LCR). In a particular real experiment from one of our e-Science applications deploying a scientific dataspace, these participants are

(a) P_{i1} - the final input datasetindexFinal input dataset (*primary data*),

(b) P_{j1} - the analytical method e.g. as Matlab scripts and functions organized in a Matlab-file (*background data*), and

(c) P_{k1} - the resulted analysis report generated using e.g. Matlab's publish function (*derived data*).

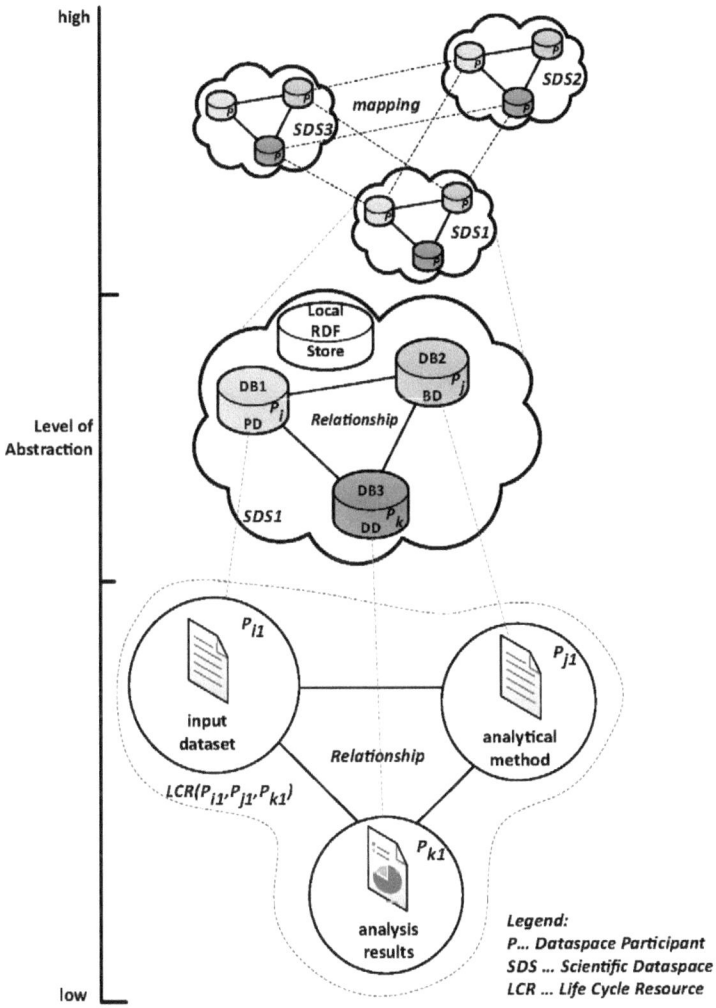

Figure 7.2: Levels of abstraction of breath gas analysis dataspace participants.

These participants are stored in corresponding databases, as depicted in Figure 7.2. The relationship among these participants is semantically rich described by individuals and properties of the e-Science life cycle ontology.

On the next abstraction level the databases DB1, DB2, and DB3 represent participants forming the scientific dataspace $SDS1$, which is an instance of a scientific dataspace as was deployed as experimental framework for one scientific application (see Chapter 8.3). On the top level we illustrate a large-scale dataspace, that arise when multiple dataspaces deployed for different organizations are interconnected e.g. multiple breath gas analysis research institutions engage research collaborations, each running their own breath gas dataspace. In this scenario the dataspaces itself represent participants of the large-scale dataspace. Such scenarios require scalability of the scientific dataspace paradigm, which is important when multiple research organizations, each having deployed their own dataspace, engage collaborations and agree on sharing their scientific dataspaces and life cycle resources, respectively.

Horizontal scalability can therefore be achieved by interconnecting multiple dataspace instances, which leads to a large-scale scientific data space infrastructure. Connecting multiple scientific dataspace instances is twofold:

1. on the physical dataset layer, the storage solution that was selected by a dataspace administrator at dataspace setup needs to be made accessible for users of other dataspace instances and

2. on the semantic markup layer, which manages the semantic relationships among dataspace participants multiple RDF stores needs to be integrated.

Security mechanisms to provide users of a dataspace instance access to dataspace participants of another dataspace instance are not addressed by this work. It is rather outsourced and currently being developed within another research project. Within the ABA-project [aba11], we are developing a framework for advanced breath analysis that includes both, preservation and advanced execution of breath gas analysis studies on a multi-institutional level. The complete life cycle from calculation of substances and concentrations in exhaled breath air up to the creation of manuscripts is being addresses. Due to protection of data privacy, as patient data is involved in the life cycle of a breath gas analysis study, all sensitive data will be stored locally at the research center and access is restricted to users with adequate permission rights. We therefore focus scalability issues on the semantic markup layer. In the very common scenario where more than one dataspace instance is set up at multiple research centers, which work together in terms of collaborative science, each center hosts their own RDF store for storing their life cycle resources. This results in a distributed RDF data environment.

There are two main approaches to handle the problem with multiple RDF stores.

1. Global centralized RDF store

2. Distributed RDF Storage

Both approaches are feasible with the architecture of jSpace described in Section 6.3. There might be use case scenarios and application domains where one approach fits better due to scale of the dataspace infrastructure or legal issues of participating institutions, etc. Also, a hybrid approach is plausible, for instance, when multiple already deployed dataspaces of homogenous application domains will be merged into a large-scale multi-disciplinary dataspace infrastructure. We discuss such a scenario in Section 7.3.4. Approach 1 (having a global centralized RDF store) was already discussed in Chapter 6 along with the architecture of jSpace. It was also implemented within a jSpace prototypical implementation described in Section 6.4. In the following we briefly discuss the second approach (distributed RDF storage) regarding the problem with addressing multiple RDF stores.

Distributed RDF Storage

This solution requires a middleware that supports federated SPARQL query processing. Currently, concepts from traditional approaches of federated query processing systems are adapted to provide integrated access to RDF data sources. Basic idea is to query a mediator, which distributes subqueries to local RDF stores and integrates the results. Figure 7.3 illustrates this approach. It shows two dataspace instances with their local RDF stores joined by an appropriate middleware that supports distributed SPARQL query processing.

SPARQL-ADERIS [LKMT10b] is an approach based on distributed query processing, where data from multiple repositories are used to construct partitioned tables that are integrated using an adaptive query processing technique supporting join reordering, which limits any reliance on statistics and meta-data about SPARQL endpoints , as such information is often inaccurate or unavailable, but is required by existing systems supporting federated SPARQL queries. SPARQL-ADERIS extends existing approaches in this area by allowing tables to be added to the query plan while it is executing, and

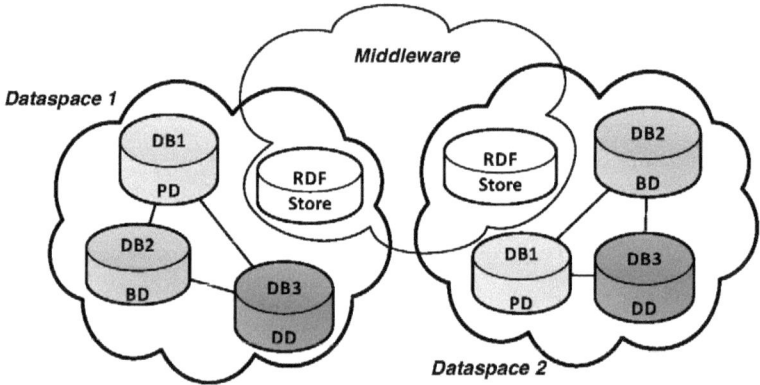

Figure 7.3: Middleware connecting two local RDF stores of two scientific dataspace instances.

shows how an approach currently used within relational query processing can be applied to distributed SPARQL query processing. SPARQL-ADERIS has been used to provide a semantic data infrastructure as discussed in Section 7.3. Other related works are described in Section 7.7 at the end of this Chapter.

A SPARQL endpoint is a SPARQL protocol service as defined in the SPARQL Protocol for RDF specification [PS08]. A SPARQL endpoint enables users to query an RDF store via the SPARQL language. Results are typically returned in one or more machine-processable formats. Therefore, a SPARQL endpoint is mostly conceived as a machine-friendly interface towards an RDF store. Both the formulation of the queries and the human-readable presentation of the results should typically be implemented by the calling software, and not be done manually by human users [sem09].

7.3 Semantic Data Infrastructure

Individual research centers often have a tendency to hold much of their data privately, however, where there is mutual benefit in doing so they may be motivated towards exposing data using standard interfaces for example in the case of RDF, using the

SPARQL query language [PS08] and protocol [C+08]. We have developed an infrastructure to support a scenario in which dataspace instances are located at multiple research centers (approach 2 discussed in Section 7.2), which work together in terms of collaborative science. In addition to functional requirements, other issues, including quality of service and security, are considered as well. In such a scenario each centre hosts their own RDF stores containing their experimental metadata, which results in a distributed RDF data environment.

Scientists are not required to interact with RDF data directly, or be aware of the details concerning how it is maintained and queried. The scientist utilizes jSpace [EB10] to construct semantic data about experiments, which hides from the scientist most of the underlying complexity involved in the process, such as working directly with RDF or writing SPARQL queries. Therefore either the e-Science life cycle composer can be used to collect information about a conducted scientific study or forms integrated into an application's portal, if available could be used as well.

In the latter case jSpace Java API is used to transform the collected information into individuals and properties of the e-Science life cycle ontology. jSpace further creates a life cycle resource and indexes it within the index server of the dataspace. jSpace finally publishes the life cycle resource into the local RDF store. These steps are hidden by jSpace. They are fulfilled for every scientific study that is being inserted into the dataspace.

7.3.1 Software Architecture Design Overview

There are many components that build the basis for the semantic data infrastructure, e.g. it is necessary to include a distributed SPARQL query processor in order to enable the system to access multiple RDF stores. In Figure 7.4 we show these components as a layered architecture.

Different user interfaces can be used to communicate with the infrastructure. The e-Science Life Cycle Composer and the jSpace Search and Query Panel are simple Java GUIs that we have described in the previous chapter. Protégé will only be used by administrators for maintenance of the e-Science Life Cycle ontology e.g. applying changes or upgrading to a newer version of the ontology. We use the Jargon Java API to communicate with the iRODS preservation system for storing and retrieving dataspace participants and the Jena Java API to access a single RDF store, which host

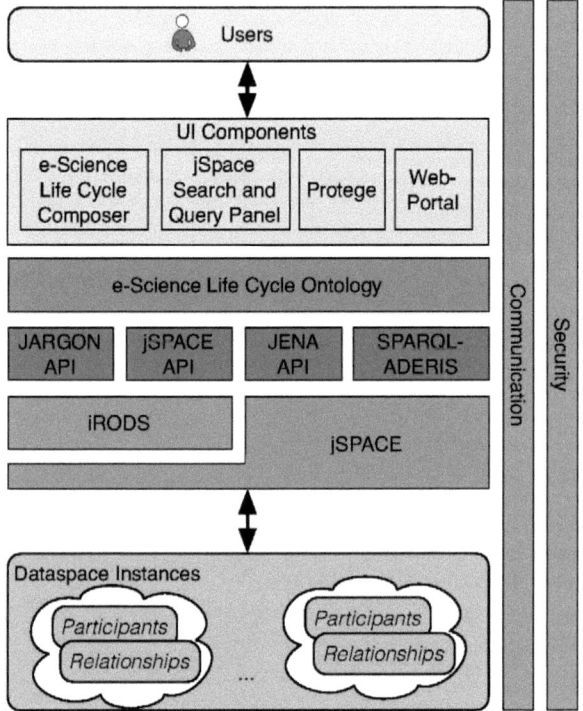

Figure 7.4: Layered architecture of the scientific dataspace support platform.

the dataspace relationships. jSpace Java API is being used to create a LCR according to the classes and properties defined by the e-Science life cycle ontology. Finally, the SPARQL-ADERIS component is being used to access multiple RDF stores.

From the UML sequence diagram shown in Figure 7.5 it can be seen that on submission of a search request to the global large-scale scientific dataspace via the jSpace Search and Query Panel, it first selects the *Home-Platform* and then forwards it to the selected platform. We distinguish *Home-* and *External Platforms*. A Home-Platform is the platform where the requesting scientist is assigned to, e.g. the dataspace platform of the research group where the scientist is working. Therefore, all other dataspace platforms are referred to as External-Platforms. The SPARQL request is then decomposed in to sub-queries and send to the SPARQL-Endpoints of all dataspace instances using the SPARQL-ADERIS component. The results are further being integrated and returned to the requestor as RDF data.

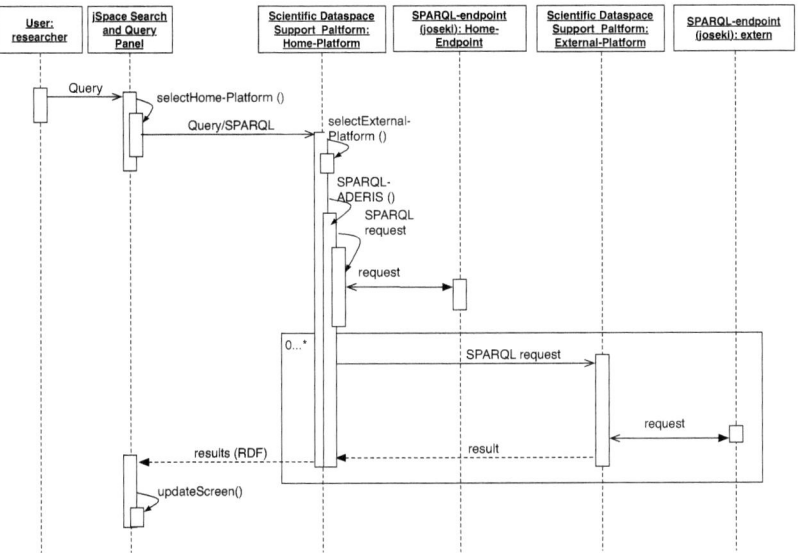

Figure 7.5: Sequence diagram showing the calls for submission of a search request.

Figure 7.6 shows on the left hand the components and their interaction of a single dataspace instance. The boxes marked in color represent existing APIs and systems that are used as part of the underlying infrastructure. On the right hand we show a second scientific dataspace support platform in order to illustrate that a large-scale scientific dataspace is consolidated of multiple local RDF stores and iRODS servers.

The heart of jSpace is the component that preserves the life cycle resources. It is named *LCR Preserver*. There are multiple interfaces to the LCR Preserver. This component is also responsible for preserving the dataspace participants.

We provide multiple tools to search and query for life cycle resources; either the jSpace Search&Query Panel, or a console, or Joseki 's SPARQL Server Web-Interface

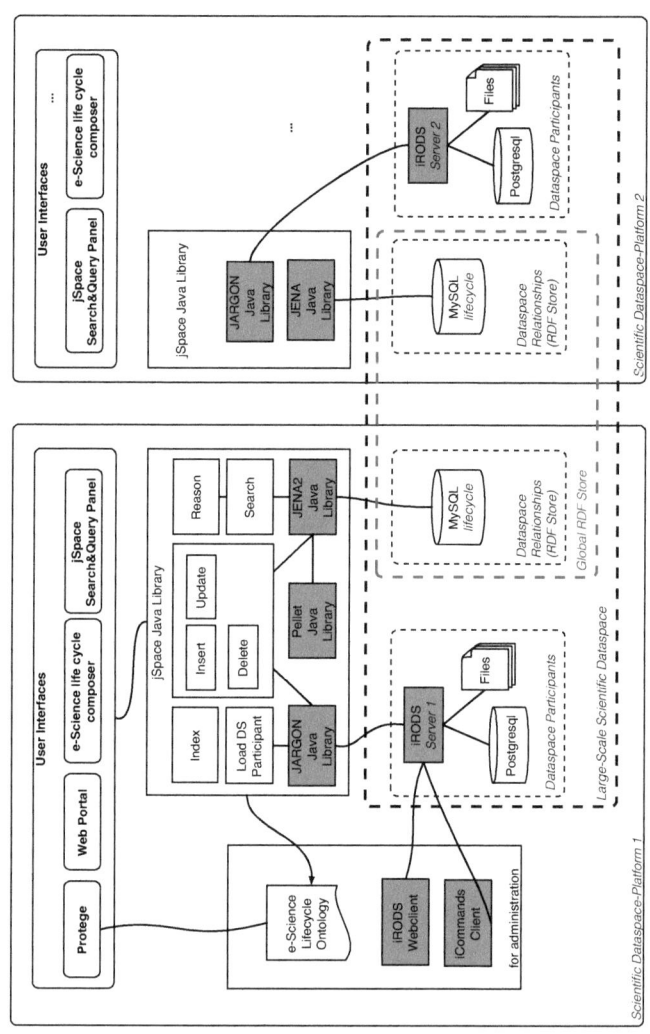

Figure 7.6: Overview of the components of a single dataspace instance.

can be used. In the latter two only SPARQL queries are supported, whereas using jSpace Search&Query Panel also keyword queries can be submitted. jSpace translates given keywords into an adequate SPARQL representation using SPARQL FILTER functions like *regex* to identify RDF literals. Different output formats such as JSON, N3, or RDF can be selected, allowing the result set to be further processed by a semantic web tool such as the Welkin RDF Visualizer presented in Section 6.3.6.

Depending on the user request the LCR Preserver queries the local or the global RDF store. In this case global RDF store stands for the single logical unit that is consolidated of the local RDF stores from multiple dataspace platform instances, as illustrated in Figure 7.6 in the colored dashed box. The global RDF store therefore is represented as multiple RDF stores, each deployed on a different dataspace instance. Therefore once the global RDF store is selected the LCR Preserver uses a distributed SPARQL query processing component that is integrated into the jSpace API. As previously mentioned, we used SPARQL-ADERIS to be this component within a prototypical implementation. The prototypical implementation is described in Section 7.3.3.

On the other side the LCR Preserver is used to store new generated life cycle resources into the local and the global RDF store. Those newly created life cycle resources from the e-Science life cycle composer are already equipped with an index key that is uniquely identifying its instances of the e-Science life cycle activities. The LCR preserver can take either an LCR object or an LCR XML file as an input. Both represent the information about a scientific study needed to create individuals and properties of the e-Science life cycle ontology, which is done by the LCR Preserver.

7.3.2 Discussion

Depending on the preservation solution chosen by the research community the dataspace is deployed to, it communicates with the preservation system using standard interfaces - for example in our prototypical implementation we use the iRODS system for storing dataset of e-Science studies. Communication with the iRODS Server is done using the Jargon iRODS client API. It basically could also talk to a single DBMS, such as MySQL where dataspace participants are stored, it could also be a collection of databases deployed using the OGSA-DAI solution for distributed data access and management. In this case LCR Preserver would use the OGSA-DAI Client toolkit [SHJ$^+$04] to communicate with the data resources. However, the underlying data preservation solution for storing dataspace participants is independent of the semantic layer meaning the preservation of semantically rich described dataspace relationships preserved by the LCR Preserver.

7.3.3 Prototypical Implementation

In a prototype of the semantic data infrastructure we set up three RDF repositories hosting real data of scientific experiments from one of our two e-Science applications at three different locations and queried them using a distributed query processor, SPARQL-ADERIS [LKMT10a], that supports federated SPARQL queries over multiple RDF data sources each of which are accessible via the SPARQL query language and protocol. The distributed query processor decomposes federated queries into subqueries that are sent to individual data resources, the results of which are processed using relational database operators (joins, unions, projections, etc.) to answer the federated query. The component requires limited metadata (e.g. statistics) about the data contained in individual RDF repositories as it is based on an adaptive approach that applies recent work on adaptive query processing in relational database systems in an RDF context. Query processing is done in an almost entirely adaptive fashion, joining data as it becomes available and modifying join order based on monitoring information gathered at runtime. We have chosen to use this component as its adaptive approach towards optimization is beneficial in this application's widely distributed, autonomous, service-based environment, where repositories may behave unpredictably and are constantly updated meaning that accurate statistics, which are required by static optimizers, are unavailable. The global RDF store in this prototype is made up of the three local RDF stores, that are accessible via an SPARQL Endpoint by the SPARQL-ADERIS component.

For this prototypical implementation we have used the LCR Preserver described in Section 7.3 to communicate with an iRODS server using the Jargon Java API. iRODS release 2.5 has been used to store basic dataset from e-Science experiments. Figure 7.7 illustrates the use of the LCR Preserver for the physical dataset and the semantic markup layer. It illustrates the three local RDF stores on the semantic markup layer. Together they form the global RDF store that is queried by the SPARQL-ADERIS component integrated into the e-Science Search&Query Panel. On the physical dataset layer we used a single iRODS server to store all datasets from the e-Science experiments

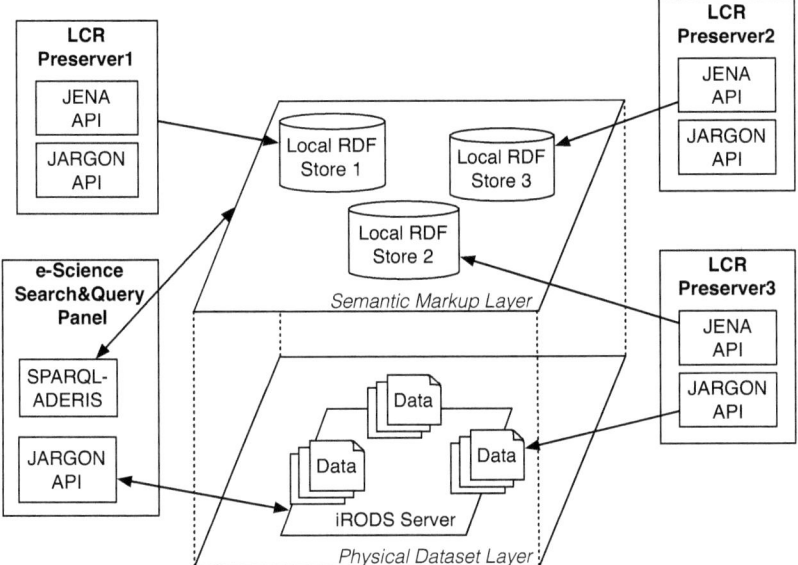

Figure 7.7: LCR Preserver and e-Science Search&Query Panel extended for large-scale dataspaces.

applied. However, with the current release 2.5 of the iRODS system it is also possible to connect multiple iRODS servers together. The focus in this work was however on the semantic markup layer, as mentioned in the introduction to this chapter.

7.3.4 Multi-Disciplinary Scientific Dataspace

In this scenario we assume that each dataspace was already deployed for a specific virtual organization where the acting scientists are feeding the dataspace continuously with their regularly running experiments. The global centralized RDF store approach was chosen to support exchange with a second virtual organization of the same domain.

Many research groups in e-Science have collaborations among each other, especially in related research areas. For example, the breath gas analysis research group, that has evaluated our scientific dataspace paradigm keeps regularly meetings with a research group that is working on breath cancer research. The idea is to exchange information and knowledge to enhance the change of discoveries in both fields. If we assume that each research group has its own dataspace instance running and since both research domains are related scientific fields, it might be the case that scientists would like to share their scientific studies among each other. In particular, it might be the case that a researcher from the breath gas analysis domain wants to share a specific scientific study along with all participating datasets (primary, background, and derived datasets) with his colleagues from the other related research field. Having on both sites a dataspace instance, as we assume for this multi-disciplinary example, it will be necessary to interconnect them in an efficient manner. This can easily be realized without concerns on heterogeneity issues, since both dataspace sites are based on top of the e-Science life cycle, that domain independently describes scientific studies. Their interconnection would lead to a multi-disciplinary large-scale scientific dataspace among the breath gas analysis and the breath cancer research domains, as illustrated in Figure 7.8.

In order to utilize this arising large-scale dataspace, it will be necessary to provide a distributed RDF storage solution on top of global RDF stores. Because we have a scenario where at least one site (breath gas analysis) has already multiple dataspace instances interconnected using the approach with a single global RDF store. LCRs that should be exchanged among different research teams are published into this global RDF store. In the example shown in Figure 7.8 the breath cancer research group has a single dataspace instance with a local and a global RDF store and the breath gas analysis domain has two dataspace instances connected with a single RDF store. In this scenario, we have set up both global RDF stores as SPARQL Endpoint and query them using the SPARQL-ADERIS distributed SPARQL query processing component, that is integrated in jSpace. We thus have a hybrid approach (merging a dataspace of the global centralized RDF store approach with the distributed RDF Storage approach) as was introduced in Section 7.2.

7.4 A Synthetic Large-Scale Dataspace

In order to test scalability we generated a synthetic large-scale dataspace on the semantic markup layer. During the Austrian Grid project we collected semantic information about a small number of different scientific studies in the breath gas analysis application. This information was used to manually generate some real LCRs using Protégé

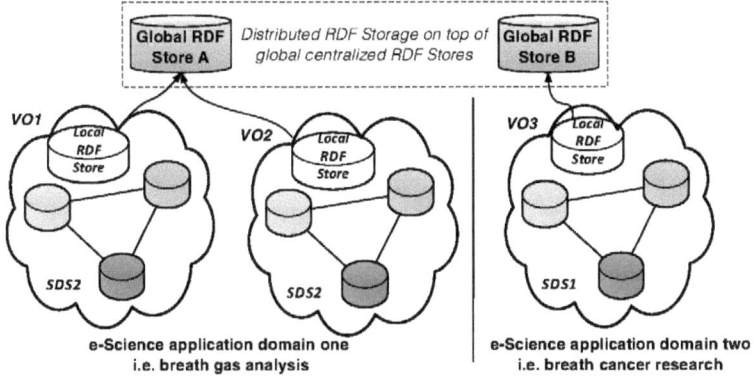

Figure 7.8: Large-scale scientific dataspace infrastructure [EB10].

[Sta10] to test the e-Science life cycle ontology and the dataspace paradigm. A concrete LCRs from the above mentioned real e-Science application is described in detail within Appendix A. However, in order to evaluate scalability and performance of the large-scale dataspace approach presented in this chapter we generated a large amount synthetic LCRs. We used the real LCRs from the breath gas analysis application (see Chapter 8.3) as templates for generating synthetic LCRs. Therefore some contents, especially literals might be duplicated. These real LCRs typically have 3 End Point References (EPRs) that point to a dataset stored in the iRODS server set up for our experimental evaluation. We generated seven different datasets containing from a single LCR with 569 triples up to 3,000 LCRs with 467,047 triples in total. Table 7.6 provides some meta information such as the number of various individuals and total number of triples and individuals about the LCR datasets generated. If we assume that the average size of a primary participant is around 10 MB[1], that an average background participant size is around 3 MB, and that an average derived dataset again is around 10 MB in size, then the scientific dataspace will have a total size of approx. 105,5 GB[2] with 3,000 LCR.

---

[1] This is a realistic average file size according to researchers from the breath gas analysis application
[2] The dataset with 3,000 LCRs generated contains 3,000 individuals of primary participants and 6,000 individuals of derived participants and 6,000 individuals of background participants. Thus 3,000*10 MB + 6,000*10 MB + 6,000* 3 MB result in 108,000 MB.

Total number of triples	569	822	1,020	1,413	10,242	98,891	467,047
Number of LCRs	1	3	6	60	300	600	3,000
Number of activities	5	15	30	300	1,500	3,000	15,000
Number of metadata individuals	11	33	66	660	3,300	6,600	33,000
Number of scientists	3	9	18	180	1,200	2,400	12,000
Number of participants (primary, background, and derived)	5	15	30	300	1500	3,000	15,000
Number of EPRs	3	9	18	180	1,200	2,400	12,000
Total number of individuals						34,200	171,000

Table 7.1: Number of individuals in the synthetic LCR datasets of different sizes.

7.5 Towards Cloud-Enabled Dataspaces

Recently ensembles of distributed, heterogeneous resources, or clouds, have emerged as popular platforms for deploying large-scale and resource-intensive applications. After grid computing [FKT01b], cloud computing [BBG11, AFG+09] has recently emerged as the paradigm for the next generation of large-scale scientific computing and data management with the main advantage in eliminating the need for hosting expensive hardware.

Some attempts to tackle the problems have been made by applying grid computing. However, grid research promised but not delivered fast, interoperable, scalable, resilient, and available systems. Grids have been used mainly in research environment; grids have not been accepted by business and industry [FA11]. Cloud computing is definitely the latest trend in computing technology. It represents a style of computing, strongly supported by major vendors and many IT service consumers, in which massively scalable high throughput/performance IT-related services are provided from the internet to multiple customers on demand [FA11]. This means that computing is done in a remote unknown location (out in the internet clouds) rather than on a local desktop. Cloud computing brings together distributed computing concepts and development outcomes, and business models. Many data center providers such as Google, Amazon, IBM, Microsoft, Salesforce had begun to establish data centers for hosting their applications in different locations to accord redundancy, reliability [BYV+09]. The infrastructures based on cloud computing concepts, enable conducting scientific as well as business studies and use of tasks addressing large-scale data management. A cloud exploits the concepts of services and Service Oriented Architectures (SOA), virtualization, and web technology and standards. Virtual Machines (VMs) are provided to the user as a service like the Amazon Elastic Cloud Compute (EC2) [Inc08a].

An approach towards cloud computing for e-Science is introduced in [WLG+08]. There an *e-Science Cloud* (Figure 7.9) is introduced, as a cloud offering core cloud services at the bottom layer followed by core e-Science cloud services such as workflow, data management, service management, etc. in the middle layer and on top of it domain specific services.

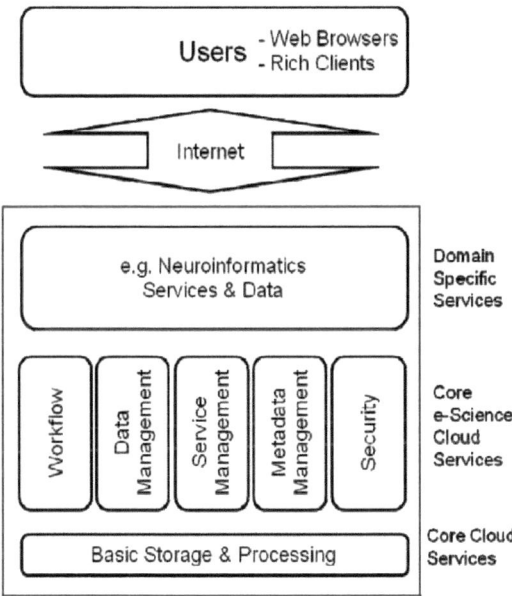

Figure 7.9: An e-Science cloud [WLG+08].

Core services of the dataspace (e.g. *Search Study, Create Study*) can be seen as an extension of the e-Science cloud introduced in [WLG+08]. In the following we discuss briefly the concepts of a cloud-enabled scientific dataspace, which we name *dataspace cloud*. However, this work has not been implemented as part of this work, it is rather an outline of what we target to investigate within our planed future works.

The Scientific Dataspace Cloud

In order to cloud-enable our scientific dataspace platform we need to establish the dataspace components described in the previous section on a data cloud. Data access services should be consequently mapped to the activities defined by the e-Science life cycle model. However, the first step towards a cloud-enabled dataspace support platform would be to follow the Software as a Service (SaaS) approach. A SaaS platform is formed by integrating an operating system, middleware, development environment, and application software, and encapsulated such that is provided to clients as a service [FA11]. jSpace belongs to the category of SaaS clouds. This implies that the dataspace features provided by the means of methods in the jSpace Java API in conjunction with a variety of third-party Java APIs and applications, need to be exposed as services. Furthermore it will be necessary to package the components of the scientific dataspace support platform on a VM and more importantly to provide a service oriented interface for client-server communication.

Figure 7.10 provides an overview of the scientific dataspace cloud. We distinguish a *Dataspace-Relationship Cloud* and a *Dataspace-Participants Cloud*. The first represents an RDF-Store where individuals and properties of the e-Science Life Cycle ontology are persistently stored in terms of LCRs and the latter one basically stores the datasets that correspond to a LCR. Key services are the dataspace services as illustrated in the figure. This group of services include services for creation, search, load, execution, management and publication of scientific studies. These dataspace services are briefly described in the following.

- Search Study - the *Search Study Service* is used to search for available studies in the dataspace. The search request has to consider available access rights of the user who submits the search request. A query is submitted to the Dataspace-Relationship Cloud, retrieving metadata about studies that match the query.

- Load study - once a study has been found and selected for further investigations, it can be loaded from the dataspace into the user interface (portal or a problem solving environment). An option could be to select which data (primary, background, and derived) should also be loaded besides the metadata of the study. This service retrieves all corresponding datasets that belong to a specific study from the Dataspace-Participants Cloud.

- Create study - this will create an empty template/structure of a study. It helps

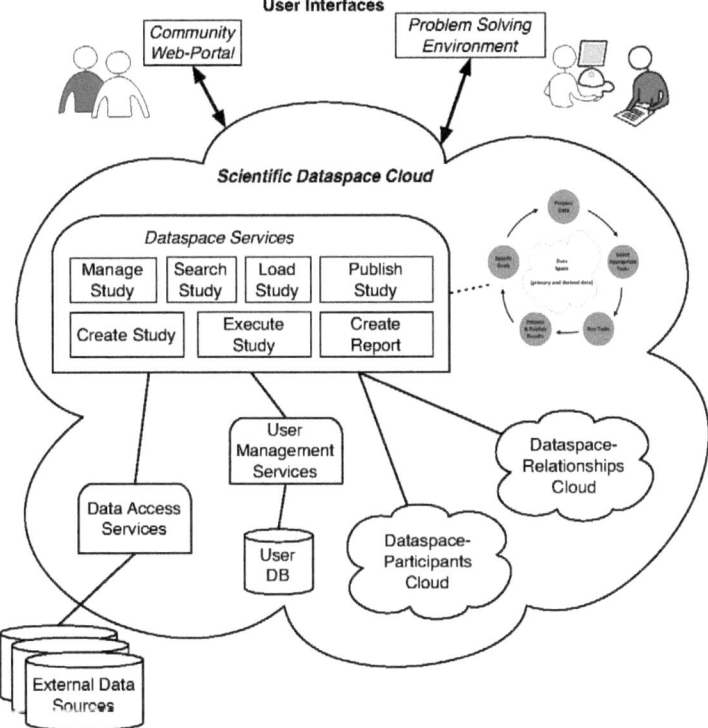

Figure 7.10: The scientific dataspace cloud.

to keep the structure of a study among the research community to which the dataspace-cloud belongs.

- Execute study - once a study is ready for execution, it can be executed using execution services on either a single computer, or a high-performance cluster (this might be provided as compute cloud services, this is not illustrated in Figure 7.10) depending on the user requirements.

- Publish study - this service allows to publish the study into the dataspace cloud, thus it will be available for the long term. Registered users who have access rights for the study will be able to search for it as well as to load it.

- Create report - a brief report of a single/multiple studies can be generated. The contents of the report need to be elaborated with a domain expert.

They above described dataspace services address the full life cycle of a study by applying the e-Science life cycle model. They map the e-Science life cycle activities to activities a scientists in doing while conducting a study.

Besides the dataspace services we also need to address user management services and standard data access services. Standard data access services are needed to provided the scientists access to the datasources he or she might be interested in. We call such a data source an external datasource, since it is outside of the dataspace cloud.

The scientific dataspace cloud will be utilized in conjunction with a problem solving environment, where scientists conduct their studies on a regular basis. The preservation of the conducted studies and their publication into the dataspace cloud has to happen on the fly with out the need to to interact with RDF data directly, or be aware of the details concerning how it is maintained and queried. Dataspace services construct semantic data about scientific studies and organize their persistent storage in the dataspace cloud (that is the dataspace-relationship and dataspace-participants cloud). However, additionally scientific studies can be searched and published into the dataspace cloud from a web portal, which usually is set up for a specific scientific community to share existing knowledge and data. Once, dataspace functions are implemented as services they can easily be called from a web portal.

7.6 Performance Evaluation

Local and global RDF stores are tested with the above described LCR datasets. The local RDF store is implemented as MySQL database with the Jena SDB triple layout. The seven LCR datasets of Table were loaded into the RDF store using Jena's Persistent Ontology Model implemented in jSpace as described in Section 6.4. For the global RDF store each LCR dataset was set up as SPARQL Endpoint to be accessible through the Joseki SPARQL Server. File and database sizes of the LCR datasets and the URIs of their corresponding ontology source files are listed in Table 7.2. Ontology source files are mapped to a locally available duplicate of the file in order to provide better performance.

LCR dataset no.	DB size (MB)	Ontology source	File size
1	0.5	http://www.gridminer.org/e-sciencelifecycle/lco-1LCR.owl	43 KB
2	0.65	http://www.gridminer.org/e-sciencelifecycle/lco-3LCR.owl	77 KB
3	0.8	http://www.gridminer.org/e-sciencelifecycle/lco-6LCR.owl	107 KB
4	1	http://www.gridminer.org/e-sciencelifecycle/lco-60LCR.owl	191 KB
5	6.8	http://www.gridminer.org/e-sciencelifecycle/lco-300LCR.owl	1.6 MB
6	57,1	http://www.gridminer.org/e-sciencelifecycle/lco-600LCR.owl	16,5 MB
7	273,7	http://www.gridminer.org/e-sciencelifecycle/lco-3000LCR.owl	82,5 MB

Table 7.2: LCR datasets file and database sizes.

To improve the load time performance for the global RDF store we transformed the OWL files into the N-Triple format, which is not smaller in size in comparison to the OWL file format, but can be processed faster by the Joseki SPARQL server due to its structure. The bar graph shown in Figure 7.11 shows load times of the LCR datasets 1 to 5 of the local and the global RDF store. For a better interpretation of the bar graph we put the load time of the last two LCR datasets (6 and 7) into a separate diagram (see Figure 7.12).

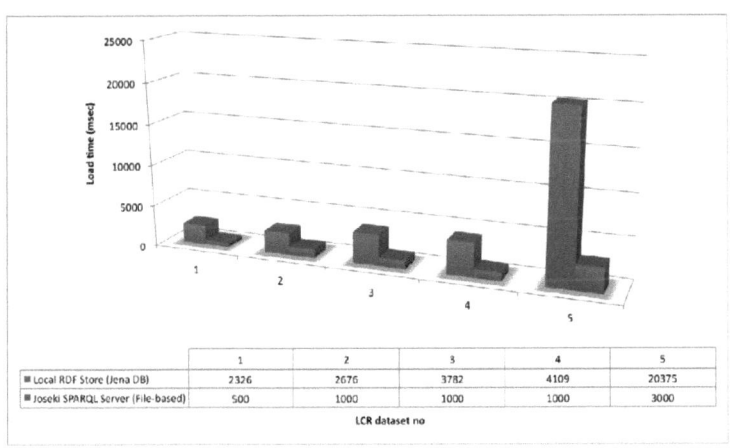

Figure 7.11: LCR dataset (1-5) load times of the local and global RDF store.

Load times of the local RDF store are much longer due to the MySQL database

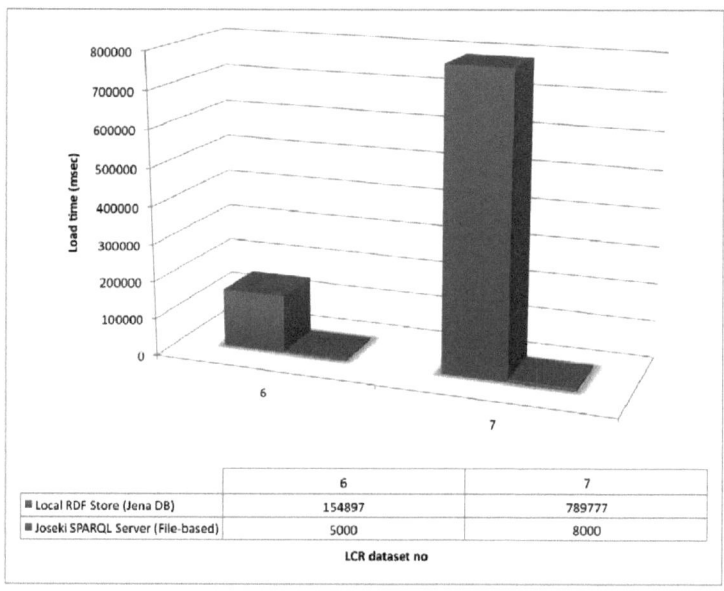

Figure 7.12: LCR dataset (6,7) load times of the local and global RDF store.

back-end, whereas the SPARQL Endpoint set up for the global RDF store work directly with the N-Triple files. The global RDF store is distributed across three sites. On each site the LCR dataset was loaded. Query answering is made up of query execution and result formatting. Both response times (query execution and result formatting) for the LCR dataset number 5 having 300 synthetic LCRs on the local RDF store is shown in the bar graph in Figure 7.13 and in Figure 7.14 for the global RDF store, respectively.

We can interpret from the response times of both RDF stores plotted in the above two bar graphs that the query execution time on the global RDF store is approx. 80% less than in the local RDF store. This is mainly due to the MySQL database backend used by the local RDF store. However, there is a time consuming load time in preface to the query execution, where information about the distributed SPARQL Endpoints is gathered before the actual query can be performed. This process accounts for 85% at an average of the query execution time. Thus, we can say that the local RDF store

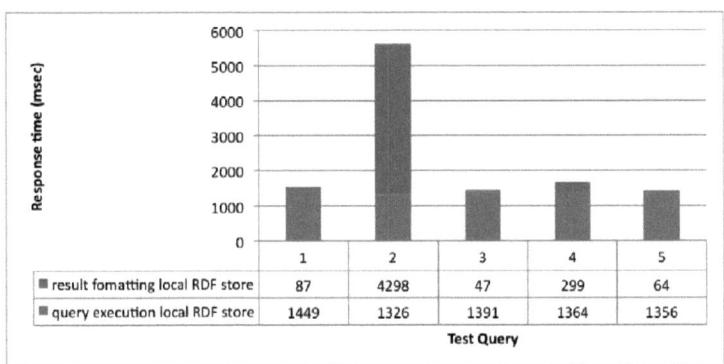

Figure 7.13: Response times of query answering in the local RDF store with the LCR dataset number 5 (300 synthetic LCRs).

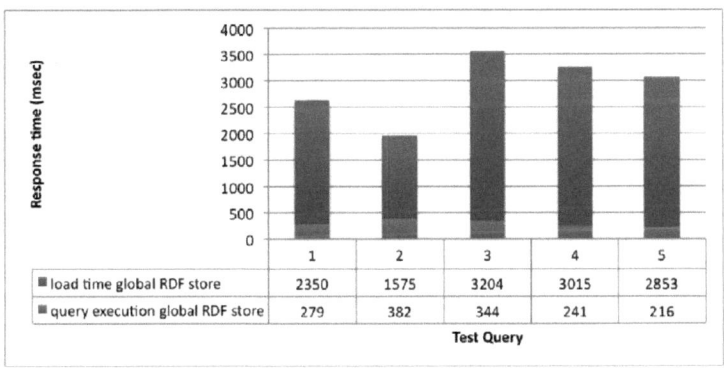

Figure 7.14: Response times of query answering in the global RDF store with the LCR dataset number 5 (300 synthetic LCRs).

provides better performance regarding an average size LCR dataset. This was actually the intention as we mentioned in Section 7.2 that local RDF stores should guarantee high performance for the local site. However, the performance provided by the global RDF store is also at a reasonable level.

Regarding larger datasets we identified that total response times of the global RDF store rises constantly still providing reasonable response times (approx. 5 seconds with the largest LCR dataset having in total 467,047 triples and 3,000 LCRs), whereas the local RDF store needs up to 16 seconds. This mainly depends on the size of the result set the query retrieves, since the result formatting is a time consuming task with large number of triples returned. Figure 7.15 shows the graph representing response times of all LCR datasets.

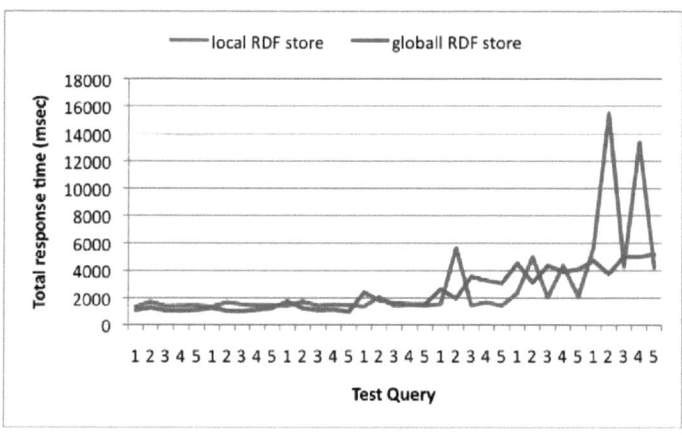

Figure 7.15: Total response times of query answering in the local and global RDF store.

7.7 Alternative Solutions for Distributed SPARQL Query Processing

In this section we briefly discuss alternative solutions for distributed SPARQL query processing. In particular, DARQ [QL08], SemWIQ [L+08], SPARQL-DQP [AAC11], and DAI-RDF [KK09].

The DARQ engine [QL08] is an extension of the Jena-embedded query engine ARQ to support federated SPARQL queries. It requires attaching a configuration file to the SPARQL query, with information about the SPARQL endpoint, vocabulary and statistics. DARQ applies logical and physical optimizations, focused on using rules for rewriting the original query planning (so as to merge basic graph patterns as soon as possible) and moving value constrains into subqueries to reduce the size of intermediate results. Unfortunately DARQ is no longer maintained. Since DARQ uses predicates to decide where to send triple patterns, no ?s ?p ?o queries are supported. Some other limitations and known issues include that joins using blank nodes and GRAPH and DESCRIBE is not supported. Also query optimization will not support many endpoints or triples.

Very similar to the DARQ approach the SemWIQ [L+08] system also contains a mediator service that distributes the execution of SPARQL queries. Heterogeneous data sources (available as CSV files, RDF datasets or related databases) are accessed by a mediator through wrappers. Queries are expressed in SPARQL and consider OWL as the vocabulary for the RDF data. SemWIQ uses the Jena's SPARQL processor ARQ to generate query plans and it applies its own optimizers. These optimizers mainly consist in rules to move down filters or unary operations in the query plan, together with join reordering based on the application of an iterative dynamic programming algorithm. The system has a registry catalog that indicates where the sources to be queried are and the vocabulary to be used is.

SPARQL-DQP [AAC11] is another approach that uses relational database DQP techniques and SQL optimization techniques to generate and optimize query plans to be executed against RDF datasets available as SPARQL endpoints. It is based on the transformation of a subset of SPARQL queries into their equivalent SQL queries, the extension of an existing relational database DQP system, named OGSA-DQP [LMC+09] to generate optimization query plans across distributed RDF datasets, and the use of the OGSA-DAI [AHH+07] framework for the robust execution of those queries and for managing direct and indirect access to datasets following the WS-DAI recommendation [AKP+06].

DAI-RDF [KK09] is a service-based RDF database middleware suite, which extends the OGSA-DAI middleware to support RDF data processing activities including SPARQL query language, ontological primitives, and reasoning functions. It basically adds a set of activities to the OGSA-DAI activity framework allowing to combine DAI-RDF activities with any existing OGSA-DAI activity, such as data compression, data conversion, and data transfer activities. DAI-RDF activities are categorized into four main groups, 1) SPARQL Activity, 2) Reasoning Activity, 3) Graph Management, and 4) Ontology Handling Activities. According to the performance results in [KK09] the middleware suite provides reasonable performance for constructing distributed RDF applications.

7.8 Summary

This work represents an important contribution for research communities that want to offer participating individuals access to semantically rich described scientific studies on a multi-institutional level. Beyond this, the experimental environment currently implemented has allowed us to investigate the scientific dataspace paradigm introduced in the previous chapters using data provided by breath gas analysis researchers. It is based on top of multiple geographically distributed data sources, taking advantage of a distributed SPARQL query processing component. This component integrates data from sources that support the SPARQL protocol, however an alternative exists in the form of the Open Grid Forum (OGF) Data Access and Integration Service (DAIS) Working Group's specifications for accessing RDF data resources [EGKMP+09], also supporting the SPARQL query language but offering a potentially more flexible set of interfaces. The application we have presented provides a scenario in which we can evaluate the use of these interfaces in a practical setting, in particular to learn lessons about how best to achieve the efficient and scalable distributed data integration that the application requires. We believe that the e-Science life cycle ontology, utilized in the context of a scientific dataspace in conjunction with the tools we have described, will provide a valuable means by which scientists from diverse e-Science applications can disseminate the results of their experiments within their community.

The performance analysis presented allowed us to evaluate the architecture on top of a synthetic large-scale scientific dataspace. However, since the synthetic LCRs within the dataspace are based on several real world scientific studies from our two e-Science applications, we believe that it represents realistic numbers regarding the performance and scale of involved datasets. Within the next chapter we introduce these two reals world e-Science applications and describe the ongoing utilization of their dataspace instances. Due to the early stage of deployment and the lack of a large amount of life cycle resources in both application domains it is however hard to provide significant numbers and bar graphs about their performance and scalability. This was actually our motivation to apply an evaluation regarding scalability and performance on a synthetic large-scale dataspace, as presented in this chapter.

Part III

Evaluation and Conclusions

Chapter 8

Experimental Evaluation in e-Science Applications

> *"In our data-centric world, the typical lifecycle of an investigation starts with the discovery of resources, followed by their acquisition. The actual conduct of the work comes next, in collaboration with project members, followed by the publication of resulting papers, data and methods - all of which then benefit from curation."*
>
> In: Realising the power of data-intensive research (Draft 1.1),
> September 2010 by
> MALCOLM ATKINSON AND DAVID DE ROURE

8.1 Introduction

The dataspace support platform presented in this book contributes to the development of methodologies and associated informatics to support preservation of the complete life cycle of scientific studies including their primary, background, and derived datasets. Within this chapter we present an experimental evaluation in two different e-Science applications including a performance evaluation of jSpace. The e-Science applications are in particular

1. Non-Invasive Health Parameter Prediction based on Traditional Chinese Medicine, and

2. Breath-Gas Analysis for Molecular-Oriented Detection of Minimal Diseases.

In the latter application the dataspace platform will be further developed within a new granted three years application driven research project [aba11]. We expect that in this application the corresponding dataspace will evolve to a large scale and semantically rich space of breath research related scientific data within the ongoing decade. Unfortunately, in the first application there is no funding to further provide maintenance and administration of the dataspace. However, we were able to elaborate and evaluate the dataspace paradigm in an early stage of development. We have learned many lessons and received valuable feedback from this first application, which was an important input for the second application.

First we introduce both e-Science applications providing some background information on each application domain and exemplify for each application a concrete scientific experiment and its mapping to an e-Science life cycle resource in jSpace.

8.2 Non-Invasive Health Parameter Prediction based on Traditional Chinese Medicine

According to the basic TCM theory, the human body has 14 acupuncture meridians, which are a secret to our biological and medical knowledge. Within the China-Austria Data Grid (CADGrid) project [cad11] investigations on how high-tech measurement and its technologies can support the exact estimation of the meridian status are observed. Therefore an e-Infrastructure supporting computation and data management services as well as access to meridian measurement databases is set up among participating research institutions in China and Austria. The analytical techniques used (electro signal and subcutaneous impedance measurement) have collected huge amounts of data referred to as meridian measurement data, which again as a result of followed data analysis, have produced a large number of derived data products. In order to use this large amount of valuable information, it was necessary to make available a space of data with semantically rich relationships accessible for other research groups targeting different research areas.

The CADGrid infrastructure provides an *Intelligence Base* offering commonly used models and algorithms as WS-I and WSRF-compliant services as well as compute and storage resources. It is equipped with WEEP [JKB08], a workflow engine allowing researchers to execute a number of pre-selected services in a controlled and efficient way.

An e-Health service aiming in the treatment of diabetic patients was the first output of commonly achieved research results within the scientific collaboration. This service, called the *Non-Invasive Blood Glucose Measurement Service*, in short NIGM-Service, was the first application on top of the CADGrid infrastructure. Non-Invasive Blood Glucose Measurement (NIGM) [EHL+08] represents a new method by measuring electro-signals in human body meridians to get blood glucose values without injuring the fingers or any other part of the body. It is a real non invasive method at all and it covers also other measurements which are necessary in internal medicine.

The NIGM workflow is described more precisely in the following Sections, as it represents the basic experiment for the creation of semantically rich relationships among dataspace participants in this application. A real NIGM study is used in order to exemplify the e-Science life cycle.

8.2.1 NIGM Use Case Scenarios

The NIGM application measures human blood glucose values accurately and conveniently by the use of a special medical meridian measurement instrument and the CADGrid infrastructure. The data obtained by this instrument is referred to as meridian measurement data and can be analyzed by the meridian electro information transmission model to derive human blood glucose values. This model is implemented as a complex grid-based computing process that executes a number of compute intensive algorithms. The controlled execution of this process is done by the Non-Invasive Blood Glucose Measurement Service (NIGM-Service) [BEH+08]. The method is based on the meridian-theory. Each of these longitudinally distributed lines on our human body has its main points called source points, totally 24 [ZJLL04].

The electro signal measurement instrument sends an electric signal (white noise) into one meridian source point and measures the corresponding signal output at another source point either on the same meridian or on another meridian.

The NIGM-Service covers the process of computing patients glucose values from these meridian measurements. The service consists of the execution of several algorithms, each one available as a standalone CADGrid service within the CADGrid Intelligence Base. Using the workflow engine WEEP [JKB08], a predefined workflow representing the NIGM workflow is deployed and available as one service within the CADGrid Intelligence Base. Figure 8.1 illustrates the NIGM-workflow.

It presents a novel non-invasive method for accurate estimation of blood glucose values based on electro-transformation measures in human body meridians. The method has two main benefits, by splitting the process of vital parameter estimation into an evolvable, personalized data mining process and a rather simple source signal emitting and recording phase: first, the infrastructure can easily be applied to other target values and second, improvements to the involved data mining services and process will directly result in a more precise and robust estimation of the values.

8.2.2 NIGM Dataspace Participants

Table 8.1 lists all datasets that are involved in a typical NIGM study as described above. These datasets are considered as dataspace participants and thus are replicated within the data preservation system iRODS. Table 8.1 also gives information about the sizes and types of the datasets and provides a brief description of its content. Each dataset is interlinked with the LCR, in particular with the corresponding activity of the LCR. The interlinking is done using the EPR-Framework, which provides an unique reference to a dataset stored in the iRODS Server.

The input dataset (fids.zip) of a typical NIGM experiment consist of input value pairs representing meridian measurements from a specific patient. The size of such an input dataset depends on the number of measurements taken from the patines. One meridian measurement generates around 1000 to 10000 value pairs. Typically for each patient 50 meridian measurements and equally many measures are applied using the conventional invasive blood glucose method. The resulting typical size of the input dataset is approx. 10MB on average. The NIGM workflow instance (NIGM.gwa) being used within the study is saved as background dataspace participant. Since the algorithms are continuously being improved, we preserve the version that was used within a specific study. The NIGM workflow is described in WS-BPEL (Web Services Business Process Execution Language) [Org07] and its size is less than 1MB. The final result of the whole workflow represents the initial model set up for predicting blood glucose values. In particular the NIGM workflow builds an individual health model for each considered person. This model is patient specific and has the form of a neural network, which is stored in a PMML file (PMMLmodel.zip) and typically not larger

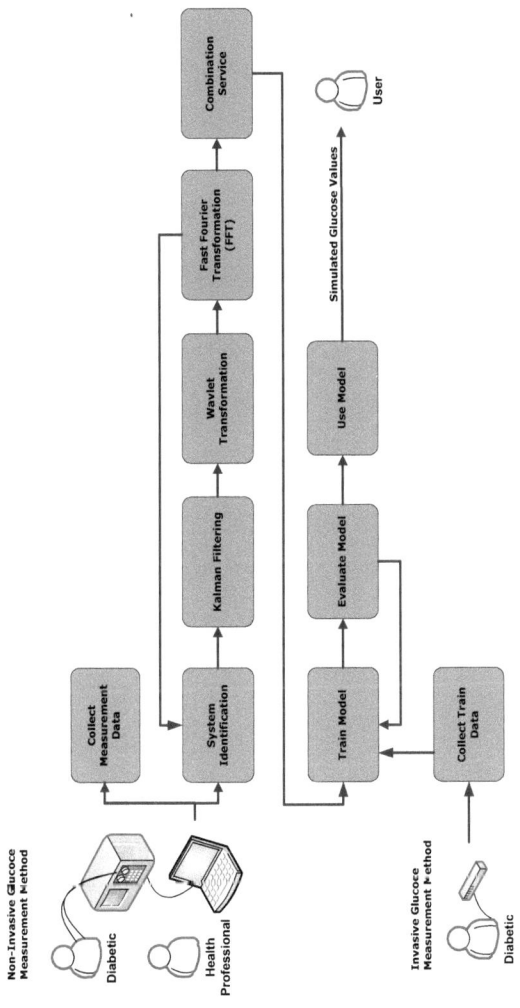

Figure 8.1: The Non-Invasive Glucose Measurement Service (NIGM-Service).

Dataset	Type	Size (kb)	Description
fids.zip	primary	10240	This represents the final input datasetindexFinal input dataset for a typical NIGM study. It is
NIGM.gwa	background	1024	NIGM workflow instance used within this study
PMMLmodel.xml	derived	2048	Patient specific model is used to predict blood glucose value for the considered particular patient.

Table 8.1: Dataspace participants in a typical NIGM study.

that 2MB on average.

8.2.3 NIGM Example Life Cycle Resource

In the following we exemplify a LCR based on a real NIGM study. In particular we show the *Goal Specification* activity of the e-Science life cycle. Figure 8.2 illustrates a graphical representation of the RDF tree regarding that activity. We describe what information is recorded as individuals and properties of the e-Science life cycle ontology in terms of a concrete NIGM study.

The green rectangles in the figure represent the values of datatype properties defined in the e-Science life cycle ontology. The dashed lines represent the datatype properties. The rounded white rectangles represent individuals of the OWL classes defined in the ontology. Solid lines are representing object properties. We can see from the figure that there is one domain specific attribute defined, which has as name *"Meridian-Name"* and corresponding value is *"HE GU"*. Since this information is too specific, we decided to include it as a domain specific attribute. Also three key words are defined, which support discovery of the LCR.

Other activities of the LCR include descriptions of the input dataset and provide related background information on the NIGM study as described above. This includes information about the algorithms used in the NIGM workflow as well as on the resulted neural network model. Table 8.2 provides counts of individual axioms for the LCR of the above described NIGM example.

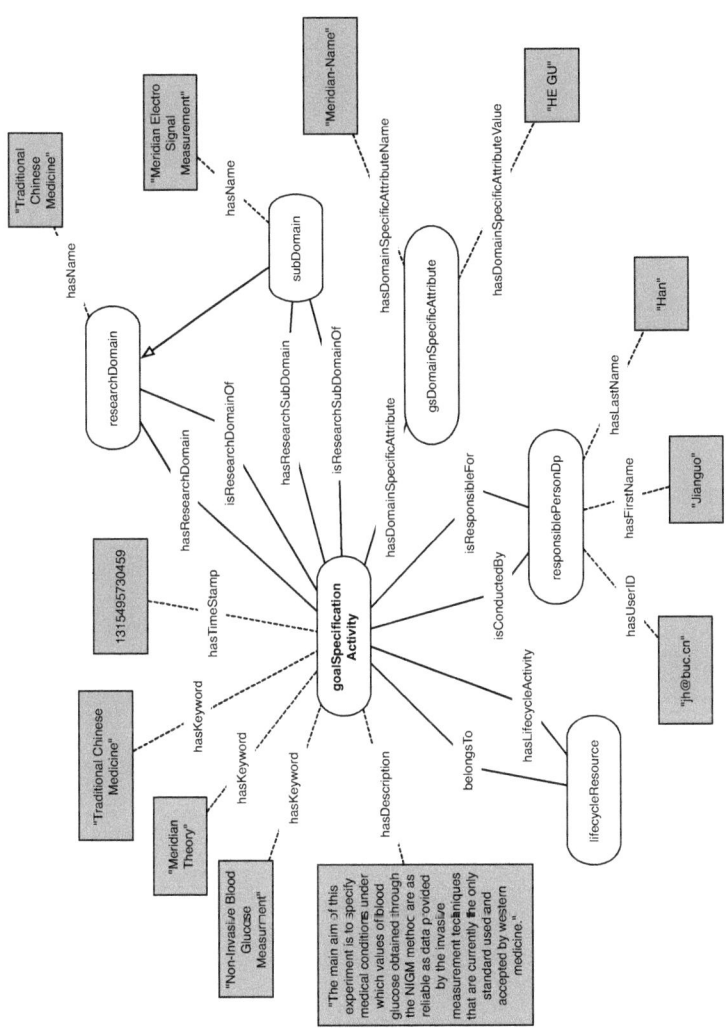

Figure 8.2: Goal specification activity of an example NIGM LCR.

Individual axiom	Count (single LCR)
ClassAssertions axioms	28
ObjectPropertyAssertion axioms	37
DataPropertyAssertion axioms	76

Table 8.2: Individual axiom counts of the NIGM LCR.

8.3 Breath Gas Analysis for Molecular-Oriented Detection of Minimal Diseases

Breath gas analysis (BGA) is an emerging new scientific field with a large scientific community spread all over the world and with a promising significant impact on many application domains. Recent results suggest that early detection of different kinds of cancer is possible by means of breath gas analysis far beyond the scope of available diagnostic methods. There is strong evidence that specific kinds of cancers can be detected using the concentration pattern of volatile compounds in exhaled air [PCC+03, Rob05].

The growing international community of gas researchers is addressing many different studies of exhaled breath including sources of endogenously-derived gases, such as skin, urine, faeces and flatulence. They are continuously developing new analytical methods, collecting pilot data for cancer and other diseases and identifying marker compounds. Breath gas researcher are investigating and screening for hundreds of compounds in the exhaled breath. The analytical instruments and techniques used include GC-MS[1], PTR-MS[2], SIFT-MS[3], IMS[4] as well as various statistical and data mining techniques supporting identification of specific markers. Currently, during the investigations – mainly performed using the common Matlab language and computing environment – a large number of new different sampling and analytical techniques for breath gas measurements are being developed.

The purpose of *breath gas analysis scientific dataspaces* [ELS+09] is to enable collaborating scientists and institutions (a) access to distributed breath gas data and analytical resources collected and developed at different research institutions around the world and (b) to easily contribute to and leverage the resources of an international-

---
[1] Gas Chromatography Mass Spectrometric
[2] Proton-Transfer-Reaction Mass Spectrometry
[3] Selected-Ion-Flow-Tube Mass Spectrometry
[4] Ion Mobility Spectrometry

and national-scale, multi-institutional environment. This will strongly support global collaborations of scientists, improve decisions and increase the chance and scope of discoveries in the breath gas research domain. In this context there is a need for a supporting information infrastructure allowing scientists to keep track of their e-Science studies and to publish corresponding results of breath gas analysis experiments linked together with their source data and semantics about the purpose of the experiments.

Source data obtained from previously mentioned analytical methods are referred to as breath gas measurement data and are saved, together with corresponding patient data, locally at each research center. These data represents the fundament for simulation and modeling by the acting research group, e.g. observation of the correlation between isoprene breath content and cholesterol level in blood. Such breath gas experiments, if evaluated on large amount of real data allow a more detailed analysis including e.g. gender-specific relation with respect to age-dependency [KAS+08]. The output of these analyses aims at defining a large number of predictions and might provoke further experimentation, which in turn may take days or weeks depending on computational and human resources available. However, the resulting *derived data*, that have arisen from the research task represent valuable information not only to the acting research group but also to other groups with respect to other main focuses.

Breath gas research specific dataspaces will be set up to serve a special subject, which is on the one hand the relationship of source data (exhaled breath measurement data) and its derived data (e.g. specific cancer markers) in breath gas analysis experiments and on the other hand to integrate scientific understandings into these applied experiments.

8.3.1 BGA Use Case Scenario

The use case scenario depicting the current sequence of events in conducting breath gas analysis experiments is illustrated in Figure 8.3, which is reproduced from the position paper [DFL+09]. It presents an overview, with the *Server* being an isle-system gathering the data. Import and export activities on this system are protected by smart card security measures. Steps 2 to 4 present the collection and subsequent transfer (i.e. manual import) of personal data to the server. Steps 5 to 7 involve the collection and preprocessing of the probands analysis data. Step 8 is the actual analysis done using a workstation employing Matlab.

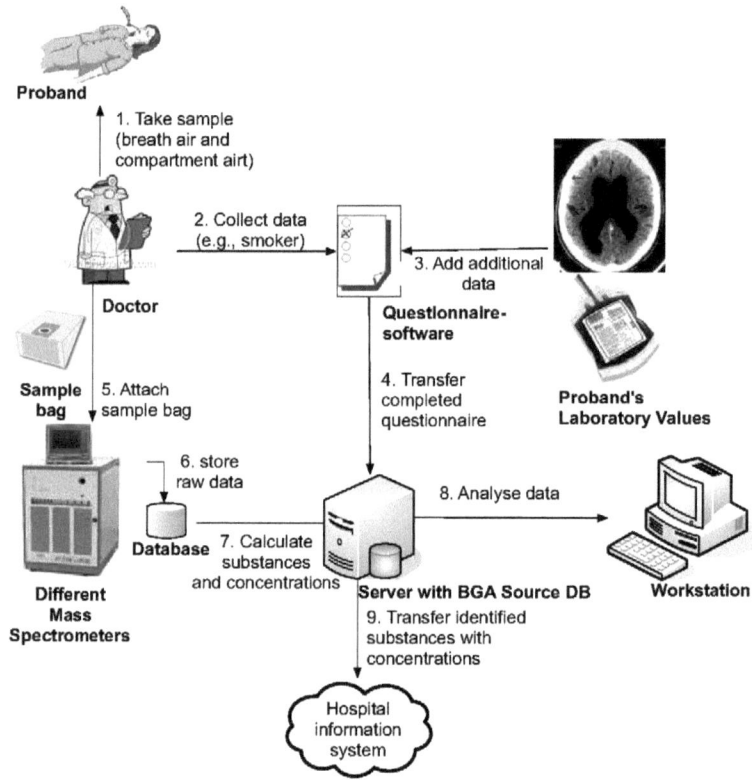

Figure 8.3: Use case depicting the current sequence of events [DFL+09].

The implementation of a secure infrastructure, which provides the needed services for breath gas researcher to efficiently and securely perform steps 1 to 7 was part of the project described in [DFL+09]. However, the work described in this chapter focuses more on the evaluation of jSpace in the breath gas scientific community and we therefore assume that a secure and isolated database storing mass spectrometer and patient data is already set up and administered by the corresponding *Regional Head Service* as described in [DFL+09]. In the following we refer to this database as the *source database.*

We are aware that in order to successfully establish a large-scale scientific dataspace for the breath gas analysis community with a large amount of well described experiments of exhaled breath, we rely on active participation of members of the scientific community. Therefore we have - in cooperation with leading breath gas researchers - defined a number of actions that a researcher is conducting during the process of performing breath gas studies. We have then mapped the specific actions to activities of the e-Science life cycle. We also indicate "where" (i.e. on the community portal or within Matlab or in the breath research lab) these actions should be taken. Actions, their corresponding e-Science life cycle activities, and the "place" or "tool" where they are taken are listed in Table 8.3.

Action	Description	e-Science life cycle activity	Place
1	Login to the system.	*GoalSpecification*	Portal
2	Definition of the goals of the study.	*GoalSpecification*	Portal
3	Collection of the probands analysis data (mass spectrometer and patient data, covers Steps 1-7).	*DataPreparation*	Lab/ Questionnaire Software
4	Formulation and submission of a query to the *source database*. This action generates the *final input dataset*, which will be included into the dataspace as participant marked with type "primary data".	*DataPreparation*	Portal
4	Selection/development of the analytical method for analyzing the prepared dataset. This action generates the analytical methods, which will be included into the dataspace as participant marked with type "background data".	*TaskSelection*	Matlab
5	Execution of the analytical methods.	*TaskExecution*	Matlab

Table continues on the next page.

Dataset	Type	Size (kb)	Description
fids.zip	primary	3072	This represents the final input datasetindexFinal input dataset.
studyMat.zip	background	1024	All analytical methods used to analyze the final input dataset
reportMat.zip	derived	3072	Matlabs publishing report.

Table 8.4: Dataspace participants in a typical BGA study.

Action	Description	e-Science life cycle activity	Place
6	Process the results and export them using Matlab's publication function into XML . This action generates the results report, which will be included into the dataspace as participant marked with type "derived data".	*ResultPublishing*	Matlab
7	Set publication mode to conducted experiment.	*ResultPublishing*	Portal

Table 8.3: Definition of breath gas analysis actions and their mapping to e-Science life cycle activities.

Based on this common understanding we have designed and implemented the tools that support the breath gas researchers in conducting their breath gas studies according to the above described actions.

8.3.2 BGA Dataspace Participants

A typical BGA study includes several datasets. Some are being accessed, others are being generated during the conduction of the study. Table 8.4 gives an overview of the types and sizes of datasets of a typical BGA study.

Final input datasets are being created after steps 1 to 7 of the use case described above. They can be retrieved by submitting a query to one of the breath gas research *source databases* available to the acting researcher. However, in order to handle the issue that data and probably also structure of the data might change over time, we replicate this dataset into the iRODS system. A typical final input dataset is less than 3 MB in its Matlab structure (.mat file), which is a binary data container format used by Matlab. It may include arrays, variables, functions, and other types of data. It is organized in three blocks as follows:

(1) patient data - includes all collected data of different test persons such as proband value (e.g. height, weight), burden (e.g. smoker/nonsmoker), labor value (e.g. blood parameter), etc.

(2) the system information block manages all system settings for the two databases like all users with their corresponding user groups, studies with their questionnaires, different mass spectrometers with status, container types with status, and

(3) the analysis data part includes all information on a specific measurement of a sample such as mass spectrometer type, used container, collection date, measurement date, data (substances with concentration and additional information), etc.

In a typical BGA-study the analytical methods include several Matlab functions, each of them is in a separate M-file (ASCII-text files containing Matlab commands and functions). Typical size of a single M-file is less that 500 KB. In the major of cases two different Matlab functions were used within a single study, resulting in a typical background dataset size of approx. 1 MB on average.

Once the breath gas researcher has accomplished his experiment, he can publish the results of his analysis. Therefore we take advantage of Matlab's publishing function, which lets you export results as plots or as complete reports. Using the Matlab editor, researchers can automatically export their Matlab results, including Matlab scripts into XML and various other file formats, e.g. HTML or LaTeX. Since typical breath gas experiments include plotting functions, this dataset usually includes images in the open PNG format. Typical size is less that 3 MB.

In addition there are special databases set up (RDF Stores) for storing individuals and properties of the e-Science life cycle ontology, which are defined in RDF [rdf04b]. Figure 8.4 gives an overview of the types and sizes of data from a single real breath

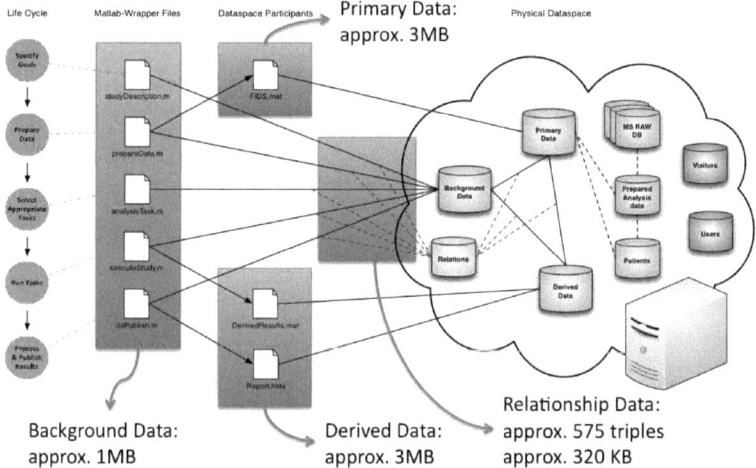

Figure 8.4: Main entities of a breath gas analysis experiment and their organization into dataspace participants and relationships.

gas analysis experiment. The figure also shows what data is considered as dataspace participant and how relationships are consolidated and semantically enriched.

Since in this application patient data is involved and due to legal requirements on such highly sensitive personal data, security and privacy issues are of utmost importance. Thus within applications in the breath gas analysis research domain all participating databases including the RDF store are isolated, monitored, and restricted to a single point of access, hence implementing strict access control. Details about the access control mechanisms and the security considerations in general are described in [DMF+09, DFL+09].

8.3.3 BGA Example Life Cycle Resource

In the following we discuss a real breath gas analysis study in the context of the e-Science life cycle and describe their outputs and how data is organized by the scientific dataspace. At first the breath gas study is described in textual form. Users can define their own attributes and add values to it, e.g. attribute *Description* contains a textual description of the goals of the study. This data is, together with information about the acting researcher (research group, department, publication mode) saved as individuals of the e-Science life cycle ontology in the RDF store. A snapshot of a simplified RDF graph of a real breath gas experiment is illustrated in Fig. 8.5. The complete RDF graph is described in Appendix A. The snapshot shows a life cycle resource, which describes the relationship of the participants depicted in the figure. Green rectangles represent the values of datatype properties and the ellipses represent individuals of corresponding OWL classes from the e-Science life cycle ontology. Table 8.5 provides counts of individual axioms of the complete LCR example. The participants represent primary, background, and derived data of the breath gas experiment. Participants are described with attributes and their values, which the acting breath gas researcher defines while conducting the experiment. In the breath gas analysis domain there is a set of attribute names predefined to be followed by scientists for a consistent description of breath gas analysis experiments.

Data access is done using the OGSA-DAI client and a certificate. In most scenarios, the researcher first loads all values of the dataset he is investigating into the Matlab structure. This is done using an implemented data load Matlab-function (`loadData.m`), which communicates with an OGSA-DAI client. Then the breath gas researcher selects the values he is interested in for the current experiment, e.g. selection of all ex-smokers. The outputs of this selection process, which is done within Matlab are twofold: (1) A new Matlab MAT-structure containing the selected data (`fids.mat`). (2) The Matlab function itself (`selectData.m`), which is responsible to select the required data.

Several analysis functions might be implemented by the breath gas researcher and applied to the final input dataset. Such Matlab functions also represent background data, thus are saved correspondingly. For easier handling we provide an empty Matlab file named `executeStudy.m`, which will be used in all experiments. Breath gas researchers may add their own implementations into it or import external analysis functions. These functions calculate the derived data, which are usually input to a plot function. Again an empty template (`plotData.m`) is prepared to be used by the researcher. Finally we provide a publish function (`dsPublish.m`), which generates an XML report of the conducted experiment including plots, if used by taking advantage of Matlab's publishing feature. This report is then zipped and stored in the preservation system, i.e. iRODS.

Based on these investigations we have created guidelines for breath gas researchers,

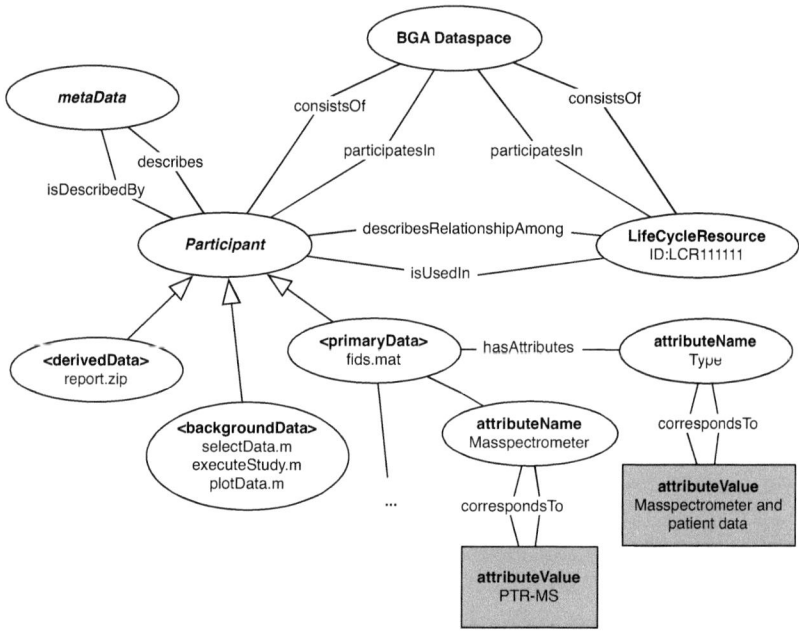

Figure 8.5: Snapshot of an RDF graph of a sample breath gas experiment.

defining concrete activities and documentation policies, which guide users through the e-Science life cycle. An empty Matlab-template with named files is also created for a better comprehension. Figure 8.6 shows Matlab m-files of the template, which are used to structure a BGA study into its representative phases according to the e-Science life cycle.

We furthermore implemented a first prototype of a web portal for the breath gas analysis application. The portal supports the features that are provided by the *e-Science Life Cycle Composer* and the *jSpace Search&Query Panel* introduced in Section 6.4. A screenshot of the web portal is shown in Figure 8.7. It is built using the GoogleWeb Toolkit (GWT), which allows to build and maintain complex yet highly performant JavaScript front-end applications in the Java programming language. It utilizes the jSpace java API to construct semantic data about experiments, which hides from the

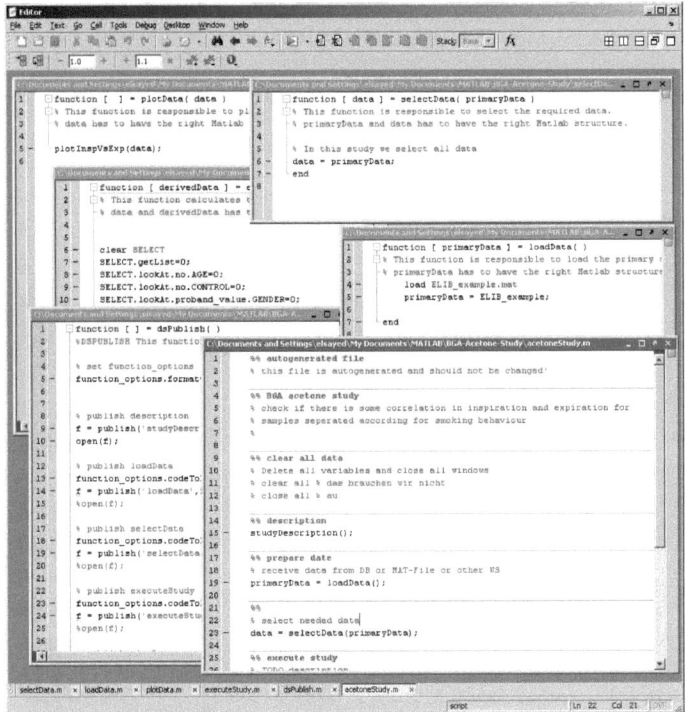

Figure 8.6: Screenshot of the Matlab-template for BGA studies.

scientist most of the underlying complexity involved in the process, such as working directly with RDF or writing SPARQL queries.

8.4 jSpace Experimental Evaluation

Creating semantically rich relationships among datasets that participant in the e-Science lifecycle is an important part of the dataspace support platform for providing well-preserved scientific experiments. The relationship creation has to be efficient to minimize perturbation of the e-Science application from which scientific experiments

Individual axiom	Count (single LCR)
ClassAssertions axioms	29
ObjectPropertyAssertion axioms	45
DataPropertyAssertion axioms	100

Table 8.5: Individual axiom counts of the BGA LCR.

should be preserved. The complete process of creating an LCR in the dataspace includes (a) the creation semantic relationships among its datasets, (b) the indexing of each activity in the LCR, and (c) the preservation of both, the individuals and properties of the experiment into the RDF Store and its participating datasets into an appropriate data preservation system such as the iRODS system. This process is referred to the *jSpace preservation process* in the following.

Since jSpace aims at providing a methodology and a Java API to support this process it has to scale with the number of clients, the size of datasets included in scientific experiments and the amount of relationships among them. The experimental evaluation uses an initial prototype of jSpace (v1.2).

The performance overhead is an important factor in determining the system scalability and acceptability. Greater the performance overhead of a system the less scalable a system is, and less scalability, among others, means less suitability for e-Infrastructure and vice versa. For these reasons, we evaluated jSpace for performance overhead on both, a real world NIGM and a BGA study and discuss the results.

8.4.1 Experimental Setup

The following setup was used for our performance evaluation on the jSpace preservation process in both application scenarios.

For the execution of the BGA study, we used a desktop computer running Windows XP x64 Edition on an Intel Core 2 Quad CPU with 2.66 GHz and 4 GB of RAM. The BGA study was executed within Matlab version 7.7.0 (R2008b). The BGA study basically checks if there is some correlation in inspiration and expiration of exhaled breath air for samples separated according for smoking behavior. It receives the data directly from within Matlab. The input dataset is represented in the Matlab data structure. The study includes three steps: (1) preparation of the data from the input data set that is in the Matlab structure, (2) execution of the tasks, which are breath gas analytical methods implemented as Matlab functions, and (3) plotting the results

Figure 8.7: Web portal for breath gas analysis researchers to interact with the scientific dataspace.

and preparing a report in the HTML format, which contains figures from plotting the results.

The NIGM performance results were elaborated on a Linux server running Fedora Core 5 on an Intel Pentium D 930 CPU with 3 GHz and 4 GB of RAM. The server hosts all the services relevant for the execution of the NIGM workflow shown in Figure 8.1. The following software versions have been used Globus Toolkit 4.05 [The11b], WEEP Version 1.2.1[JKB08], OGSA-DAI WSRF 2.2 [AHH+07] exposing a MySQL 4 database with the meridian measurement test datasets collected with the meridian measurement instrument. A detailed performance evaluation on the NIGM application was conducted in [BEH+08], on top of which Prewe build our jSpace performance

Description	Best Time	Worst Time	Avg. Overhead (time)	% Overhead
With jSpace PP	159380ms	162425ms	1623ms	1.64%
Without jSpace PP	156800ms	158453ms	-	-

Table 8.6: Performance overhead of the jSpace preservation process in the NIGM application.

evaluation for that application. The NIGM service consists of the following algorithms, deployed as WS-I and WSRF-compliant CADGrid services: (1) System Identification, (2) Kalman Filtering, (3) Fast Fourier Transformation, (4) Combination Service, and finally (5) Back Propagation Neural Network.

The performance of the jSpace preservation process was tested on a macbook pro running Mac OS X version 10.7.1 on an 2.4 GHz Intel Core 2 Duo processor with 5 GB of RAM. The installed software components include iRODS 2.4.1 [iRO11], Jargon 2.4 [jar11], Jena 2.6.4 [jen11] and the current version of the jSpace API which is 1.2.

8.4.2 jSpace Performance Evaluation on NIGM

For the performance overhead of the jSpace preservation process (jSpace PP) in the NIGM application, the NIGM service as explained in Section 8.2 was executed with the dataspace system and without. The jSpace preservation process was conducted subsequent to the NIGM workflow. A comparison of the results of the execution was performed. The results of the performance overhead are shown in Table 8.6, which reflects that jSpace has on average 1.64% performance overhead. *Best Time* and *Worst Time* in Table 8.6 are the total execution times including the execution time of the NIGM-workflow. In the worst case a performance overhead of 2660ms was recorded and in the best case the overhead was 1301ms.

Figure 8.8 shows how the performance overhead of the jSpace preservation process is consolidated into its three phases. The creation of semantic relationships takes the greatest part, almost 50% of the total time needed to preserve an NIGM study, directly followed by the preservation phase with approx. 40%. The indexing phase accounts for approx. 10%.

In some application scenarios, it might be not so important to replicate the input dataset, since the end point references defined by jSpace might be sufficient. However, in this experiment we have chosen to replicate the data from the dataspace participants layer, which include the input dataset as well as the result dataset and the NIGM workflow. The performance overhead of the preservation phase is mainly caused by replicating the input dataset into the iRODS system. The input dataset used in this experiment had the typical size of 10 MB, whereas all other participating datasets where in all not larger that 3 MB on average.

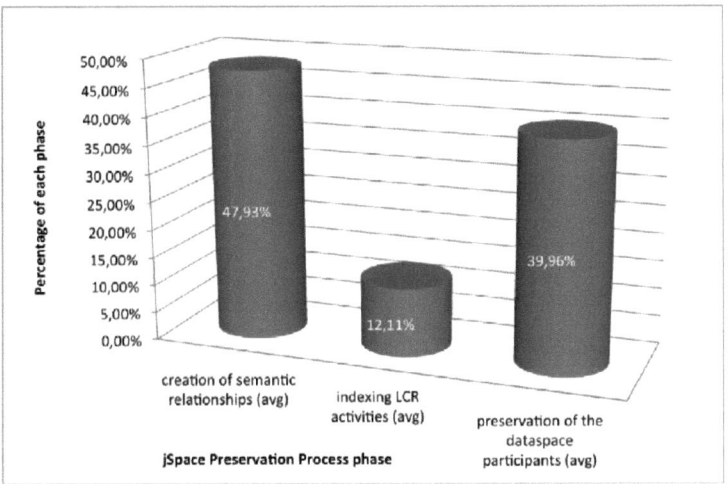

Figure 8.8: Distribution of the performance overhead among the phases of the jSpace preservation process (average on preservation of 100 NIGM-LCRs).

8.4.3 jSpace Performance Evaluation on BGA

For the second application domain we have executed a typical breath gas analysis experiment with the jSpace preservation process subsequently to the study execution and without it. The study has been executed one hundred times in order to elaborate significant average performance results. The performance overhead is shown in Table 8.7, which reflects a performance overhead of approx. 11.63% on average.

We argue that the performance results presented in Table 8.7 represents a remarkable low performance overhead, which is most likely due to the relatively small sizes of dataspace participants in this application. Therefore the preservation phase of the jSpace preservation process is quite small. Dealing with larger datasets we are facing

Description	Best Time	Worst Time	Avg. Overhead (time)	% Overhead
With jSpace	9855ms	12078ms	1275ms	12.14%
Without jSpace	7915ms	8001ms	-	-

Table 8.7: Performance overhead of jSpace in the BGA application.

a great increase in the performance overhead which is mainly the result of a longer preservation phase time. This is discussed in more detail with larger test datasets in further experiments in the Section 8.4.4. The distribution of the performance overhead to the three phases of the jSpace preservation process is given in Figure 8.9 and in Figure 8.10 we illustrate the performance overhead in relation to the total execution time of the BGA study.

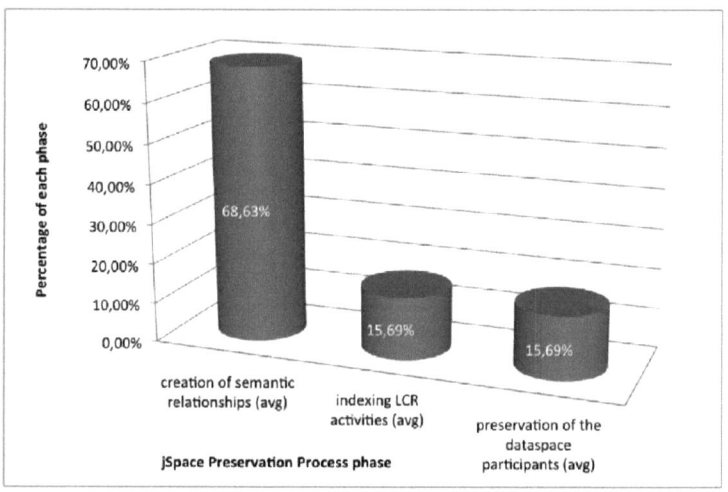

Figure 8.9: Distribution of the performance overhead among the phases of the jSpace preservation process (average on preservation of 100 BGA-LCRs).

Another important factor, which influences the performance results is the amount of reused Life Cycle Activities (LCA) within the LCR that is being inserted to the dataspace. In another experiment where we have been successively reusing the five e-Science life cycle activities in the BGA study starting with only one refused activity until all five activities of the randomly generated LCR represented reused activities.

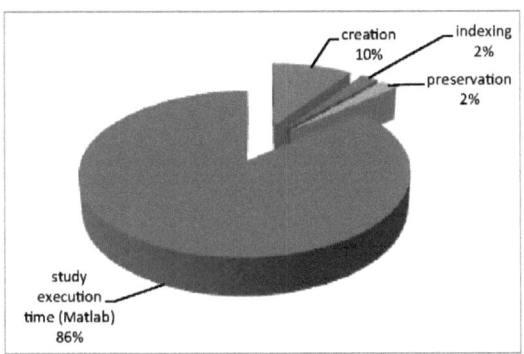

Figure 8.10: Distribution of the performance overhead among the phases of the jSpace Preservation Process (average on preservation of 100 LCR) in relation to the total execution time of the BGA study.

No reused LCA	Best Time	Worst Time	Avg. Overhead (time)	% Overhead
1	8769ms	9389ms	1078ms	13.55%
2	8612ms	9146ms	813ms	10.23%
3	8540ms	8981ms	733ms	9.22%
4	8370ms	8971ms	524ms	6.6%
5	8229ms	8549ms	337ms	4.25%

Table 8.8: Performance overhead of jSpace in the BGA application with reused LCA.

We executed the BGA study for each LCR one hundred times. Table 8.8 shows the performance overhead for this experiment.

The graph in Figure 8.11 clearly shows that the performance overhead reduces with an increasing number of reused life cycle activities. This is due to the fact that jSpace does not store duplicates of the same life cycle activity. Once an activity is identified as a reused one, jSpace queries for the corresponding activity individual from the RDF Store, compares it with the activity to be inserted and in case its attributes are equal, jSpace reuses the activity that is already stored in the RDF Store. This reused actually means that only the object properties to and from the activity are being created. The individual of the activity itself is not created again. The same is true for the indexing of that activity and the preservation of its datasets. Therefore the total time of the jSpace preservation process is shorter when using reused activities within an LCR. In the last run, we generated a LCR that is reusing all five LCA, which means that no new LCR

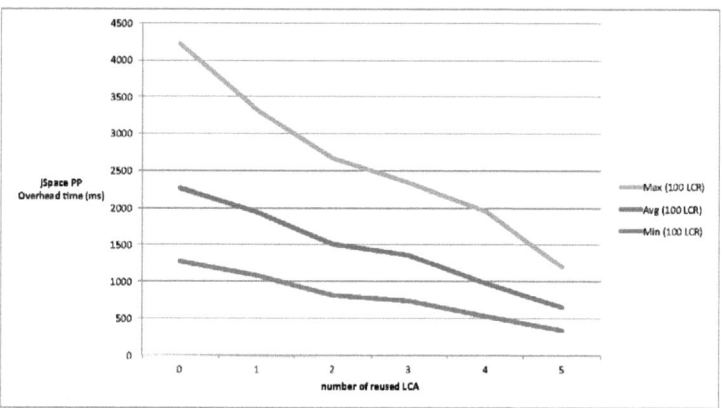

Figure 8.11: Performance overhead of the jSpace preservation process with different number of reused LCA.

individual will be created. The average performance overhead after conducting the jSpace preservation process one hundred times with that LCR is 337ms. This number represent the time needed for (a) retrieving the corresponding individuals from the RDF store, and (b) the comparison of its attributes with the attributes of the activity to be inserted.

8.4.4 Impact of Large Values of Dataspace Participants in jSpace

Scientific experiments can be data-intensive and involve complex computation over large volumes of input data. It is important for any data preservation system to perform well in such scenarios. The iRODS system that is used in conjunction with jSpace for the persistent storage of dataspace participants provides great performance in handling large-data sets.

However, the semantic markup layer provided by jSpace, allows to answers search requests without accessing initial dataspace participants based on the semantic relations described by individuals of the ontology. We can reason from this that there is no direct relation or impact on the jSpace performance regarding the volume of dataspace participants being processed on the semantic markup layer. The semantic markup layer and the dataspace participants layer is introduced in Figure 6.7 in Section 6.4 The reason for this no impact/relation is that jSpace stores a reference in particular an end point reference to the dataspace participant being used and persistently stored in iRODS. This makes the jSpace system ideal for scientific experiments consuming data where the original data resource might not be modified or removed frequently. On the other side dealing with remarkably large values of primary datasets, one should consider the overhead in replicating the data into the preservation system iRODS. This however is important since the experiment would otherwise not be preserved for a rerun in the future. We have shown in the performance evaluation with two different applications that the overall performance overhead is little significant in relation to the total study execution time. In both experiments we have included the replication of the data into the iRODS system. The performance results showed that the percentage of the preservation phase, which is doing the replication of the datasets into iRODS is approx. 40% for the NIGM study and approx. 2% in the BGS study of the complete jSpace preservation process. So it might make sense up to a certain size of input data to replicate the dataset into the iRODS system. We have conducted some further experiments in order to show how jSpace in conduction with the iRODS system scales with the size of datasets from the dataspace participants layer. A number of randomly generated LCR were executed with different input data sizes ranging from 10 MB up to 2.5 GB. Each LCR was inserted multiple times in order to get solid average performance numbers. The results are presented in Figure 8.12.

It is important to mention that in both applications the maximum dataset accessed did not exceed 100 MB. We are aware that this situation might change over time in particular in the breath gas analysis domain as new mass spectrometer instruments have emerged, which can calculate much faster the volatile compound in exhaled breath. However, we believe that the overhead in replicating the input dataset still pays off, since it enables researcher to rerun a BGA study even after a long time period, when the original data source might have been changed or is not available anymore.

8.4.5 Dataspace Reusability Measures

In general the examination of dataspace measures allows to monitor system usage and thus helps improving the system.

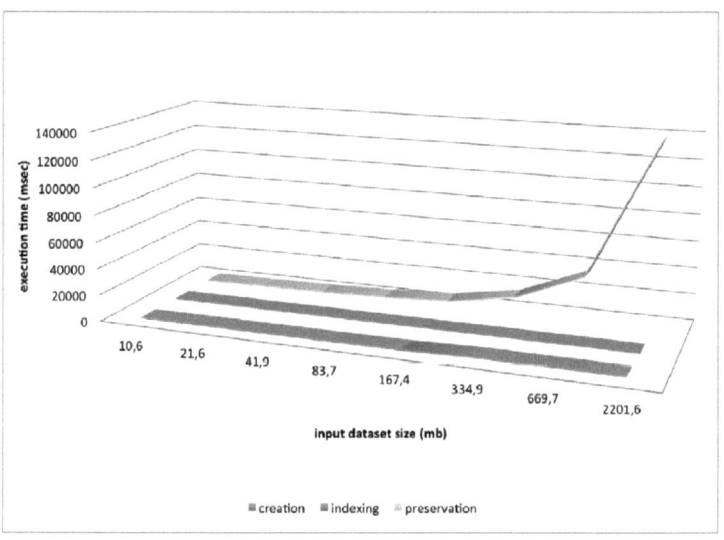

Figure 8.12: Performance overhead of the jSpace preservation process with different input dataset sizes.

The dataspace reusability measure is an important measure to express how useful the scientific dataspace might be for an acting research group in the application area to which the dataspace is deployed. In order to measure it, we first have to elaborate the number of reused Life Cycle Activities (LCA) using the dataspace indexer introduced in Section 6.3.4. In order to do this, we request the *current indexKey* from the dataspace indexer. An *indexKey* has the form of an LCR key as exemplified in Section 6.2.3 in Listing 6.1 The current indexKey represents the key of the last LCR inserted into the dataspace. Its indexes therefore represent the highest indexes in each lifecycle activity. Having the key we simply retrieve the total number of LCRs in the dataspace from the highest index or directly from the index table, which is described in Section 6.3.4. If we define $LcrKeys$ as the set of all keys, the cardinality of this set represents the total number of LCRs in the dataspace and thus is equal to the highest index i of all lifecycle activities in the current indexKey:

$$LCR_{Count} = |LcrKeys| = (max)i_{LcrKeys}$$

where $(max)i_{LcrKeys}$ represents the maximum of all indexes in the set of LcrKeys. For the calculation of the reusability measure we further need the amount of distinct life cycle activities in the dataspace. We therefore define $LCA\text{-}Ind_{count}(x)$ as the sum of all distinct LCA individuals of x, where x is one activity from the set of e-Science life cycle activities: $x \in LCA = \{GS, DP, TS, TE, RP\}$.

$$LCA\text{-}Ind_{Count} = \sum_{i=0}^{n}(distinct)LCA\text{-}Ind(x)$$

For example $LCA\text{-}Ind_{Count}(GS)$ represents the total number of distinct individuals of the e-Science life cycle activity *GoalSpecification*. The $LCA\text{-}Ind_{Count}$ values in each activity must be equal to the highest index of the corresponding activity in the *current indexKey* that we derive from the dataspace indexer because it contains the last added LCR including its either reused or new generated LCAs to the dataspace.

Having this two important measures, LCR_{Count} and $LCA\text{-}Ind_{Count}$ defined, we can further define the dataspace reusability for an e-Science life cycle activity as following:

$$DS_{Reusability}(LCA(x)) = \frac{LCA\text{-}Ind_{Count}(x)}{LCR_{Count}}$$

The value this measure can receive will always be in the interval $[0, 1]$ since the relation of the two counts is always that:

$$LCA\text{-}Ind_{Count}(x) \leq LCR_{Count}$$

The $DS_{reusability}(LCA(x))$ measure can be interpreted in such a way that the closer the value is to 1, the less reused activities and the more distinct activities are in the corresponding LCA. Furthermore the closer the value is to 0 the more LCAs are reused and the less distinct LCAs are in the corresponding LCA.

The above measure represents the data space measure for a single LCA. We furthermore define the global dataspace reusability $DA_{reusability}$, as a measure to express how much the activities in general are being reused in the dataspace independent from a specific LCA. We define this measure as follows:

$$DS_{Reusability} = \frac{\sum DS_{Reusability}(LCA(x))}{|LCA|}$$

where $|LCA|$ represents the cardinality of the set of LCA, which is five in the current version of the e-Science life cycle model. Again this measure will always be in the interval $[0,1]$ since $\sum DS_{Reusability}(LCA(x))$ will not exceed 5.

We argue that an optimal value for this measure is around 0.5 in general. This would indicate that there is a fair division of reused and newly generated LCAs in the dataspace. A too high value would indicate that LCAs are being reused too often, which has the effect that not much new data is added to the dataspace and a too low value would indicate that the amount of available studies in the dataspace is high but the LCRs are too different from each other. However, we believe that the values for the dataspace reusability in each LCA should be interpreted differently. For example having a low dataspace reusability measure in the data preparation activity, gives an indication that the initial input datasets used for the studies are quite similar to each other whereas a high value would indicate that they are different from each other. Therefore we think that the global dataspace reusability measure is differently to interpret than the corresponding values for each LCA. However, the real interpretation of this measures can only be done after a longer period of time in which the dataspace is intensively used by an acting research group. Currently this is being faced within a new three years research project in cooperation with a leading breath gas analysis institution as previously mentioned.

8.4.6 Experiences

A brief discussion on the experiences that were learned from the development and performance evaluation of the jSpace system is provided as follows:

- The methodology jSpace is using to preserve LCR into the dataspace is fairly lightweight in the sense that it only captures minimal information from the researcher who accomplishes the scientific experiment and all other processing like the creation of semantically rich relationships with individuals and properties of the e-Science life cycle ontology and their organization within an RDF store is done automatically. Furthermore, it promises to be performance efficient as it does not have an impact on the volumes of the dataspace participants involved in regard of the semantic markup layer.

- Since the semantical layer containing the dataspace relationships is independent from the physical storage of the dataspace participant, jSpace can work with different data preservation systems and storage solutions.

- Since the e-Science life cycle ontology is kept domain independently and included a way to describe domain-specific metadata separately from the core concepts of the e-Science life cycle model, jSpace can be deployed to many application domains.

- Many scientist are already used to some tools and therefore might not want to change their analysis environment. Since we were considering in our architecture to make the interface to the scientific dataspace independent of any analysis tool, we can support different tools available for scientific investigations (e.g. Matlab, Octave, GridMiner, etc.). Through the jSpace Java API we provide interfaces for accessing data from and publishing data into the dataspace for almost any application scenario.

- During our evaluation of jSpace in the BGA application we have identified that experiments on exhaled breath gas are being successively refined [*iterations of action 4-6 in Table 8.3*], by the acting researcher until the study either shows a significant result (i.e. definition of accurate methods for estimation of blood gas levels of certain biomarker values from breath gas samples) [*prepare action 7*] or ends up in a modification of the intended defined goal specification for that experiment [*modify goals and restart action 2*]. However, in both cases several iterations of the e-Science life cycle are being performed. Some instances of e-Science life cycle activities have been reused in another iteration of the life cycle, for instance when a breath gas researcher executes the same *final input dataset* on a slightly refined analytical method. In this case the goals defined and the data prepared for that experiment did not change, therefore its corresponding instances of the e-Science life cycle activities have been reused within new iterations of the life cycle. This led us to the definition of dataspace reusability measures.

8.5 Summary

In the previous part of this book we have introduced the e-Science life cycle ontology, whose major goal was to semantically enrich the existing relationship among primary, derived, and background datasets that emerge during the life cycle of scientific data. We have also introduced the architecture of jSpace, which is dataspace-based support platform and provided details about the implementation as well as its realization for large-scale scientific dataspaces. A performance evaluation on a synthetic large scale dataspace was also provided testing existing technologies in conjunction with the jSpace API.

In this Chapter we have described two promising new e-Science applications, whose collaborating organizations have deployed the scientific dataspace paradigm. We elaborated how the scientific experiments are consolidated, what actions are involved in terms of data access, analysis, and publication. We have also showed how the full life cycle of data of the experiments is organized by the corresponding scientific dataspace.

The jSpace system was experimentally validated using the two applications with multiple real scientific experiments. NIGM experiments use different services and activities to access and pre-process data in comparison to the scientific experiments from the breath gas analysis application. First, in this chapter, an introduction on each application domain was given. Performance overhead of the jSpace system and its components were investigated, and it was shown that the overhead is reasonable according to the benefits the scientists have with an evolving scientific dataspace.

Generally the performance overhead of the jSpace preservation process is quite static, since it mainly depends on the semantic descriptions provided by the user and the sizes of participating datasets. In relation to the execution time of a scientific study, it actually is of little significance. As we have seen in several experiments the overhead done is always lower than 15% in the BGA application where experiments are quite fast. This is because currently breath gas analysis researcher mainly perform their experimentations within Matlab and the typical size of input datasets is not larger that 3MB directly imported into Matlab. Therefore the total execution time of a typical BGA study does not exceed the one minute upper limit.

In the NIGM application this is a bit differently, since web services are invoked remotely to execute the NIGM-workflow, and input data size is larger and is obtained from a database. However, even with a greater performance overhead that with the

BGS study, it is still of little significance in relation to the total execution time for an NIGM study. The average performance overhead with less than 2% in our experiments show an even lower overhead in comparison to the BGS study.

The impact on the performance of jSpace for large values of dataspace participants was investigated as well. It proved that there is no relation between the volume of dataspace participants and the semantic markup layer provided by jSpace, if the input dataset is not replicated into the iRODS system. Since jSpace generates a reference, in particular an End-Point Reference (EPR) organized by the EPR-Framework to the input dataset, it is in fact not necessary to do the replication, which as the performance results have show, can be time intensive for large datasets. We argued that dataspace participants up to a certain size should be replicated into a preservation system such as iRODS in order to be independent on possible changes that might happen to the datasource.

There are many different tools available for scientific investigations (e.g. Matlab, Octave, GridMiner, etc.). Many scientist are already used to some tools and therefore might not want to change their analysis environment. Therefore, we were considering in our architecture to make the interface to the scientific dataspace independent of any analysis tool. We provided interfaces for accessing data from and publishing data into the dataspace.

Chapter 9

Conclusions

> *"Religion hinges upon faith, politics hinges upon who can tell the most convincing lies or maybe just shout the loudest, but science hinges upon whether its conclusions resemble what actually happens"*
>
> IAN STEWART

9.1 Summary of the Research

Central to the work described in this book is the scientific dataspace paradigm called jSpace, which is a novel approach to scientific data preservation since it preserves datasets from scientific studies including their background and derived datasets and interrelates them by individuals and properties of the e-Science life cycle ontology. Our research has resulted in an approach, which allows to address the full data life cycle in order to provide well preserved replicas of scientific studies in any e-Science application. jSpace therefore supports the interaction among specific research groups by the means of advanced scientific data management in e-Infrastructures. A key goal of the research conducted in this work has been to investigate an approach to invent a suitable relationship paradigm for the creation, representation and advanced searching of relationships among primary, background, and derived datasets in scientific studies. Mainly because of the nature of datasets participating in scientific studies we considered semantic web technologies such as OWL [owl04], RDF [rdf04b], and the SPARQL query language and protocol [PS08] as underlying technology for creation and management of semantically rich described relationships among those interrelated but disparately managed datasets.

Semantically rich described relationships among datasets of scientific studies and in an higher level of abstraction among participants of a distributed dataspace is the key to the scientific dataspace paradigm introduced in this work. To support the thesis that a scientific dataspace environment can deliver significant value to distributed research groups that collaborate in terms of collaborative science we have:

- invented a suitable relationship paradigm for the creation, representation and advanced searching of relationships among participants of a scientific dataspace,
- developed an OWL ontology that addresses the full data life cycle in scientific studies considering accessed and derived, as well as background datasets,
- proposed an appropriate indexing mechanism for uniform organization of scientific data life cycle resources, and
- experimentally implemented large-scale dataspaces with geographically distributed scientific data and collaborating scientists on top of two different real world e-Science applications.

The dataspace paradigm presented in [FHM05] is further developed by considering its major research challenge "managing relationships among participants" in order to explicitly support the existing relationship among primary, background, and derived data in scientific collaborations. In the rest of this chapter we detail the results of our research, indicate directions for possible future extensions, and list publications that have resulted from our research on topics related to this work.

9.2 Research Contributions

Within this work we identified and addressed several research challenges related to the vision of dataspaces that were introduced in [FHM05]. However, during our research we somehow drifted away from the mainstream driven dataspace research and considered to follow a slightly different vision, which is the realization of a scientific dataspace paradigm that considers dataspace concepts and semantic web technologies. The scientific dataspace paradigm supports the phases of the e-Science life cycle and integrates them to an advanced scientific dataspace support platform. Figure 9.1 depicts the realization of the proposed components presented in this book by concrete results of our

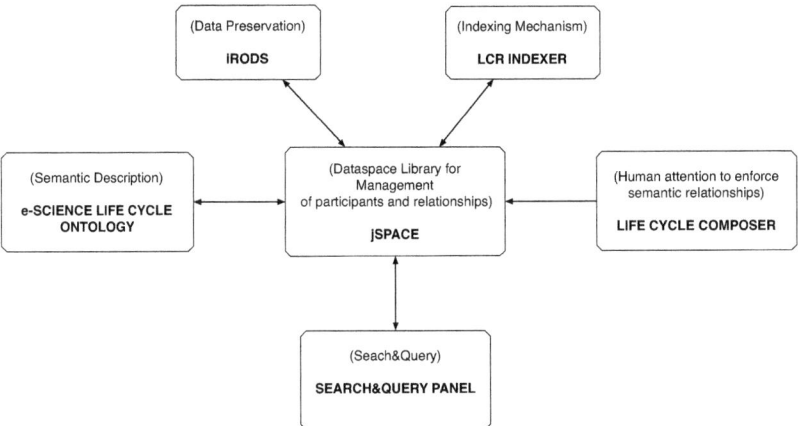

Figure 9.1: Realization of the scientific dataspace paradigm.

work except the preservation system, which is supplemented by the open-source data grid software iRODS [iRO11], because it is to our best knowledge the best standard component for digital preservation.

The jSpace scientific dataspace framework developed has been designed and developed domain independently without having any e-Science application in perspective. The experiments and evaluations have been in the CADGrid [agr10] and the Austrian Grid [cad11] project [agr10]. The results of the evaluation show the applicability of the system in these domains.

In the following we list the major contributions of the work presented in this book.

- **e-Science Life Cycle Ontology** - We developed a specialized model, named the e-Science life cycle for semantic enrichment of dataspace relationships by the use of an OWL ontology.

  The intelligence of the proposed e-Science life cycle lies in its capability as customizable relationship model for scientific dataspaces, as it covers the creation, representation and searching of semantically rich relationships among participants of a dataspace. It enables researchers to find not only relevant primary data in connection with its derived data, but also lots of semantics about what was initially done with the data, such as which data preprocessing methods have been applied, which data mining and analysis models have been used, which result visualizations are available etc. Furthermore it points to relevant background and ontological data, such as descriptions of applied services, models, research domains etc.

All this information is meant to be the semantically rich relationship among primary and derived data described by the e-Science life cycle ontology. Additionally scientists will retrieve information about the goals specified, which domain it corresponds, and whom to contact in case of interest for engaging collaborations, in short, users will understand for what reason a specific e-Science life cycle was applied, which we summarize be the meaning of *e-Science Understanding*.

- **Long-Term Preservation Framework for Scientific Studies** - To support long-term preservation the complete life cycle of data in e-Science applications is addressed and a framework for their intelligent storage and management has been designed and prototypically implemented. The framework has been evaluated on top of two real world e-Science applications. The framework also includes an intelligent indexing mechanism that uniquely identifies dataspace participants and their relationships as they are participating in multiple life cycle resources. The indexing mechanism also supports a large-scale scenario as described below. The profound knowledge of iterations of the e-Science life cycle consolidated within individuals and properties of the ontology has allowed us to provide well-preserved RDF-trees that form together with their liked dataspace participants a rich preservation framework for scientific studies.

The preservation framework allows to preserve scientific studies almost domain independently. It can easily be ported to any e-Science application, since the e-Science life cycle ontology is being kept domain independent. Tools for the creation of life cycle resources (e-Science life cycle composer) as well as for searching and querying the dataspace (e-Science life cycle Search and Query panel) have been developed as Java stand alone applications. Their Java classes and methods were organized into a Java dataspace API (see below). In the second real world e-Science application the prototypical implementation of a web portal has been done in order to prototype a web based interface to the framework.

- **Large-Scale Scientific Dataspace Platform** - The idea to support multiple domains, multiple disciplines and to enable secure but verified access to research data have become the leading motivation for the development of our large-scale scientific dataspace platform. The intelligent interconnection of multiple dataspace instances, where each dataspace instance is acting as a single participant of a larger dataspace has allowed us to realize large-scale dataspaces.

  Local RDF stores hosting semantically enriched relationships of locally available dataspace participants provide high performance on local requests and at the same time are available to be combined and interconnected with other local RDF stores, thus form a distributed RDF data environment, that is the global RDF store. Using the SPARQL-ADERIS distributed SPARQL query processing component we, were able to support search and query interfaces on top of this large-scale dataspace. A prototypical jSpace implementation with multiple geographically distributed RDF stores has been developed. To evaluate scalability of the prototype several synthetic large-scale dataspaces with up to 3000 LCRs with approx. 460,000 triples have been generated. A performance evaluation on top of that architecture was applied showing a performance results at reasonable level.

- **jSpace Java API** - A Java API providing all needed methods to construct semantic data about experiments, which hides from the scientist most of the underlying complexity involved in the process, such as working directly with RDF or writing SPARQL queries is provided. The Java dataspace API provides a model for management of life cycle resources (LCRs) within a distributed data environment. In particular, methods for creation, representation, maintenance, and advanced searching of LCRs is supported. The API included methods to set up a local RDF store based on a relational database. The store can be used to permanently store life cycle resources.

- **Applicability to Domains** - The jSpace Scientific Dataspace platform developed has been designed and developed domain independently without having any e-Science application in perspective. The experiments and evaluations have been in the CADGrid and the Austrian Grid project with two different e-Science applications. The results of the evaluation show the applicability of the system in these domains.

9.3 Open Issues and Future Research Directions

During the research in this dissertation, several possibilities for expanding this work have been observed. While these do not detract from the conclusion of the dissertation, they do provide suggestions for improving the system to make it more elastic regarding scalability as well as practicable and user-friendly in a typical e-Science application. In this section we briefly describe our proposals for future work.

Generally, there are many potential extensions of this work towards a comprehensive, productive, and high-performance scientific dataspace infrastructure for research collaborations among multi-disciplinary research groups. Below we outline two promising future research avenues and discuss a third one more precisely. The first is an adaption of provenance related approaches to support full automatically creation of relationships among dataspace participants and the second is an ability to provide autonomous based analyses on top of relationships and participants from existing scientific studies in the dataspace. The latter one is currently being addressed in the context of a new three years research project funded by the Federal Ministry for Transport, Innovation and Technology (BMVIT) and Austrian Science Fund (FWF) called *Dataspace Support Platform for Breath Gas Analysis*. Within this new project the dataspace support platform presented in this book will be further developed and deployed to a core of early adopters from a leading Breath Gas Analysis research group.

The third potential extension of this work, which is described in the following paragraph more precisely deals with a modern approach to address scalability of the scientific dataspace in an elastic manner.

Elastic Large-Scale Dataspaces

This work was mainly undertaken in the context of the Austrian Grid and the China-Austria Data Grid project, both research projects in the field of grid technology. Anyhow, the work presented in this book is kept more or less independent from any grid-specific middleware, which was a major design criteria. For example, we have chosen the iRODS data grid solution as underlying data preservation system to preserve dataspace participants for the long run, instead of selecting an architecture that is based on the grid middleware Globus toolkit [The11b] in conjunction with the de facto standard for grid-based database access and integration software OGSA-DAI [AHH+07], which is a common architectural pattern in many grid-based e-Infrastructures. Grid technology had a strong impact on many computer science research institutions around the world. Many e-Science applications have been build on the grid technology. Recently ensembles of distributed, heterogeneous resources, or clouds, have emerged as popular platforms for deploying large-scale and resource-intensive applications. After grid computing, cloud computing has now emerged as the paradigm for the next generation of large-scale scientific computing and data management with the main advantage in eliminating the need for hosting expensive hardware.

Scientists still have their grid environments in place and can benefit from them using leased cloud resources whenever needed [OPF10]. This paradigm shift that emerged recently affected many grid service and infrastructure providers in both data and computational respects and opened new challenges that need to be analyzed, such as the integration of the new paradigm into existing environments, applications on them, and security.

Within the uprising cloud computing initiative we identified that elasticity (e.g. how elastic the need for cloud-based resources can be handled) represents a future research direction within both data and compute cloud applications. The extension of the large-scale dataspace approach presented in this book to support a cloud-based infrastructure represents therefore a potential future research direction to be investigated at our research group.

The *CloudMiner* [The11a] is the follow-up project from the successful GridMiner project [BJT05]. Data management within CloudMiner will be based on the scientific dataspace concepts presented in this book and an elastic large-scale dataspace approach will be investigated. In this context the cloud simulation framework presented in [CRB+11] might be used for validating various scheduling and optimization strategies at a larger scale.

9.4 Research Publications

Below is a list of publications that have resulted from our research on topics related to the work presented in this book (order by: most recent comes first):

- Ibrahim Elsayed, Gregory Madey, and Peter Brezany. *"Portals for collaborative research communities: two distinguished case studies."* Concurrency and Computation: Practice and Experience, volume 23, Issue 3, pages 269-278, March

2011.

- Ibrahim Elsayed and Peter Brezany. *"Towards large-scale scientific dataspaces for e-Science applications."* In M. Yoshikawa, X. Meng, T. Yumoto, Q. Ma, L. Sun, and C. Watanabe, editors, DASFAA Workshops, volume 6193 of Lecture Notes in Computer Science, pages 69-80, Tsukuba, Japan, 2010. Springer.

- Ibrahim Elsayed, Thomas Ludescher, Philip Masser, Thomas Feilhauer, and Peter Brezany. *"Grid-based scientific dataspace support platform for breath gas analysis."* In J. Volkert, T. Fahringer, D. Kranzlmueller, R. Kobler, and W. Schreiner, editors, Proceedings of the 3rd Austrian Grid Symposium, volume 269, pages 154-168, Linz, Austria, 2010. Austrian Computer Society.

- Ibrahim Elsayed, Steven Lynden, Isao Kojima, and Peter Brezany. *"Semantic data infrastructure to support a scientific dataspace for breath gas analysis."* In Proceedings of the UK e-Science All Hands Meeting, Cardiff, UK, 2010.

- Marco Descher, Thomas Feilhauer, Thomas Ludescher, Philip Masser, Bernd Wenzel, Peter Brezany, Ibrahim Elsayed, Alexander Whrer, A Min Tjoa, and David Huemer. *"Position paper: Secure infrastructure for scientific data life cycle management."* In ARES '09: Proceedings of the 2009 International Conference on Availability, Reliability and Security, pages 606-611, Washington, DC, USA, 2009. IEEE Computer Society.

- Ibrahim Elsayed, Thomas Ludescher, Konrad Schwarz, Thomas Feilhauer, Anton Amann, and Peter Brezany. *"Towards realization of scientific dataspaces for the breath gas analysis research community."* In IWPLS '09: Proceedings of the 1st International Workshop on Portals for Life Sciences, UK, 2009. CEUR Workshop Proceedings, ISSN 1613-0073, UK, September 14-15.

- Peter Brezany, Ibrahim Elsayed, Yuzhang Han, Ivan Janciak, Alexander Whrer, Lenka Novakova, Olga Stepankova, Monika Zakova, Jianguo Han, and Ting Liu. *"Inside the NIGM Grid Service: Implementation, Evaluation and Extension."* In SKG '08: Proceedings of the 2008 Fourth International Conference on Semantics, Knowledge and Grid, pages 314-321, Washington, DC, USA, 2008. IEEE Computer Society.

- Ibrahim Elsayed, Jianguo Han, Ting Liu, Alexander Whrer, Fakhri A. Khan, and Peter Brezany. *"Grid-Enabled Non-Invasive Blood Glucose Measurement."* In ICCS '08: Proceedings of the 8th international conference on Computational Science, Part I, pages 76-85, Berlin, Heidelberg, 2008. Springer-Verlag.

- Ibrahim Elsayed, Adnan Muslimovic, and Peter Brezany. *"Intelligent dataspaces for e-science."* In Proceedings of the 7th WSEAS international conference on Computational intelligence, man-machine systems and cybernetics, pages 94-100, Stevens Point, Wisconsin, USA, 2008. World Scientific and Engineering Academy and Society (WSEAS).

- Ibrahim Elsayed, Peter Brezany, and A Min Tjoa. *"Towards Realization of Dataspaces."* In DEXA '06: Proceedings of the 17th International Conference on Database and Expert Systems Applications, pages 266-272, Washington, DC, USA, 2006. IEEE Computer Society.

Bibliography

[AAC11]   Carlos Buil Aranda, Marcelo Arenas, and Oscar Corcho, *Semantics and optimization of the sparql 1.1 federation extension*, Extended Semantic Web Conference (ESWC2011), 2011.

[AAS07]   Yair Amit, Danny Allan, and Adi Sharabani, *Overtaking google desktop - a security analysis*, Watchfire Whitepaper, 2007.

[aba11]   *Dataspace-Based Support Platform for Breath Gas Analysis*, Website, 2011, http://aba.cloudminer.org/.

[ACD04]   Nagrai Alur, YunJung Chang, and Barry Devlin, *Patterns: Information aggregation and data integration with db2 information integrator*, IBM Redbooks, 9 2004.

[AFG+09]   Michael Armbrust, Armando Fox, Rean Griffith, Anthony D. Joseph, Randy H. Katz, Andrew Konwinski, Gunho Lee, David A. Patterson, Ariel Rabkin, Ion Stoica, and Matei Zaharia, *Above the clouds: A berkeley view of cloud computing*, Tech. Report UCB/EECS-2009-28, EECS Department, University of California, Berkeley, Feb 2009.

[agr10]   *The Austrian Grid Project*, Website, 2010, http://www.austriangrid.at/.

[AHH+07]   M. Antonioletti, N. P. Chue Hong, A. C. Hume, M. Jackson, K. Karasavvas, A. Krause, J. M. Schopf, M. P. Atkinson, B. Dobrzelecki, M. Illingworth, N. McDonnell, M. Parsons, and E. Theocharopoulous, *Ogsa-dai 3.0 - the what's and whys*, UK e-Science All Hands Meeting, 2007.

[AKP+06]   Mario Antonioletti, Amy Krause, Norman W. Paton, Andrew Eisenberg, Simon Laws, Susan Malaika, Jim Melton, and Dave Pearson, *The wsdai family of specifications for web service data access and integration*, SIGMOD Rec. **35** (2006), 48–55.

[Ale08]   Sergejs Aleksejevs, *Contribution model - myexperiment developer documentation*, Website, 2008, http://wiki.myexperiment.org/.

[AR10]   Malcolm Atkinson and David De Roure, *Data-intensive research: making best use of research data*, 2010.

[BAB+03]   Paolo Bruni, Francis Arnaudies, Amanda Bennett, Susanne Englert, and Gerhard Keplinger, *Data federation with ibm db2 information integrator v8.1*, first ed., IBM Corp., Riverton, NJ, USA, 2003.

[BBG11]   Rajkumar Buyya, James Broberg, and Andrzej M. Goscinski (eds.), *Cloud computing principles and paradigms (wiley series on parallel and distributed computing)*, Wiley, 3 2011.

[BEH+08]   Peter Brezany, Ibrahim Elsayed, Yuzhang Han, Ivan Janciak, Alexander Wöhrer, Lenka Novakova, Olga Stepankova, Monika Zakova, Jianguo Han, and Ting Liu, *Inside the nigm grid service: Implementation, evaluation and extension*, Proceedings of the 2008 Fourth International Conference on Semantics, Knowledge and Grid (Washington, DC, USA), IEEE Computer Society, 2008, pp. 314–321.

[BFO11]   *Basic Formal Ontology*, Website, 2011, http://www.ifomis.org/bfo.

[BGS06]   Gordon Bell, Jim Gray, and Alex Szalay, *Petascale computational systems*, Computer **39** (2006), 110–112.

[BHBL09]   Christian Bizer, Tom Heath, and Tim Berners-Lee, *Linked data - the story so far.*, International Journal on Semantic Web and Information Systems **5** (2009), no. 3, 1–22.

[BJT05]   Peter Brezany, Ivan Janciak, and A Min Tjoa, *Gridminer: A fundamental infrastructure for building intelligent grid systems*, Web Intelligence, IEEE/WIC/ACM International Conference on **0** (2005), 150–156.

[BKT01]   Peter Buneman, Sanjeev Khanna, and Wang Chiew Tan, *Why and where: A characterization of data provenance*, Proceedings of the 8th International Conference on Database Theory (London, UK), ICDT '01, Springer-Verlag, 2001, pp. 316–330.

[BLHL01]   Tim Berners-Lee, James Hendler, and Ora Lassila, *The semantic web*, Scientific American **284** (2001), no. 5, 34–43.

[BpDG+07]   Lukas Blunschi, Jens peter Dittrich, Olivier Ren Girard, Shant Kirakos, Karakashian Marcos, and Antonio Vaz Salles, *A dataspace odyssey: The iMeMex personal dataspace management systems*, In Third Biennial Conference on Innovative Data Systems Research, CIDR, 2007, pp. 114–119.

[BRA05]   Jonathan Bard, Seung Rhee, and Michael Ashburner, *An ontology for cell types*, Genome Biology **6** (2005), no. 2, R21+.

[BS09]   Christian Bizer and Andreas Schultz, *The berlin sparql benchmark.*, International Journal on Semantic Web and Information Systems (IJSWIS) **5** (2009), no. 2, 1–24.

[BSS08]   Uri Braun, Avraham Shinnar, and Margo Seltzer, *Securing provenance*, Proceedings of the 3rd conference on Hot topics in security (Berkeley, CA, USA), USENIX Association, 2008, pp. 4:1–4:5.

[BW45]   Vannevar Bush and Jingtao Wang, *As we may think*, Atlantic Monthly **176** (1945), 101–108.

[BYV+09]   Rajkumar Buyya, Chee Shin Yeo, Srikumar Venugopal, James Broberg, and Ivona Brandic, *Cloud computing and emerging it platforms: Vision, hype, and reality for delivering computing as the 5th utility*, Future Gener. Comput. Syst. **25** (2009), 599–616.

[C+08]   Kendall G. Clark et al., *SPARQL Protocol for RDF*, Tech. report, W3C, 2008.

[cad11]   *The China-Austria Data Grid (CADGrid) project*, Website, 2011, http://www.par.univie.ac.at/project/cadgrid/.

[cal11]　　　*Calais*, Website, Mai 2011, http://www.opencalais.com/.

[CCK+00]　　Pete Chapman, Julian Clinton, Randy Kerber, Thomas Khabaza, Thomas Reinartz, Colin Shearer, and Rudiger Wirth, *Crisp-dm 1.0 step-by-step data mining guide*, Tech. report, The CRISP-DM consortium, August 2000.

[CDH+05]　　Yuhan Cai, Xin Dong, Alon Halevy, Jing Michelle Liu, and Jayant Madhavan, *Personal information management with semex*, SIGMOD, June 2005, pp. 921–923.

[CFK+99]　　Ann Chervenak, Ian Foster, Carl Kesselman, Charles Salisbury, and Steven Tuecke, *The data grid: Towards an architecture for the distributed management and analysis of large scientific datasets*, J Network and Computer Applications **23** (1999), 187–200.

[CHST04]　　Philipp Cimiano, Andreas Hotho, Gerd Stumme, and Julien Tane, *Conceptual knowledge processing with formal concept analysis and ontologies*, Proceedings of the The Second International Conference on Formal Concept Analysis (ICFCA 04), LNCS, vol. 2961, Springer, 2004.

[CKS+00]　　Michael J. Carey, Jerry Kiernan, Jayavel Shanmugasundaram, Eugene J. Shekita, and Subbu N. Subramanian, *Xperanto: Middleware for publishing object-relational data as xml documents*, Proceedings of the 26th International Conference on Very Large Data Bases (San Francisco, CA, USA), VLDB '00, Morgan Kaufmann Publishers Inc., 2000, pp. 646–648.

[Con05]　　Andy Conigliaro, *Ibm websphere information integrator portfolio overview: Integrating data and content on demand*, IBM Software Goup, White Paper, January 2005.

[CRB+11]　　Rodrigo N. Calheiros, Rajiv Ranjan, Anton Beloglazov, Cesar A. F. De Rose, and Rajkumar Buyya, *Cloudsim: a toolkit for modeling and simulation of cloud computing environments and evaluation of resource provisioning algorithms*, Softw. Pract. Exper. **41** (2011), 23–50.

[CRDS06]　　Edward Cutrell, Daniel Robbins, Susan Dumais, and Raman Sarin, *Fast, flexible filtering with phlat*, Proceedings of the SIGCHI conference on

Human Factors in computing systems (New York, NY, USA), CHI '06, ACM, 2006, pp. 261–270.

[CWW+08] Paolo Ciccarese, Elizabeth Wu, Gwen Wong, Marco Ocana, June Kinoshita, Alan Ruttenberg, and Tim Tim Clark, *The swan biomedical discourse ontology*, J. of Biomedical Informatics **41** (2008), 739–751.

[Dat08] Data Mining Group, *The Predictive Model Markup Language (PMML)*, Website, July 2008, http://www.dmg.org/v3-2/.

[dbx02] *DBXplorer: A system for keyword-based search over relational databases*, Proceedings of the 18th International Conference on Data Engineering (Washington, DC, USA), ICDE '02, IEEE Computer Society, 2002, pp. 5–16.

[DCM04] DCMI-Libraries Working Group, *Dc-library application profile (dc-lib)*, Website, September 2004, http://dublincore.org/documents/2004/09/10/library-application-profile/.

[DCM11] DCMI community, *Dublin core metadata initiative*, Website, May 2011, http://www.dublincore.org/.

[DFL+09] Marko Descher, Thomas Feilhauer, Thomas Ludescher, Philip Masser, Bernd Wenzel, Peter Brezany, Ibrahim Elsayed, Alexander Woehrer, A Min Tjoa, and David Huemer, *Position paper: Secure infrastructure for scientific data life cycle management*, Proceedings of the International Conference on Availability, Reliability and Security (Los Alamitos, CA, USA), IEEE Computer Society, 2009, pp. 606–611.

[DH05] Xin Dong and Alon Y. Halevy, *A Platform for Personal Information Management and Integration*, Second Biennial Conference on Innovative Data Systems Reasearch (CIDR), 2005, pp. 119–130.

[Dit06] Jens-Peter Dittrich, *imemex: A platform for personal dataspace management*, August 2006.

[DMF+09] Marco Descher, Philip Masser, Thomas Feilhauer, A Min Tjoa, and David Huemer, *Retaining data control to the client in infrastructure*

	clouds, Proceedings of the International Conference on Availability, Reliability and Security (Los Alamitos, CA, USA), IEEE Computer Society, 2009, pp. 9–16.
[doi11]	*The DOI System*, Website, 2011, http://www.doi.org/.
[DS06]	Jens-Peter Dittrich and Marcos Antonio Vaz Salles, *idm: a unified and versatile data model for personal dataspace management*, Proceedings of the 32nd international conference on Very large data bases, VLDB '06, VLDB Endowment, 2006, pp. 367–378.
[DSDH08]	Anish Das Sarma, Xin Dong, and Alon Halevy, *Bootstrapping pay-as-you-go data integration systems*, Proceedings of the 2008 ACM SIGMOD international conference on Management of data (New York, NY, USA), SIGMOD '08, ACM, 2008, pp. 861–874.
[DSp11]	*Dspace open source software enables open sharing of content that spans organizations, continents and time.*, Website, 2011, http://www.dspace.org/.
[EB10]	Ibrahim Elsayed and Peter Brezany, *Towards large-scale scientific dataspaces for e-science applications*, Proceedings of the 15th international conference on Database systems for advanced applications (Berlin, Heidelberg), DASFAA'10, Springer-Verlag, 2010, pp. 69–80.
[EBT06]	Ibrahim Elsayed, Peter Brezany, and A Min Tjoa, *Towards realization of dataspaces*, Proceedings of the 17th International Conference on Database and Expert Systems Applications (Washington, DC, USA), IEEE Computer Society, 2006, pp. 266–272.
[EGKMP+09]	Miguel Esteban Gutiérrez, Isao Kojima, Said Mirza Pahlevi, Óscar Corcho, and Asunción Gómez-Pérez, *Accessing RDF(S) data resources in service-based grid infrastructures*, Concurrency and Compututation : Practice and Experience **21** (2009), no. 8, 1029–1051.
[EHL+08]	Ibrahim Elsayed, Jianguo Han, Ting Liu, Alexander Wöhrer, Fakhri Alam Khan, and Peter Brezany, *Grid-enabled non-invasive blood glucose measurement*, Proceedings of the 8th international conference on

Computational Science, Part I (Berlin, Heidelberg), ICCS '08, Springer-Verlag, 2008, pp. 76–85.

[ELS+09] Ibrahim Elsayed, Thomas Ludescher, Konrad Schwarz, Thomas Feilhauer, Anton Amann, and Peter Brezany, *Towards realization of scientific dataspaces for the breath gas analysis research community*, IWPLS '09: Proceedings of the 1st International Workshop on Portals for Life Sciences, CEUR Workshop Proceedings, ISSN 1613-0073, UK, September 14-15, 2009.

[EMB08] Ibrahim Elsayed, Adnan Muslimovic, and Peter Brezany, *Intelligent dataspaces for e-science*, Proceedings of the 7th WSEAS international conference on Computational intelligence, man-machine systems and cybernetics (Stevens Point, Wisconsin, USA), World Scientific and Engineering Academy and Society (WSEAS), 2008, pp. 94–100.

[FA11] Sandro Fiore and Giovanni Aloisio (eds.), *Grid and cloud database management*, 1st edition. ed., Springer, 7 2011.

[FHM05] Michael Franklin, Alon Halevy, and David Maier, *From databases to dataspaces: a new abstraction for information management*, SIGMOD Rec. **34** (2005), 27–33.

[FKNT02a] I. Foster, C. Kesselman, J. Nick, and S. Tuecke (eds.), *The physiology of the grid: An open grid services architecture for distributed systems integration*, 2002.

[FKNT02b] Ian Foster, Carl Kesselman, Jeffrey M. Nick, and Steven Tuecke, *Grid services for distributed system integration*, Computer **35** (2002), 37–46.

[FKT01a] Ian Foster, Carl Kesselman, and Steven Tuecke, *The anatomy of the grid: Enabling scalable virtual organizations*, Int. J. High Perform. Comput. Appl. **15** (2001), no. 3, 200–222.

[FKT01b] Ian Foster, Carl Kesselman, and Steven Tuecke, *The anatomy of the grid: Enabling scalable virtual organizations*, Int. J. High Perform. Comput. Appl. **15** (2001), 200–222.

[Fon11]   DSpace Fondation, *Dspace 1.7.1 system documentation*, Website, 2011, https://wiki.duraspace.org/display/DSDOC.

[Fos01]   Ian Foster, *The anatomy of the grid: Enabling scalable virtual organizations*, Cluster Computing and the Grid, IEEE International Symposium on **0** (2001), 6.

[FVWZ02]   Ian Foster, Jens-S. Vöckler, Michael Wilde, and Yong Zhao, *Chimera: A virtual data system for representing, querying, and automating data derivation*, Proceedings of the 14th International Conference on Scientific and Statistical Database Management (Washington, DC, USA), SSDBM '02, IEEE Computer Society, 2002, pp. 37–46.

[GDR07]   Carole Anne Goble and David Charles De Roure, *myexperiment: social networking for workflow-using e-scientists*, Proceedings of the 2nd workshop on Workflows in support of large-scale science (New York, NY, USA), WORKS '07, ACM, 2007, pp. 1–2.

[GF95]   M. Grüninger and M. Fox, *Methodology for the Design and Evaluation of Ontologies*, IJCAI'95, Workshop on Basic Ontological Issues in Knowledge Sharing, April 13, 1995, 1995.

[GLM04]   P Groth, M Luck, and L Moreau, *A protocol for recording provenance in service-oriented grids*, The 8th International Conference on Principles of Distributed Systems (OPODIS'04), 2004.

[GLNS+05]   Jim Gray, David T. Liu, Maria Nieto-Santisteban, Alex Szalay, David J. DeWitt, and Gerd Heber, *Scientific data management in the coming decade*, SIGMOD Rec. **34** (2005), 34–41.

[GM02]   Robert Grossman and Marco Mazzucco, *Dataspace: A data web for the exploratory analysis and mining of data*, Computing in Science and Engg. **4** (2002), 44–51.

[GPC+08]   Dennis Gannon, Beth Plale, Marcus Christie, Yi Huang, Scott Jensen, Ning Liu, Suresh Marru, Sangmi Lee Pallickara, Srinath Perera, Satoshi Shirasuna, Er Slominski, Yiming Sun, and Nithya Vijayakumar, *Building grid portals for e-science: a service-oriented architecture*, Advances in Parallel Computing **16** (2008).

[GPFLC04] Asunción Gómez-Pérez, Mariano Fernández-López, and Oscar Corcho, *Ontological engineering*, Springer, Berlin, 2004.

[GSBS03] Lin Guo, Feng Shao, Chavdar Botev, and Jayavel Shanmugasundaram, *Xrank: ranked keyword search over xml documents*, Proceedings of the 2003 ACM SIGMOD international conference on Management of data (New York, NY, USA), SIGMOD '03, ACM, 2003, pp. 16–27.

[Hal05] Alon Halevy, *Why your data won't mix*, Queue **3** (2005), 50–58.

[Har03] Richard Harada, *Are you prepared for long-term data preservation? - first in/first out*, Computer Technology Review (2003).

[HB11] Tom Heath and Christian Bizer, *Linked data: Evolving the web into a global data space*, 1st ed., Morgan & Claypool, 2011.

[HFM06] Alon Halevy, Michael Franklin, and David Maier, *Principles of dataspace systems*, Proceedings of the twenty-fifth ACM SIGMOD-SIGACT-SIGART symposium on Principles of database systems (New York, NY, USA), PODS '06, ACM, 2006, pp. 1–9.

[HKF+09] Cornelia Hedeler, Belhajja Khalid, Alvaro A. Fernandes, Suzanne M. Embury, and Norman W. Paton, *Dimensions of dataspaces*, Proceedings of the 26th British National Conference on Databases: Dataspace: The Final Frontier (Berlin, Heidelberg), BNCOD 26, Springer-Verlag, 2009, pp. 55–66.

[HKP06] Jiawei Han, Micheline Kamber, and Jian Pei, *Data mining: Concepts and techniques, second edition (the morgan kaufmann series in data management systems)*, 2 ed., Morgan Kaufmann, 1 2006.

[HP02] Vagelis Hristidis and Yannis Papakonstantinou, *Discover: keyword search in relational databases*, Proceedings of the 28th international conference on Very Large Data Bases, VLDB '02, VLDB Endowment, 2002, pp. 670–681.

[HQZW04]   Qinming He, Ling Qiu, Guotao Zhao, and Shenkang Wang, *Text categorization based on domain ontology*, Web Information Systems - WISE 2004 (Xiaofang Zhou, Stanley Su, Mike P. Papazoglou, Maria E. Orlowska, and Keith G. Jeffery, eds.), Lecture Notes in Computer Science, vol. 3306, Springer Berlin/Heidelberg, 2004, pp. 319–324.

[HT05]   Tony Hey and Anne E Trefethen, *Cyberinfrastructure for e-science*, Science **308** (2005), no. 5723, 817–821.

[HTT09]   Tony Hey, Stewart Tansley, and Kristin Tolle (eds.), *The fourth paradigm: Data-intensive scientific discovery*, Microsoft Research, Redmond, Washington, 2009.

[IEE08]   IEEE, *The world's leading professional association for the advancement of technology*, Website, 2008, http://www.ieee.org/.

[IG99]   Tomasz Imieliński and Samir Goel, *Dataspace - querying and monitoring deeply networked collections in physical space*, Proceedings of the 1st ACM international workshop on Data engineering for wireless and mobile access (New York, NY, USA), MobiDe '99, ACM, 1999, pp. 44–51.

[Inc08a]   Amazon Inc, *Amazon elastic compute cloud (Amazon EC2)*, Amazon Inc., Published on the web, 2008, http://aws.amazon.com/ec2/.

[Inc08b]   Google Inc., *Google desktop features*, Website, 2008, http://desktop.google.com/en/features.html.

[Inc10]   Liferay Inc., *Liferay portal overview*, Website, 2010, http://www.liferay.com/products/liferay-portal/overview.

[iRO11]   iRODS, *Irods:data grids, digital libraries, persistent archives, and real-time data systems*, Website, January 2011, https://www.irods.org/.

[jar11]   *Jargon, a java client api for the datagrid*, Website, 2011, https://www.irods.org/index.php/Jargon.

[jen11]   *Jena - A Semantic Web Framework for Java*, Project Website, 2011, http://jena.sourceforge.net/.

[JKB08]   Ivan Janciak, Christian Kloner, and Peter Brezany, *Workflow enactment engine for wsrf-compliant services orchestration*, Proceedings of the 2008 9th IEEE/ACM International Conference on Grid Computing (Washington, DC, USA), GRID '08, IEEE Computer Society, 2008, pp. 1–8.

[JZY08]   Lei Jin, Yawei Zhang, and Xiaojun Ye, *An extensible data model with security support for dataspace management*, HPCC '08: Proceedings of the 2008 10th IEEE International Conference on High Performance Computing and Communications (Washington, DC, USA), IEEE Computer Society, 2008, pp. 556–563.

[KAA+05]   Konstantinos Karasavvas, Mario Antonioletti, Malcolm Atkinson, Neil Chue Hong, Tom Sugden, Alastair Hume, Mike Jackson, Amrey Krause, and Charaka Palansuriya, *Introduction to ogsa-dai services*, Scientific Applications of Grid Computing (Pilar Herrero, Mara S. Prez, and Vctor Robles, eds.), Lecture Notes in Computer Science, vol. 3458, Springer Berlin/Heidelberg, 2005, pp. 291–294.

[KAS+08]   Ievgeniia Kushch, Barbora Arendack, Svorad Stolc, Pawel Mochalski, Wojciech Filipiak, Konrad Schwarz, Lukas Schwentner, Alex Schmid, Alexander Dzien, Monika Lechleitner, Viktor Witkovsk, Wolfram Miekisch, Jochen Schubert, Karl Unterkofler, and Anton Amann, *Breath isoprene - aspects of normal physiology related to age, gender and cholesterol profile as determined in a proton transfer reaction mass spectrometry study*, Clin Chem Lab Med **46(7)** (2008), 1011–8.

[KC04]   Graham Klyne and Jeremy J. Carroll, *Resource Description Framework (RDF): Concepts and Abstract Syntax*, Tech. report, W3C, 2004.

[KCKN04]   Rajasekar Krishnamurthy, Venkatesan T. Chakaravarthy, Raghav Kaushik, and Jeffrey F. Naughton, *Recursive xml schemas, recursive xml queries, and relational storage: Xml-to-sql query translation*, Proceedings of the 20th International Conference on Data Engineering (Washington, DC, USA), ICDE '04, IEEE Computer Society, 2004, pp. 42–.

[kep11]   *The Kepler Project*, Website, 2011, http://www.kepler-project.org/.

[KK09] Isao Kojima and Masahiro Kimoto, *Implementation of a service-based grid middleware for accessing rdf databases.*, OTM Workshops (Robert Meersman et al., eds.), LNCS, vol. 5872, Springer, 2009, pp. 866–876.

[Kri04] Arun Krishnan, *A survey of life sciences applications on the grid*, New Generation Computing **22** (2004), no. 2.

[L+08] Andreas Langegger et al., *A semantic web middleware for virtual data integration on the web*, ESWC'08, June 2008, pp. 493–507.

[LKMT10a] Steven Lynden, Isao Kojima, Akiyoshi Matono, and Yusuke Tanimura, *Adaptive integration of distributed semantic web data*, Databases in Networked Information Systems (Shinji Kikuchi, Shelly Sachdeva, and Subhash Bhalla, eds.), Lecture Notes in Computer Science, vol. 5999, Springer Berlin/Heidelberg, 2010, pp. 174–193.

[LKMT10b] _____, *Aderis: Adaptively integrating rdf data from sparql endpoints*, Database Systems for Advanced Applications (Hiroyuki Kitagawa, Yoshiharu Ishikawa, Qing Li, and Chiemi Watanabe, eds.), Lecture Notes in Computer Science, vol. 5982, Springer Berlin/Heidelberg, 2010, pp. 400–403.

[LL05] Clifford A. Lynch and Joan K. Lippincott, *Institutional Repository Deployment in the United States as of Early 2005*, D-Lib Magazine **11** (2005), no. 9.

[LM08] Yukun Li and Xiaofeng Meng, *Research on personal dataspace management*, Proceedings of the 2nd SIGMOD PhD workshop on Innovative database research (New York, NY, USA), IDAR '08, ACM, 2008, pp. 7–12.

[LMC+09] Steven Lynden, Arijit Mukherjee, Hu Alastair C., Alvaro A. A. Fernandes, Norman W. Paton, Rizos Sakellariou, and Paul Watson, *The design and implementation of ogsa-dqp: A service-based distributed query processor*, Future Gener. Comput. Syst. **25** (2009), 224–236.

[LME09] Ken Laskey, Francis McCabe, and Jeff Estefan, *Oasis soa reference model tc*, Tech. report, OASIS, 2009.

[Lyn08] Clifford Lynch, *Big data: How do your data grow?*, Nature **455** (2008), no. 7209, 28–29, 10.1038/455028a.

[MBDH05] Jayant Madhavan, Philip A. Bernstein, AnHai Doan, and Alon Halevy, *Corpus-based schema matching*, Proceedings of the 21st International Conference on Data Engineering (Washington, DC, USA), ICDE '05, IEEE Computer Society, 2005, pp. 57–68.

[MC04] Stefano Mazzocchi and Paolo Ciccarese, *Welkin - a graph-based rdf visualizer*, Website, 2004, http://www.simile.mit.edu/welkin/.

[MCD+07] Jayant Madhavan, Shirley Cohen, Xin L. Dong, Alon Y. Halevy, Shawn R. Jeffery, David Ko, and Cong Yu, *Web-Scale Data Integration: You can afford to Pay as You Go*, CIDR, www.crdrdb.org, 2007, pp. 342–350.

[MCS+06a] Reagan Moore, Sheau-Yen Chen, Wayne Schroeder, Arcot Rajasekar, Michael Wan, and Arun Jagatheesan, *Production storage resource broker data grids*, International Conference on e-Science and Grid Computing (2006), 147.

[MCS+06b] _____, *Production storage resource broker data grids*, e-Science, 2006, p. 147.

[MRW05] Reagan Moore, Arcot Rajasekar, and Michael Wan, *Data grids, digital libraries, and persistent archives: An integrated approach to sharing, publishing, and archiving data*, Proceedings of the IEEE **93** (2005), no. 3, 578–588.

[MWR05] Reagan Moore, Michael Wan, and Arcot Rajasekar, *Storage resource broker; generic software infrastructure for managing globally distributed data*, Proceedings of the 2005 IEEE International Symposium on Mass Storage Systems and Technology (Washington, DC, USA), IEEE Computer Society, 2005, pp. 65–69.

[n311] *Notation3 (N3): A readable RDF syntax*, Website, 2011, http://www.w3.org/TeamSubmission/n3/.

[Nat07a]   National Institute for Environmental eScience, *The NIEeS wiki for grid information*, Website, 2007, `http://gridinfo.niees.ac.uk/index.php/InQ`.

[Nat07b]   National Science Foundation, *Cyberinfrastructure vision for 21st century discovery*, National Science Foundation, Cyberinfrastructure Council, Arlington, VA, 2007.

[OBI11]   *The OBI Consortium*, Website, 2011, `http://purl.obolibrary.org/obo/obi`.

[Ock07]   John Mark Ockerbloom, *Toward the next generation: Recommendations for the next dspace architecture*, Tech. report, University of Pennsylvania, 2007.

[ont11]   *Ontos*, Website, May 2011, `http://www.ontos.com/`.

[OPF10]   Simon Ostermann, Radu Prodan, and Thomas Fahringer, *Resource management for hybrid grid and cloud computing*, Cloud Computing (Nick Antonopoulos and Lee Gillam, eds.), Computer Communications and Networks, vol. 0, Springer London, 2010, pp. 179–194.

[Org07]   Organization for the Advancement of Structured Information Standards (OASIS), *Web services business process execution language (WS-BPEL) version 2.0*, April 2007.

[owl04]   *Web Ontology Language (OWL)*, Website, 2004, `http://www.w3.org/2004/OWL/`.

[PCC+03]   Michael Phillips, Renee N. Cataneo, Andrew R.C. Cummin, Anthony J. Gagliardi, Kevin Gleeson, Joel Greenberg, Roger A. Maxfield, and William N. Rom, *Detection of Lung Cancer With Volatile Markers in the Breath*, Chest **123** (2003), no. 6, 2115–2123.

[pel11]   *Pellet: OWL 2 Reasoner for Java*, Website, 2011, `http://clarkparsia.com/pellet/`.

[PS08]   Eric Prudhommeaux and Andy Seaborne, *SPARQL Query Language for RDF*, Tech. report, W3C, 2008.

[QL08]   Bastian Quilitz and Ulf Leser, *Querying distributed rdf data sources with sparql*, 5th European Semantic Web Conference (ESWC2008), June 2008, pp. 524–538.

[RBJS03]   David De Roure, Mark A. Baker, Nicholas R. Jennings, and Nigel R. Shadbolt, *The evolution of the grid*, Grid Computing: Making The Global Infrastructure a Reality (F. Berman, A. J. G. Hey, and G. Fox, eds.), John Wiley & Sons, 2003, pp. 65–100.

[rdf04a]   *RDF Vocabulary Description Language 1.0: RDF Schema*, Website, 2004, http://www.w3.org/TR/rdf-schema/.

[rdf04b]   *Resource Description Framework (RDF)*, Website, February 2004, http://www.w3.org/RDF/.

[rdf08]   *RDFizers Project*, Website, August 2008, http://simile.mit.edu/wiki/RDFizers/.

[rdf11]   *RDF/XML Syntax Specification (Revised)*, Website, 2011, http://www.w3.org/TR/REC-rdf-syntax/.

[RGS07]   David De Roure, Carole Goble, and Robert Stevens, *Designing the myexperiment virtual research environment for the social sharing of workflows*, Proceedings of the Third IEEE International Conference on e-Science and Grid Computing (Washington, DC, USA), IEEE Computer Society, 2007, pp. 603–610.

[RJS03]   David De Roure, Nicholas R. Jennings, and Nigel R. Shadbolt, *The semantic grid: A future e-science infrastructure*, Grid Computing - Making the Global Infrastructure a Reality (F. Berman, G. Fox, and A.J.G. Hey, eds.), John Wiley and Sons Ltd, 2003, pp. 437–470.

[RMH+10]   Arcot Rajasekar, Reagan Moore, Chien-Yi Hou, Christopher A. Lee, Richard Marciano, Antoine de Torcy, Michael Wan, Wayne Schroeder, Sheau-Yen Chen, Lucas Gilbert, Paul Tooby, and Bing Zhu, *irods primer: Integrated rule-oriented data system*, vol. 2, Synthesis Lectures on Information Concepts, Retrieval, and Services, no. 1, Morgan & Claypool Publishers, 2010.

[Rob05]   Roberto F. M. et al., *Detection of Lung Cancer by Sensor Array Analyses of Exhaled Breath*, Am. J. Respir. Crit. Care Med. **171** (2005), no. 11, 1286–1291.

[RSP07]   Lavanya Ramakrishnan, Yogesh Simmhan, and Beth Plala, *Realization of Dynamically Adaptive Weather Analysis and Forecasting in LEAD: Four Years Down the Road*, Dynamic Data-Driven Application Systems Workshop at ICCS, 2007.

[RWM02]   Arcot Rajasekar, Michael Wan, and Reagan Moore, *MySRB & SRB: Components of a Data Grid*, Proceedings of the 11th IEEE International Symposium on High Performance Distributed Computing (Washington, DC, USA), HPDC '02, IEEE Computer Society, 2002, pp. 301–310.

[SAB+03]   York Sure, H. Akkermans, Jeen Broekstra, John Davies, Y. Ding, A. Duke, Robert Engels, Dieter Fensel, Ian Horrocks, Victor Iosif, A Kampman, A. Kiryakov, Michel Klein, T. Lau, D. Ognyanov, Ulrich Reimer, K. Simov, Rudi Studer, J. Meer, and F. van Harmelen, *On-to-knowledge: Semantic web enabled knowledge management*, Web Intelligence (N. Zhong, J. Liu, and Y. Yao, eds.), Springer-Verlag, 2003, pp. 277–300.

[sem09]   *SPARQL endpoint*, Website, January 2009, http://www.semanticweb.org/wiki/SPARQLendpoint/.

[SES02]   York Sure, Michael Erdmann, and Rudi Studer, *Ontoedit: Collaborative engineering of ontologies*, On-To-Knowledge: Semantic Web enabled Knowledge Management (F. van Harmelen (eds.) J. Davies, D. Fensel, ed.), Wiley, 2002.

[She00]   Colin Shearer, *The crisp-dm model: the new blueprint for data mining*, Journal of Data Warehousing **15(4)** (2000), 13–19.

[She08]   Jerry Sheehan, *Research intelligence: A social networking toolset supporting multidisciplinary e-science*, ESCIENCE '08 (Washington, DC, USA), IEEE Computer Society, 2008, p. 331.

[SHJ+04]   Tom Sugden, Alastair Hume, Mike Jackson, Mario Antonioletti, Neil Chue Hong, Amy Krause, and Martin Westhead, *Protecting application developers - a client toolkit for ogsa-dai*, Proceedings of the UK e-Science All Hands Meeting, September 2004.

[SK06]   Larisa N. Soldatova and Ross D. King, *An ontology of scientific experiments*, Journal of The Royal Society Interface **3** (2006), no. 11, 795–803.

[SPG05]   Yogesh L. Simmhan, Beth Plale, and Dennis Gannon, *A survey of data provenance in e-science*, SIGMOD Rec. **34** (2005), 31–36.

[ST05]   Latha Srinivasan and Jem Treadwell, *An overview of service-oriented architecture, web services and grid computing*, Hewlett-Packard White Paper, 2005.

[Sta05]   IBM Staff, *Rational unified process - best practices for software development teams*, Rational Software White Paper, TP026B, Rev 11/01, 2005.

[Sta10]   Stanford Center for Biomedical Informatics Research, *Protege ontology editor and knowledge-base framework*, Website, 2010, http://protege.stanford.edu/.

[Ste08]   Lincoln D. Stein, *Wiki features and commenting - towards a cyberinfrastructure for the biological sciences: progress, visions and challenges*, Nature Reviews Genetics **9** (2008), no. 9, 678–688.

[SUM11]   *Suggested Upper Merged Ontology (SUMO)*, Website, 2011, http://www.ontologyportal.org/.

[Tan08]   Val Tannen, *Provenance and annotation of data and processes*, Springer-Verlag, Berlin, Heidelberg, 2008.

[tav11]   *Taverna Workflow Management System*, Website, 2011, http://taverna.sourceforge.net/.

[TDG06]   Ian J. Taylor, Ewa Deelman, and Dennis B. Gannon, *Workflows for e-Science: Scientific workflows for grids*, Springer, December 2006.

[The10]   The @neurIST Project, *Integrated Biomedical Informatics for the Management of Cerebral Aneurysms*, Website, 2010, http://www.aneurist.org/.

[The11a]   The CloudMiner Team, *The cloudminer project*, Website, May 2011, http://www.cloudminer.org/.

[The11b]   The Globus Alliance, *Globus toolkit*, Website, May 2011, http://www.globus.org/toolkit/.

[UML11]   *Unified Medical Language System (UMLS)*, Website, 2011, http://www.nlm.nih.gov/research/umls/.

[Usc96]   Mike Uschold, *Building Ontologies: Towards a Unified Methodology*, 16th Annual Conf. of the British Computer Society Specialist Group on Expert Systems (Cambridge, UK), 1996.

[vis11]   *The Vis Trails Project*, Website, 2011, http://www.vistrails.org/.

[W3C04]   W3C, *Web ontology language (owl)*, 2004.

[W3C10]   _____, *OWL 2 Web Ontology Language, Direct Semantics*, Website, 2010, http://www.w3.org/TR/2009/REC-owl2-direct-semantics-20091027/.

[WLG+08]   Paul Watson, Phillip Lord, Frank Gibson, Panayiotis Periorellis, and Georgios Pitsilis, *Cloud computing for e-science with carmen*, In 2nd Iberian Grid Infrastructure Conference Proceedings, 2008, pp. 3–14.

[xml11]   *Extensible Markup Language (XML)*, Website, 2011, http://www.w3.org/xml/.

[Yua10]   Jonas X. Yuan, *Liferay portal 6 enterprise intranets*, Packt Publishing, 5 2010.

[ZCL09]   Jing Zhang, Adriane Chapman, and Kristen Lefevre, *Do you know where your data's been? — tamper-evident database provenance*, Proceedings of the 6th VLDB Workshop on Secure Data Management (Berlin, Heidelberg), SDM '09, Springer-Verlag, 2009, pp. 17–32.

[ZJLL04] W. B. Zhang, D. M. Jeong, Y. H. Lee, and M. S. Lee, *Measurement of subcutaneous impedance by four-electrode method at acupoints located with single-power alternative current.*, Am J Chin Med **32** (2004), no. 5, 779–788.

[ZXS08] Hai Zhuge, Yunpeng Xing, and Peng Shi, *Resource space model, owl and database: Mapping and integration*, ACM Trans. Internet Technol. **8** (2008), 20:1–20:31.

Part IV

Appendices

Appendix A

A concrete Life Cycle Resource from a real Breath Gas Analysis Study

Within this Appendix we exemplify a life cycle resource (LCR) from a real breath gas analysis application. A visual illustration of OWL classes and properties of a single slightly simplified LCR is given in Figure A.1. The figure shows selected OWL classes and their object and datatype properties of the e-Science life cycle ontology that correspond to an LCR. It gives an overview of the semantic relationships organized within a LCR. Ellipses represent the values of datatype properties. Rounded rectangles represent the OWL classes and the edges among them represent object properties. In order to give a clear abstract overview of the main concepts of an LCR and to avoid crossing edges we are not illustrating all object properties defined in the e-Science life cycle ontology.

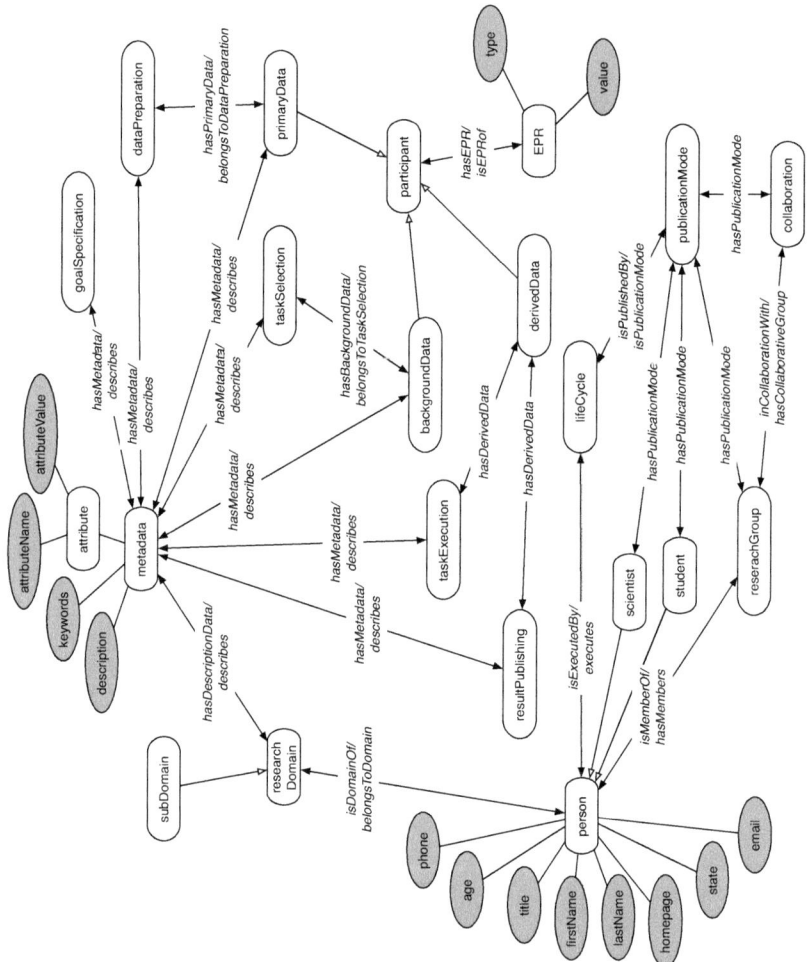

Figure A.1: Classes and properties of a single LCR.

A.1 Life Cycle Activities

In the following we provide for each activity of the e-Science life cycle in own figure illustrating the instance of the activity of a concrete LCR from the BGA application. Figure A.2 illustrates the goal specification activity. Figure A.3 illustrates the data preparation activity. Figure A.4 illustrates the task selection activity. Figure A.5 illustrates the task execution activity. Figure A.6 illustrates the result publishing activity.

A.2 Individuals of the e-Science life cycle ontology

Selected individuals of the e-Science life cycle ontology describing the above introduced LCR resource are listed in the following in the Notation3 (N3) RDF syntax [n311]. Prior to the listing of the individuals we give selected classes and their corresponding object and datatype properties defined in the ontology. The listing is organized into groups separated by comments. We choose the N3 syntax since it is much more compact and readable than the XML RDF syntax [rdf11].

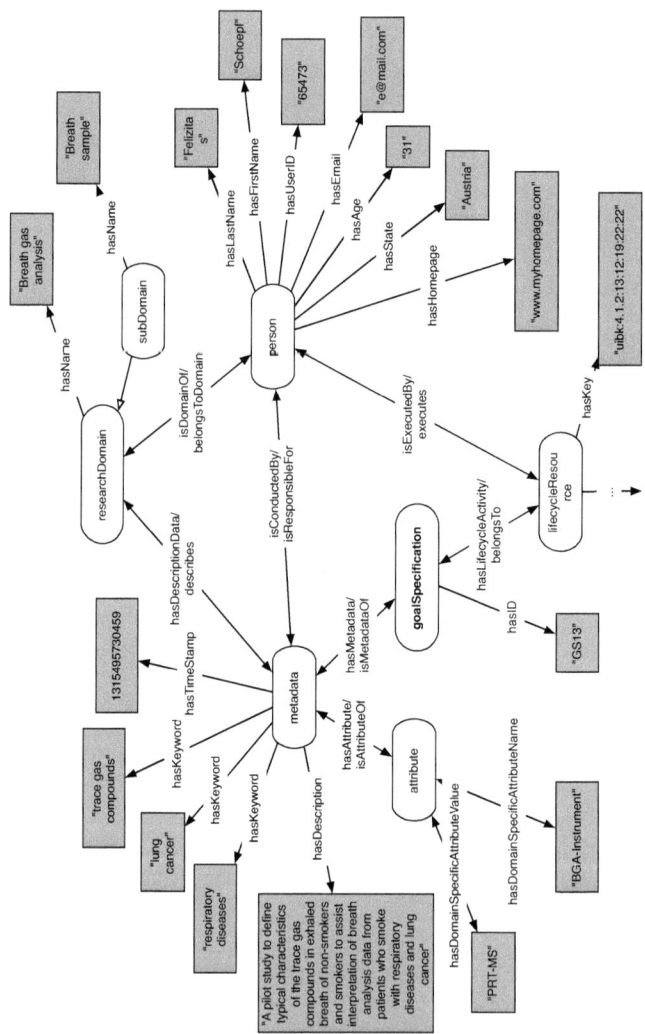

Figure A.2: Classes and properties of the goal specification activity of a concrete BGA LCR.

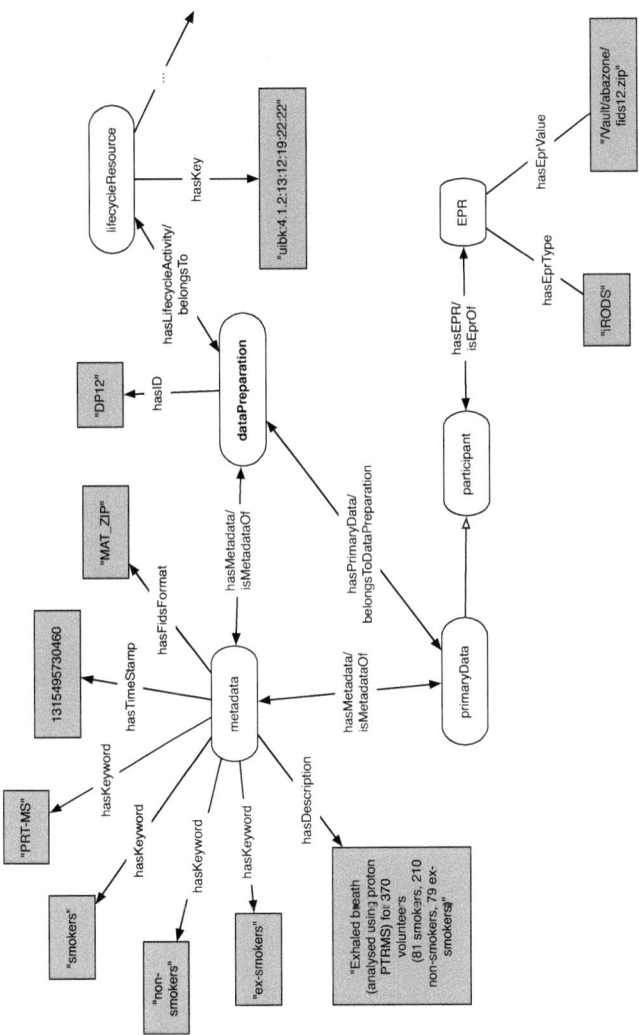

Figure A.3: Classes and properties of the data preparation activity of a concrete BGA LCR.

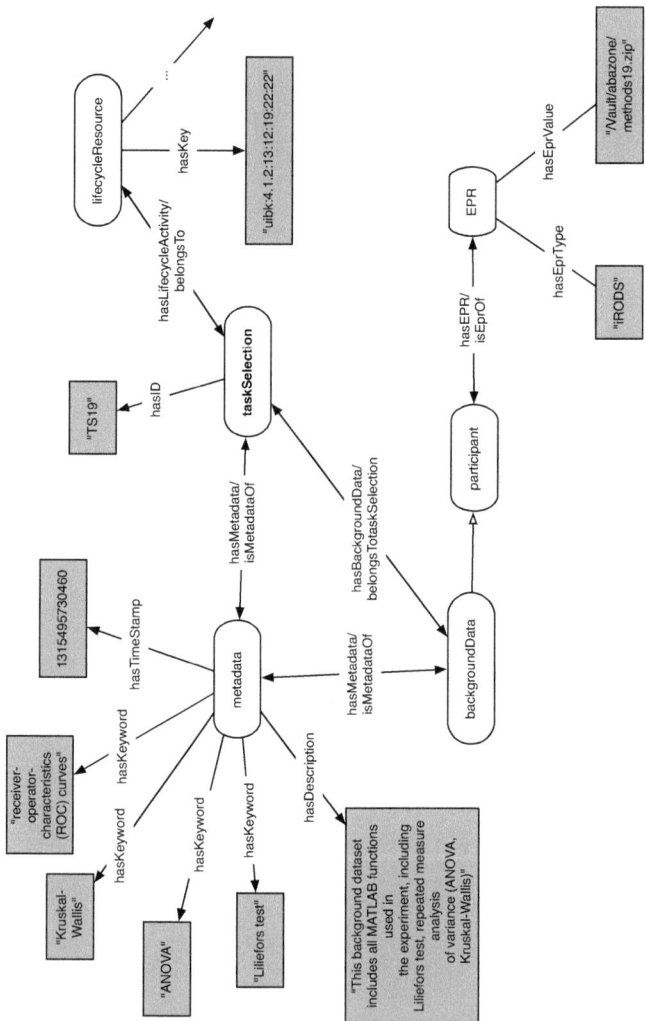

Figure A.4: Classes and properties of the task selection activity of a concrete BGA LCR.

257

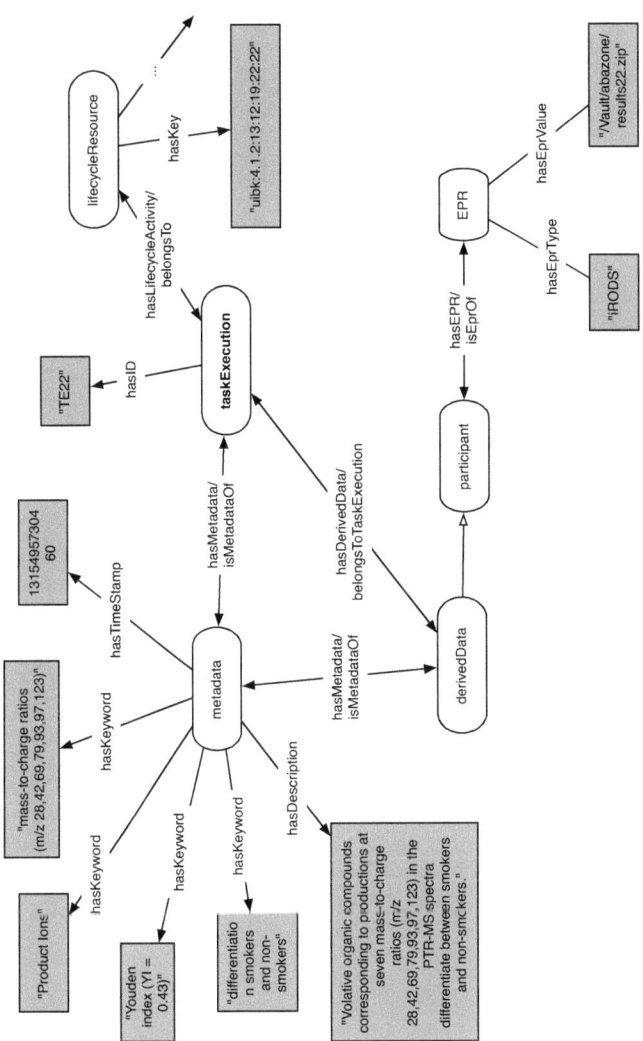

Figure A.5: Classes and properties of the task execution activity of a concrete BGA LCR.

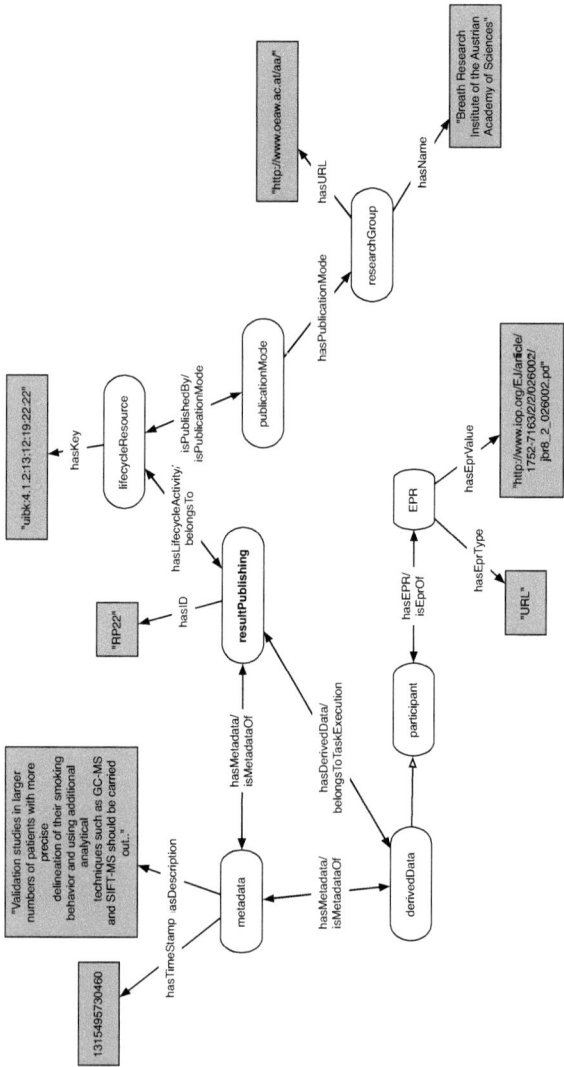

Figure A.6: Classes and properties of the result processing activity of a concrete BGA LCR.

```
#################################################################
# Class representing a lifecycle resource
#################################################################

default:lifeCycle
        a       owl:Class ;
        rdfs:subClassOf owl:Thing ;
        rdfs:subClassOf
                [ a       owl:Restriction ;
                  owl:maxCardinality "1"^^xsd:int ;
                  owl:onProperty default:hasResultPublishing
                ] ;
        rdfs:subClassOf
                [ a       owl:Restriction ;
                  owl:maxCardinality "1"^^xsd:int ;
                  owl:onProperty default:hasTaskSelection
                ] ;
        rdfs:subClassOf
                [ a       owl:Restriction ;
                  owl:maxCardinality "1"^^xsd:int ;
                  owl:onProperty default:hasGoalSpecification
                ] ;
        rdfs:subClassOf
                [ a       owl:Restriction ;
                  owl:maxCardinality "1"^^xsd:int ;
                  owl:onProperty default:hasDataPreparation
                ] ;
        rdfs:subClassOf
                [ a       owl:Restriction ;
                  owl:maxCardinality "1"^^xsd:int ;
                  owl:onProperty default:hasTaskExecution
                ] ;
        rdfs:subClassOf
                [ a       owl:Restriction ;
                  owl:onProperty default:isPublishedBy ;
                  owl:someValuesFrom default:publicationMode
                ] ;
        rdfs:subClassOf
                [ a       owl:Restriction ;
                  owl:allValuesFrom default:scientist ;
                  owl:onProperty default:isExecutedBy
                ] .

#################################################################
# Classes representing the e-Science life cycle activities
#################################################################

default:activity
        a       owl:Class .

default:goalSpecification
        a       owl:Class ;
```

```
        rdfs:comment "The goalSpecification activity of the e-science life cycle.";
        rdfs:subClassOf default:activity ;
        rdfs:subClassOf
                [ a         owl:Restriction ;
                  owl:onProperty default:hasMetadata ;
                  owl:someValuesFrom default:metadata
                ] ;
        owl:disjointWith default:resultPublishing , default:taskExecution ,
          default:dataPreparation , default:taskSelection .

default:dataPreparation
        a       owl:Class ;
        rdfs:comment "The dataPreparation activity of the e-science life cycle.";
        rdfs:subClassOf default:activity ;
        rdfs:subClassOf
                [ a         owl:Restriction ;
                  owl:onProperty default:hasMetadata ;
                  owl:someValuesFrom default:metadata
                ] ;
        rdfs:subClassOf
                [ a         owl:Restriction ;
                  owl:onProperty default:hasEPR ;
                  owl:someValuesFrom default:EPR
                ] ;
        owl:disjointWith default:resultPublishing , default:taskExecution ,
          default:goalSpecification , default:taskSelection .

default:taskSelection
        a       owl:Class ;
        rdfs:comment "The taskSelection activity of the e-science life cycle." ;
        rdfs:subClassOf default:activity ;
        owl:disjointWith default:resultPublishing , default:taskExecution ,
          default:goalSpecification , default:dataPreparation .

default:taskExecution
        a       owl:Class ;
        rdfs:comment "The taskExecution activity of the e-science life cycle." ;
        rdfs:subClassOf default:activity ;
        rdfs:subClassOf
                [ a         owl:Restriction ;
                  owl:onProperty default:hasMetadata ;
                  owl:someValuesFrom default:metadata
                ] ;
        owl:disjointWith default:resultPublishing , default:goalSpecification ,
          default:dataPreparation , default:taskSelection .

default:resultPublishing
        a       owl:Class ;
        rdfs:comment "The resultPublishing activity of the e-science life cycle." ;
        rdfs:subClassOf default:activity ;
        owl:disjointWith default:taskExecution , default:goalSpecification ,
          default:dataPreparation , default:taskSelection .
```

```
#################################################################
# Classes for managing dataspace participants
#################################################################

default:participant
        a       owl:Class .

default:primaryData
        a       owl:Class ;
        rdfs:subClassOf default:participant .

default:backgroundData
        a       owl:Class ;
        rdfs:subClassOf default:participant .

default:derivedData
        a       owl:Class ;
        rdfs:subClassOf default:participant .

default:EPR
        a       owl:Class ;
        rdfs:subClassOf owl:Thing ;
        rdfs:subClassOf
                [ a       owl:Restriction ;
                  owl:onProperty default:isEPRof ;
                  owl:someValuesFrom default:primaryData
                ] ;
        rdfs:subClassOf
                [ a       owl:Restriction ;
                  owl:onProperty default:isEPRof ;
                  owl:someValuesFrom default:backgroundData
                ] ;
        rdfs:subClassOf
                [ a       owl:Restriction ;
                  owl:onProperty default:isEPRof ;
                  owl:someValuesFrom default:derivedData
                ] .


#################################################################
# Classes for managing publication modes
#################################################################

default:researchDomain
        a       owl:Class ;
        rdfs:subClassOf owl:Thing ;
        rdfs:subClassOf
                [ a       owl:Restriction ;
                  owl:onProperty default:hasMetadata ;
                  owl:someValuesFrom default:metadata
```

```
            ] ;
    rdfs:subClassOf
            [ a       owl:Restriction ;
              owl:onProperty default:isDomainOf ;
              owl:someValuesFrom default:scientist
            ] .

default:subDomain
    a       owl:Class ;
    rdfs:subClassOf default:researchDomain .

default:researchGroup
    a       owl:Class ;
    rdfs:subClassOf owl:Thing ;
    rdfs:subClassOf
            [ a       owl:Restriction ;
              owl:onProperty default:hasMetadata ;
              owl:someValuesFrom default:metadata
            ] ;
    rdfs:subClassOf
            [ a       owl:Restriction ;
              owl:onProperty default:inCollaborationWith ;
              owl:someValuesFrom default:collaboration
            ] .

default:collaboration
    a       owl:Class ;
    rdfs:subClassOf owl:Thing ;
    rdfs:subClassOf
            [ a       owl:Restriction ;
              owl:onProperty default:hasCollaborativeGroup ;
              owl:someValuesFrom default:researchGroup
            ] .

default:publicationMode
    a       owl:Class ;
    rdfs:subClassOf owl:Thing ;
    rdfs:subClassOf
            [ a       owl:Restriction ;
              owl:onProperty default:hasPublicationMode ;
              owl:someValuesFrom default:collaboration
            ] ;
    rdfs:subClassOf
            [ a       owl:Restriction ;
              owl:onProperty default:hasPublicationMode ;
              owl:someValuesFrom default:researchDomain
            ] ;
    rdfs:subClassOf
            [ a       owl:Restriction ;
              owl:onProperty default:hasPublicationMode ;
              owl:someValuesFrom default:person
            ] ;
```

```
        rdfs:subClassOf
                [ a       owl:Restriction ;
                  owl:onProperty default:hasPublicationMode ;
                  owl:someValuesFrom default:researchGroup
                ] .

default:scientist
        a       owl:Class ;
        rdfs:subClassOf default:person ;
        rdfs:subClassOf
                [ a       owl:Restriction ;
                  owl:onProperty default:isMemberOf ;
                  owl:someValuesFrom default:researchGroup
                ] ;
        rdfs:subClassOf
                [ a       owl:Restriction ;
                  owl:onProperty default:belongsToDomain ;
                  owl:someValuesFrom default:researchDomain
                ] ;
        rdfs:subClassOf
                [ a       owl:Restriction ;
                  owl:onProperty default:executes ;
                  owl:someValuesFrom default:lifeCycle
                ] .

default:metadata
        a       owl:Class ;
        rdfs:comment "This class describes any individual according to the self-defined attributes." ;
        rdfs:subClassOf owl:Thing ;
        rdfs:subClassOf
                [ a       owl:Restriction ;
                  owl:onProperty default:describes ;
                  owl:someValuesFrom default:researchDomain
                ] ;
        rdfs:subClassOf
                [ a       owl:Restriction ;
                  owl:onProperty default:describes ;
                  owl:someValuesFrom default:researchGroup
                ] ;
        rdfs:subClassOf
                [ a       owl:Restriction ;
                  owl:onProperty default:describes ;
                  owl:someValuesFrom default:participant
                ] ;
        rdfs:subClassOf
                [ a       owl:Restriction ;
                  owl:onProperty default:describes ;
                  owl:someValuesFrom default:dataPreparation
                ] ;
        rdfs:subClassOf
                [ a       owl:Restriction ;
                  owl:onProperty default:describes ;
```

```
                        owl:someValuesFrom default:taskExecution
                    ] ;
        rdfs:subClassOf
                [ a        owl:Restriction ;
                  owl:onProperty default:describes ;
                  owl:someValuesFrom default:goalSpecification
                ] .


###################################################################
# Selected object properties
###################################################################

default:hasAttribute
        a       owl:ObjectProperty ;
        rdfs:domain default:metadata ;
        rdfs:range default:attribute .

default:isExecutedBy
        a       owl:ObjectProperty ;
        rdfs:domain default:lifeCycle ;
        rdfs:range default:scientist ;
        owl:inverseOf default:executes .

default:hasMetadata
        a       owl:ObjectProperty ;
        rdfs:domain
                [ a       owl:Class ;
                  owl:unionOf ( default:goalSpecification
                    default:researchDomain
                    default:dataPreparation
                    default:researchGroup
                    default:taskExecution
                    default:participant
                    default:taskSelection)
                ] ;
        rdfs:range default:metadata ;
        owl:inverseOf default:describes .

default:hasResearchDomain
        a       owl:ObjectProperty .

default:hasMembers
        a       owl:ObjectProperty ;
        rdfs:domain default:researchGroup ;
        rdfs:range default:scientist ;
        owl:inverseOf default:isMemberOf .

default:isPublicationModeOf
        a       owl:ObjectProperty ;
        rdfs:domain default:publicationMode ;
        rdfs:range default:lifeCycle ;
```

```
        owl:inverseOf default:isPublishedBy .

default:hasTaskSelection
        a       owl:FunctionalProperty , owl:ObjectProperty ;
        rdfs:domain default:lifeCycle ;
        rdfs:range default:taskSelection .

default:isEPRof
        a       owl:ObjectProperty ;
        rdfs:domain default:EPR ;
        rdfs:range default:participant ;
        owl:inverseOf default:hasEPR .

default:hasPrimaryData
        a       owl:ObjectProperty ;
        rdfs:domain default:dataPreparation ;
        rdfs:range default:primaryData ;
        owl:inverseOf default:belongsToDataPreparation .

default:isDomainOf
        a       owl:ObjectProperty ;
        rdfs:domain default:researchDomain ;
        rdfs:range default:scientist ;
        owl:inverseOf default:belongsToDomain .

default:isMemberOf
        a       owl:ObjectProperty ;
        rdfs:domain default:scientist ;
        rdfs:range default:researchGroup ;
        owl:inverseOf default:hasMembers .

default:hasBackgroundData
        a       owl:ObjectProperty ;
        rdfs:domain default:taskSelection ;
        rdfs:range default:backgroundData ;
        owl:inverseOf default:belongsToTaskSelection .

default:inCollaborationWith
        a       owl:ObjectProperty ;
        rdfs:domain default:researchGroup ;
        rdfs:range default:collaboration ;
        owl:inverseOf default:hasCollaborativeGroup .

default:hasResultPublishing
        a       owl:FunctionalProperty , owl:ObjectProperty ;
        rdfs:domain default:lifeCycle ;
        rdfs:range default:resultPublishing .

default:EPRvalue
        a       owl:DatatypeProperty ;
        rdfs:domain default:EPR ;
        rdfs:range xsd:string .
```

```
default:belongsToDataPreparation
        a       owl:ObjectProperty ;
        owl:inverseOf default:hasPrimaryData .

default:hasDataPreparation
        a       owl:FunctionalProperty , owl:ObjectProperty ;
        rdfs:domain default:lifeCycle ;
        rdfs:range default:dataPreparation .

default:belongsToTaskSelection
        a       owl:ObjectProperty ;
        owl:inverseOf default:hasBackgroundData .

default:hasCollaborativeGroup
        a       owl:ObjectProperty ;
        rdfs:domain default:collaboration ;
        rdfs:range default:researchGroup ;
        owl:inverseOf default:inCollaborationWith .

default:isPublishedBy
        a       owl:ObjectProperty ;
        rdfs:domain default:lifeCycle ;
        rdfs:range default:publicationMode ;
        owl:inverseOf default:isPublicationModeOf .


default:hasEPR
        a       owl:ObjectProperty ;
        rdfs:domain default:participant ;
        rdfs:range default:EPR ;
        owl:inverseOf default:isEPRof .

default:executes
        a       owl:ObjectProperty ;
        rdfs:domain default:scientist ;
        rdfs:range default:lifeCycle ;
        owl:inverseOf default:isExecutedBy .

default:describes
        a       owl:ObjectProperty ;
        rdfs:domain default:metadata ;
        rdfs:range
                [ a       owl:Class ;
                  owl:unionOf ( default:dataPreparation
                    default:researchDomain
                    default:goalSpecification
                    default:researchGroup
                    default:taskExecution)
                ] ;
        owl:inverseOf default:hasMetadata .
```

```
default:belongsToDomain
        a       owl:ObjectProperty ;
        rdfs:domain default:scientist ;
        rdfs:range default:researchDomain ;
        owl:inverseOf default:isDomainOf .

default:keywords
        a       owl:DatatypeProperty ;
        rdfs:domain default:metadata ;
        rdfs:range xsd:string .

default:hasGoalSpecification
        a       owl:FunctionalProperty , owl:ObjectProperty ;
        rdfs:domain default:lifeCycle ;
        rdfs:range default:goalSpecification .

default:hasTaskExecution
        a       owl:FunctionalProperty , owl:ObjectProperty ;
        rdfs:domain default:lifeCycle ;
        rdfs:range default:taskExecution .

default:lastName
        a       owl:DatatypeProperty ;
        rdfs:domain default:person .

default:hasDerivedData
        a       owl:ObjectProperty ;
        rdfs:domain
                [ a       owl:Class ;
                  owl:unionOf (default:taskExecution default:resultPublishing)
                ] ;
        rdfs:range default:derivedData .

default:hasPublicationMode
        a       owl:ObjectProperty ;
        rdfs:domain default:publicationMode ;
        rdfs:range
                [ a       owl:Class ;
                  owl:unionOf ( default:researchDomain
                    default:researchGroup
                    default:collaboration
                    default:person)
                ] .


####################################################################
# Selected datatype properties  ##
####################################################################

default:attributeValue
        a       owl:DatatypeProperty ;
        rdfs:domain default:attribute ;
```

```
        rdfs:range xsd:string .

default:country
        a       owl:DatatypeProperty .

default:EPRtype
        a       owl:DatatypeProperty ;
        rdfs:domain default:EPR ;
        rdfs:range xsd:string .

default:homepage
        a       owl:DatatypeProperty ;
        rdfs:domain default:person .

default:Name
        a       owl:DatatypeProperty ;
        rdfs:domain default:metadata ;
        rdfs:range xsd:string .

default:firstName
        a       owl:DatatypeProperty ;
        rdfs:domain default:person ;
        rdfs:range xsd:string .

default:description
        a       owl:DatatypeProperty ;
        rdfs:domain default:metadata ;
        rdfs:range xsd:string .

default:email
        a       owl:DatatypeProperty ;
        rdfs:domain default:person .

default:state
        a       owl:DatatypeProperty ;
        rdfs:domain default:person .

default:age
        a       owl:DatatypeProperty ;
        rdfs:domain default:person .

default:attributeName
        a       owl:DatatypeProperty ;
        rdfs:comment "The name of an attribute."^^xsd:string ;
        rdfs:domain default:attribute ;
        rdfs:range xsd:string .


####################################################################
# Selected individuals of a concrete LCR
####################################################################
```

```
### The LCR individual ###

default:lifeCycle_1
        a       default:lifeCycle ;
        rdfs:comment "This class forms the e-science life cycle by connecting the five e-science
        life cycle activities and attaching a publication mode and a reference to the scientists
        who executed the study."^^xsd:string ;
        default:hasDataPreparation
                default:dataPreparation_12 ;
        default:hasGoalSpecification
                default:goalSpecification_13 ;
        default:hasResultPublishing
                default:resultPublishing_22 ;
        default:hasTaskExecution
                default:taskExecution_22 ;
        default:hasTaskSelection
                default:taskSelection_19 ;
        default:isExecutedBy
                <http://localhost/LifeCycleOntology.owl#f.schoepf> ;
        default:isPublishedBy
                default:publicationMode_1 .

### Individuals of the five life cycle activities and their corresponding descriptions ###

default:goalSpecification_13
        a       default:goalSpecification ;
        rdfs:comment "The goalSpecification activity of an e-science life cycle." ;
        default:hasMetadata default:metadata_3 .

default:metadata_3
        a       default:metadata ;
        rdfs:comment "Metadata about a goalSpecification activity" ;
        default:describes default:goalSpecification_13 ;
        default:description " A pilot study to define typical characteristics of the trace gas
         compounds in exhaled breath of non-smokers and smokers to assist
         interpretation of breath analysis data from  patients who smoke
         with respiratory diseases and lung cancer."@en ;
        default:keywords    "trace gas compounds"@en ,
         "respiratory diseases"@en ,
         "lung cancer"@en .

default:dataPreparation_12
        a       default:dataPreparation ;
        rdfs:comment "The dataPreparation activity of an e-science life cycle." ;
        default:hasMetadata default:metadata_4 ;
        default:hasPrimaryData
                default:primaryData_1 .

default:metadata_4
        a       default:metadata ;
        rdfs:comment "Metadata about a dataPreparation activity" ;
```

```
        default:describes default:primaryData_1 , default:dataPreparation_12 ;
        default:description " Exhaled breath (analyzed using proton PTRMS) for 370 volunteers
          (81 smokers, 210 non-smokers, 79 ex-smokers)"@en ;
        default:keywords  "smokers"@en ,
          "ex-smokers"@en ,
          "non-smokers"@en ,
          "PTR-MS"@en .

default:taskSelection_19
        a       default:taskSelection ;
        rdfs:comment "The taskSelection activity of an e-science life cycle." ;
        default:hasBackgroundData
                default:backgroundData_1 ;
        default:hasMetadata default:metadata_6 .

default:metadata_6
        a       default:metadata ;
        default:describes default:backgroundData_1 , default:taskSelection_19 ;
        default:description " This background dataset includes all MATLAB functions used in the
          experiment, including  Liliefors test, repeated measure analysis
          of variance (ANOVA, Kruskal-Wallis)."@en ;
        default:keywords  "receiver-operator-characteristics (ROC) curves"@en ,
          "Liliefors test"@en ,
          "Kruskal-Wallis"@en ,
          "ANOVA"@en .

default:taskExecution_22
        a       default:taskExecution ;
        rdfs:comment "The taskExecution activitiy of an e-science life cycle." ;
        default:hasDerivedData
                default:derivedData_1 ;
        default:hasMetadata default:metadata_7 .

default:metadata_7
        a       default:metadata ;
        rdfs:comment "The metadata about a taskExecution activity." ;
        default:describes default:taskExecution_22 , default:derivedData_1 ;
        default:description " Volatile organic compounds corresponding to product ions at
          seven mass-to-charge  ratios (m/z 28,42,69,79,93,97,123) in
          the PTR-MS spectra differentiate between smokers
          and non-smokers"@en ;
        default:keywords  "differentiation smokers and non-smokers"@en ,
          "Youden index (YI = 0.43)"@en ,
          "product ions"@en ,
          "mass-to-charge ratios (m/z 28,42,69,79,93,97,123)"@en .


default:resultPublishing_22
        a       default:resultPublishing ;
        rdfs:comment "The resultPublishing activity of an e-science life cycle." ;
        default:hasDerivedData
                default:derivedData_2 , default:derivedData_1 .
```

```
default:f.schoepf
        a       default:scientist ;
        rdfs:comment "A scientists affiliation and contact details."@en ;
        default:age "31"^^xsd:string ;
        default:belongsToDomain
                default:breathGasAnalysis ;
        default:email "e@mail.com" ;
        default:homepage "http://www.myhomepage.com" ;
        default:executes default:lifeCycle_1 ;
        default:firstName "Felizitas" ;
        default:lastName "Schoepf" ;
        default:state "Austria" .

### Individuals related to datasets of the LCR ###

default:primaryData_1
        a       default:primaryData ;
        rdfs:comment ""^^xsd:string ;
        default:belongsToDataPreparation
                default:dataPreparation_12 ;
        default:hasEPR default:EPR_1 ;
        default:hasMetadata default:metadata_4 .

default:EPR_1
        a       default:EPR ;
        rdfs:comment "The EPR to a primary dataset from a dataPreparation activity." ;
        default:EPRtype "iRODS"@en ;
        default:EPRvalue "Vault/abazone/fids12.zip"@en ;
        default:isEPRof default:primaryData_1 .

default:backgroundData_1
        a       default:backgroundData ;
        rdfs:comment "A backgroundData set from the taskSelection activity." ;
        default:belongsToTaskSelection
                default:taskSelection_19 ;
        default:hasEPR default:EPR_2 ;
        default:hasMetadata default:metadata_6 .

default:EPR_2
        a       default:EPR ;
        rdfs:comment "The EPR of a background data set." ;
        default:EPRtype "iRODS"@en ;
        default:EPRvalue "Vault/abazone/methods.zip" ;
        default:isEPRof default:backgroundData_1 .

default:derivedData_1
        a       default:derivedData ;
        rdfs:comment "The derived data participant of a life cycle." ;
        default:hasEPR default:EPR_3 ;
        default:hasMetadata default:metadata_7 .
```

```
default:EPR_3
        a       default:EPR ;
        rdfs:comment "The EPR of a derived data set." ;
        default:EPRtype "iRODS"@en ;
        default:EPRvalue "/Vault/abazone/results22.zip"@en ;
        default:isEPRof default:derivedData_1 .

default:derivedData_2
        a       default:derivedData ;
        rdfs:comment "This is the derived data participant representing the manuscript";
        default:hasEPR default:EPR_4 ;
        default:hasMetadata default:metadata_8 .

default:EPR_4
        a       default:EPR ;
        rdfs:comment "The EPR to a scientific publication representing the
          output of a specific study." ;
        default:EPRtype "URL"@en ;
        default:EPRvalue "http://www.iop.org/EJ/article/1752-7163/2/2/026002/jbr8_2_026002.pdf"@en ;
        default:isEPRof default:derivedData_2 .

### Individuals regarding the scientific domain of the LCR ###

default:breathGasAnalysis
        a       default:researchDomain ;
        rdfs:comment "A research area/scientific domain."@en ;
        default:hasMetadata default:metadata_1 ;
        default:isDomainOf default:f.schoepf ;
        ...
    defautl:isDomainOf default:otherUsers.

default:metadata_1
        a       default:metadata ;
        rdfs:comment "This is a brief description of the breath gas analysis domain." ;
        default:describes default:breathGasAnalysis ;
        default:description " Breath Gas Analysis is an emerging new scientific field with
          a growing international scientific community addressing many
          different breath gas studies in terms of investigating and
          screening of hundreds of compounds in exhaled breath gas." ;
        default:keywords  "breath gas analysis"@en ,
          "volatile organic compound"@en ,
          "exhaled breath gas"@en .
```

Index

A
ABA-project, 157
Advanced Breath Analysis, 8
Application repository, 25
Austrian Grid, 8, 168, 214, 216, 217

B
Back propagation neural network, 201
Background data, 5, 9, 23, 64, 83, 88, 89, 102, 155
Basic Formal Ontology (BFO), 117
Breath gas analysis, 13, 84, 87, 99, 106, 130, 190, 196, 206, 215, 217
    action, 193
    application, 168, 198, 210
    community, 192
    experiment, 8, 191, 195, 196, 202
    institution, 209
    measurements, 103
    research group, 166, 217
    researcher, 180, 200, 211
    scientific dataspace, 190
    study, 92, 141, 173, 196
    task, 86

C
CADGrid, 185
    infrastructure, 186
    intelligence base, 186
    service, 186, 201
Catalog, 24, 179

Cell type ontology, 116
Chimera, 44, 45, 63, 64
Cloud computing, 16, 18, 169, 217, 218
CloudMiner, 218
Combination service, 201
CoreSpace framework, 65
CRISP, 22
Cyberinfrastructures, *see* e-Infrastructures

D
DAI-RDF, 178, 179
DAIS, 180
DARQ, 178
Data
    center provider, 169
    grid, 10, 33, 37, 38, 45, 71, 213, 217
    interchange, 5
    management, 18, 37, 57, 169, 217
        community, 5, 28, 70, 71
        extension, 24
        facilities, 44
        mechanisms, 19
        services, 185
        solution, 5, 7, 26
        system, 27, 62, 152
    preservation, 124
        spaces, 9
        system, 131, 142, 143, 145, 165, 187, 199, 205, 209, 217
        publication, 22, 23

replication, 35, 36, 39, 71
store, 4
web, 14
Data provenance, *see* Provenance
Dataspace, 4, 6–9, 14, 15, 23, 25, 26, 28, 49, 51, 63, 64, 71–74, 80, 86, 102, 123, 127, 140, 185, 199
  browser, 129, 139
  cloud, 174
  components, 24
  concepts, 6, 15, 63, 71, 72, 213, 218
  entity, 155
  environment, 23, 90, 146, 147, 213
  features, 28, 29, 62, 63, 65, 66
  functions, 172
  indexer, 128, 129, 137, 207
  instance, 128, 145–147, 149, 154, 155, 157–159, 163, 165–167, 180, 215
  management approach, 65
  management system, 24, 56, 63, 65
  measure, 139, 207
  paradigm, 8, 22, 25, 63, 85, 90, 92, 102, 122, 152, 154–156, 166, 168, 180, 185, 210, 212–214
  participants, 7, 9, 24, 25, 70, 71, 83–88, 97, 98, 102, 104, 105, 122, 124, 125, 128, 130, 142, 143, 145, 147, 155, 157, 162, 164, 165, 186, 195, 215–217
  layer, 144
  proposal, 63
  realization, 64
  relationships, 71, 84, 124, 127, 146, 155, 164, 214
  research, 6, 7, 213
  reusability measure, 207
  service, 174

Support Platform, 6, 9–11, 23, 28, 80, 94, 97, 107, 110, 113, 128, 143, 176, 184, 213, 217, 218
  system, 6, 23, 28, 62, 71, 90, 126, 130
DBMS, 4, 32, 102, 131, 149, 164
Derived data, 5, 16, 22, 27, 44, 73, 83, 88, 92, 102, 126, 155, 174, 191, 197
Digital Object Identifier, 87
Digital object identifier, 87
Distributed
  computing, 17, 169
  dataspace, 153
DSpace, 29, 31, 63, 64
Dublin core, 31–33, 117

E

e-Infrastructure, 5, 15, 73, 185, 199, 212, 217
e-Science, 4, 15, 27, 28, 72
  application, 4, 8–10, 15, 25, 46, 72, 73, 82, 83, 85, 86, 97, 98, 106, 122, 141, 152, 155, 164, 180, 184, 210, 213, 215–217
  application domain, 6
  cloud, 169
  experiment, 90, 122, 123, 130, 142, 165
  life cycle, 22, 64, 71, 72, 74–76, 79, 80, 82, 88, 90, 92–94, 97, 99, 101, 105, 111, 115, 122, 123, 125, 126, 128, 133, 134, 139, 140, 149, 167, 186, 188, 193, 196, 210, 213–215
  activity, 73, 75, 76, 82, 86, 90, 127, 128, 133, 135, 136, 140, 193, 210
  composer, 86, 133, 135, 144, 145, 149, 159, 163, 215
  model, 22
  ontology, 71, 72, 83, 84, 88, 92–94, 96, 97, 99, 102, 104–106, 110, 111, 113–115, 122, 127, 130, 133, 135, 141–143,

145, 155, 159, 163, 168, 180, 188, 195, 210, 212, 215
  resource, 129, 133, 134, 140, 141
  search and query panel, 86, 215, 241
  visualizer, 139, 140
  portal, 16, 21, 23
  understandings, 83
End point reference, 86, 117, 168, 201
EXPO, 116, 117

F
Fast fourier transformation, 201
Final input dataset, 86

G
GC-MS, 190
Global
  catalog, 41
  RDF store, 163–167, 174–177, 216
Globus toolkit, 200, 217
Google desktop search, 59
Grid, 16
  computing, 16–18, 169, 217
  environment, 217
  service, 218
  technology, 217
GridMiner, 209, 211, 218

I
iMeMex, 50
IMS, 190
Index key, 127, 207
Information
  extraction, 24
  gathering task, 130
  retrieval, 24
Institutional repositories, 5

iRODS, 37–40, 63, 106, 125, 131, 142–146, 160, 162, 164, 165, 168, 213, 217
  architecture, 38

J
Jargon Java API, 160, 165
Jena, 54, 113, 135, 141, 149, 161, 174, 178
Joseki SPARQL server, 149, 162, 175
JSON, 148, 162
jSpace, 62, 63, 124, 125, 128–131, 133, 135, 141, 143, 145–149, 154, 157–160, 162, 167, 170, 212, 214
  Java API, 159, 161, 170, 198, 201, 209, 210
  preservation process, 199, 201–206, 210

K
Kalman filtering, 201
Knowledge
  discovery, 14, 119
  exchange, 19, 64
  grid, 71
  management
    solution, 10
    technologies, 7

L
Large-scale
  dataspace, 8, 10, 65, 153, 168
  science, 4
  scientific
    dataspace, 147, 152, 153
    scientific dataspace, 139
LCR preserver, 162, 164, 165
Liferay portal platform, 17
Linked data, 49, 51, 63, 64
Local
  RDF store, 146, 147, 149, 158, 159

store, 25, 145

M
Matlab, 102, 103, 126, 145, 155, 173, 174
Meridian, 185, 186
    electro information, 186
    measurement, 185–187
        instrument, 186, 201
    name, 188
    theory, 186
Metadata catalog, 33, 39, 40, 63
myExperiment, 46, 47, 63, 64
MySQL, 102, 141, 149, 164, 174, 176, 201

N
N-Triples, 29
N3, 29, 162, 258
NIGM, 107, 199
    analysis, 108
    application, 201
    experiment, 210
    LCR, 190
    service, 74, 201
    study, 189, 201, 206
    workflow, 190, 200, 201

O
OASIS group, 17
OBI, 117
Octave, 209, 211
OGSA-DAI, 73, 80, 164, 179, 196, 217
On-to-knowledge, 94
Open grid forum, 180
Open group, 17
OrientSpace, 65
OWL, 8, 9, 29, 71, 94, 99, 125, 179, 212

P

Pay-as-you-go
    data
        management, 47
        integration, 6
    principle, 47
PAYGO, 47, 49, 63
    architecture, 48
Pellet reasoner, 99, 113
Persistent ontology model, 141, 174
Phlat, 59
PMML, 74, 80, 126, 188
Prepare Data, 73, 75, 80, 86, 128
Primary data, 5, 7, 16, 27, 83, 88, 102, 214
Problem solving environment, 172, 173
Process and Publish Results, 74, 75, 80
Protégé ontology editor, 95, 106, 107, 160, 168
Provenance, 16, 20, 217
    data, 5, 64
    metadata, 32
PRT-MS, 190

R
Rational unified process, 22
RDF, 49, 71, 84
    graph, 77, 84
    schema, 29
    store, 54, 84, 85, 88, 104, 126–129, 131–133, 137, 139, 141, 142, 145–149, 154, 157–159, 162–165, 167, 174–178, 196, 216, 241, 242
    tree, 82, 84
RDF/XML, 29, 258
RDFizing tools, 51
Relational database to RDF wrappers, 51
Replication, 24, 35, 39, 57, 206, 211
    process, 102
    storage, 25

Resource view catalog, 57
Rule oriented programming, 37
Run Tasks, 74, 75, 80, 86

S
SaaS, 170
Scientific
    dataspace model, 71
    data
        management, 20–22, 153, 212
        preservation, 212
        dataspace, 6, 25, 71, 74, 75, 81, 83, 102, 126, 141, 154, 196, 210, 213
        cloud, 170, 171
        support platform, 40, 153
        dataspace model, 72, 75, 90, 92, 97, 104
        instrument, 4
        resource space model, 74
Select Appropriate Tasks, 73–75, 80, 86
Semantic
    data, 125, 150, 159, 172, 216
        infrastructure, 147, 154, 159, 164
        model, 88
    description, 93, 127, 210
    explorer, 54
    heterogeneity, 70
    information, 25, 44, 128
    integration, 15, 26, 65
    level, 113
    mapping, 6, 47
    markup layer, 143, 144, 157, 163, 165, 205, 209
    model, 92
    relationship, 7, 9, 65, 70, 83–85, 88, 95, 199, 201
    repository, 96
    search, 63

web application, 149
web technologies, 29, 174, 212, 213
web tool, 162
web wiki, 118
Semex, 54, 63
SemWIQ, 178, 179
Service Oriented Architecture, 15, 17, 169
SIFT-MS, 190
SPARQL
    endpoint, 158, 159, 164, 167, 174, 176, 178, 179
    protocol, 29, 180
SPARQL-ADERIS, 158, 163, 167, 216
SPARQL-DQP, 178, 179
Specify Goals, 73, 75, 80
SQL, 5, 126
    facilities, 41
    language, 46
    optimization techniques, 179
    query, 41, 42, 46, 132, 179
    query statements, 43
    statements, 43, 44
Storage resource broker, 33, 63
Subdataspace, 81
SUMO, 117
System identification, 201

T
Traditional Chinese Medicine, 8, 108, 184, 185
Turtle, 29

U
UML, 125, 131, 133, 135

V
Virtual
    data
        applications, 44

    catalog, 44, 64
    language, 44
    system, 44, 64
  database, 40
  machines, 169
  organization, 7, 10, 16, 166
  research platform, 46, 64
  scientific
    communities, 16
    activities, 16
  team, 16

W

Web resource space model, 88
Webshpere Information Integrator, 40, 63
WEEP, 185, 186, 200
Welkin, 141, 162
Windows desktop serach, 59
WS-I, 185, 201
WSRF, 185, 201

X

XML, 5, 40, 44, 57, 71, 103, 148, 163, 193, 195, 197
  data, 73
  databases, 24
  documents, 43
  files, 41, 51
  metadata document, 32
  schema, 43
  sources, 43
XQuery, 126

i want morebooks!

Buy your books fast and straightforward online - at one of world's fastest growing online book stores! Environmentally sound due to Print-on-Demand technologies.

Buy your books online at
www.get-morebooks.com

Kaufen Sie Ihre Bücher schnell und unkompliziert online auf einer der am schnellsten wachsenden Buchhandelsplattformen weltweit! Dank Print-On-Demand umwelt- und ressourcenschonend produziert.

Bücher schneller online kaufen
www.morebooks.de

 VDM Verlagsservicegesellschaft mbH
Heinrich-Böcking-Str. 6-8 Telefon: +49 681 3720 174 info@vdm-vsg.de
D - 66121 Saarbrücken   Telefax: +49 681 3720 1749 www.vdm-vsg.de

Printed by Books on Demand GmbH, Norderstedt / Germany